TERROR ON THE PITCH

TERROR ON THE PITCH

HOW BIN LADEN TARGETED BECKHAM AND THE ENGLAND FOOTBALL TEAM

ADAM ROBINSON

First published in Great Britain in 2002 by
MAINSTREAM PUBLISHING COMPANY (EDINBURGH) LTD
7 Albany Street
Edinburgh EH1 3UG

ISBN 1 84018 613 5

A catalogue record for this book is available from the British Library

Typeset in Janson and Frutiger
Printed and bound in Great Britain by Mackays of Chatham

Contents

Preface

To most of us, the name Osama bin Laden conjures up images of a one-dimensional figure, a terrorist with a Kalashnikov who has corrupted all the peaceful tenets of Islam into a twisted manifesto of hatred and death.

But for a monster, he is also uncomfortably like you and me.

Bin Laden adores his children. He loves his mother. He suffered emotionally from the break-up of his parents' relationship. He likes to be appreciated and loved. He has been known to enjoy drinking whisky and champagne. He went to school and university, laughed with friends, enjoyed fast cars and riding horses, has been on foreign sightseeing holidays . . . all simple pleasures that 'normal' people hold dear.

It should therefore not have come as much of a shock to learn that he loves football, although it might be more surprising to learn that he supports Arsenal Football Club.

Football is the world's most popular sport, is it so strange that a man who played as a youngster still follows the game as an adult? Billions of people around the world have done so throughout their lives and hundreds of millions have formed attachments to clubs outside of their own countries – witness the global support base for Manchester United.

The similarity between Bin Laden and the average person's interest in the beautiful game ends here, however. Far from being a benign supporter, Bin Laden's interest has been proven to extend in an unthinkably evil direction. Where others campaign for the sanctity of sport for the benefit of humanity, Bin Laden sees it only as a vehicle for his perverted ends. He is a fan of football, has a history of involvement and affection for the game, yet has worked for years to use its greatest event as a platform for his twisted vision of apocalypse.

As a youngster, Bin Laden was an aspiring goalkeeper. Although there was no formal youth set-up in Saudi Arabia, he joined the Under-12s youth team attached to Ittihad Club, a Saudi Arabian First Division side and the biggest sports club in his home city, Jeddah. He later graduated to playing with the Under-14s and Under-16s. After being forced to leave Jeddah to study in Lebanon, he reached the fringes of the team at Nejmeh Sporting Club, a club which in the early 1970s was as dominant in the Lebanese First Division as the David Beckham-inspired Manchester United are in the English Premiership today.

As he got older, Bin Laden turned his back on the sport for a time, but then sponsored a club side in Sudan during the early 1990s and even stood in the Clock End at Highbury to see his heroes Arsenal in action during the early months of 1994.

Then came 1998. This was the year of the World Cup in France, an event second in size only to the Olympics. Bin Laden sought to use the event as the centrepiece of a terrible series of simultaneous terrorist attacks, aiming to bolster the cause of Islamic fundamentalism and damage his prime enemies – the United States and England. For four years his Al-Qaeda terror network and its allies in the Algerian Armed Islamic Group (GIA) schemed against the tournament.

Chillingly, as new research for this book has uncovered, Bin Laden had personally ordered the Algerians to plan for David Beckham's murder, along with that of Alan Shearer, Michael Owen, David Seaman and Glenn Hoddle, while England were playing Tunisia in Marseilles on 15 June.

Now, four years on from the planned attack, the World Cup competition moves to Japan and South Korea. The world has turned, for better and for worse. In 1998, Bin Laden plotted a horrendous series of attacks on France. He did not have to leave Afghanistan to do this and indeed Al-Qaeda had only peripheral involvement. Instead Bin Laden used the GIA, a terror group blamed for a large proportion of the killing in an Algerian civil war that has cost 100,000 lives. Its interests matched his own.

In the wake of 11 September, Bin Laden's world of safe havens and safe houses has come crashing down on him. Nothing is known of his plans, if any, regarding the 2002 World Cup, but what is clear, from past experience, is that if he had set his sights on interrupting this festival of sport, Al-Qaeda cells, or those of convenient allies in the Far East such as the Japanese Red Army or Abu Sayyaf, will probably be well-enough organised not to require his personal input at this late stage in the game.

Bin Laden's twisted passion for football has not suddenly gone away and the 2002 World Cup presents him with another opportunity to strike a blow for his twisted version of Islam.

This is a cautionary tale.

One

Osama's World Cup

The Nightmare Scenario . . .

Marseilles had seen its share of history, had been kicked about through the centuries by invaders who each left their mark, but it had never encountered anything quite like the events surrounding the 1998 World Cup. As the days progressed towards mid-June, the one million inhabitants of this sprawling metropolis on France's Mediterranean coast witnessed an invasion unlike any that had gone before. This new advancing army danced to dozens of different drumbeats, wore the uniforms and flew the flags of what seemed like half the nations on earth. Tens of thousands of them flooded Marseilles by road and rail. Disparate though they were, they shared a common passion for football that enveloped the city in a party atmosphere. In all, the visitors numbered nearly 70,000, part of an extraordinary celebration of humanity and sport.

Very quickly, the bistros and bars clustered on the rocky coastline around the old harbour were teeming with fans young and old, all intent on having a good time. They ate the traditional bouillabaisse and drank pastis, talked football and cheered as the televised games of the world championships lifted spirits and set the scene for a sporting classic. The match they were most anticipating was to be played right here, in Marseilles, on 15 June – England versus Tunisia.

As the city partied, behind the scenes the French authorities were finalising their strategy for match day. They expected nothing less than a clash of Titans, an emotionally charged game that would test the mettle of many both on the pitch and off. The police knew enough about

English and Tunisian fans to understand that small elements of each would act out their intense competitive spirit in violence on the streets; that keeping them apart was essential if they were to maintain a semblance of peace. During these lead-up days, however, there were few arrests and Englishmen and Tunisians celebrated side by side.

By 15 June, the World Cup would be five days into its five-week programme, a summer fiesta of football that commentators claimed would eventually attract a cumulative global television audience of 37 billion people for the 64 televised games. Hundreds of thousands more had gathered in France to see the games live, soaking in the atmosphere of what was billed as the second greatest sporting spectacle on the face of the earth, surpassed only by the Olympics. Thirty-two national teams from five continents had reached the finals, after a two-year qualifying campaign that had encompassed 652 matches between 145 teams. Seldom had the attention of the world been so singularly focused.

For France's politicians and spin doctors, the championships represented an opportunity to bask in the warmth of global attention, to display the country's best face on a world stage and earn billions of dollars from the foreign visitors who had made the journey. Football was once again demonstrating its pulling power as one of the world's richest industries.

Marseilles is the Mediterranean gateway to France and, like most southern French cities, it has a large and colourful immigrant population from the former French colonies of Africa. The city fathers of Marseilles, looking to boost their city's regeneration, had welcomed the cheap labour that immigrants represented. Mainly Central and North Africans, these newcomers were attracted to the big city by the promise of employment and a better life. A significant number were from the former French colony of Algeria, just across the azure waters of the Mediterranean from Marseilles. For them, France also represented a refuge from a terrible civil war.

Resembling a vast cultural melting pot, Marseilles is home to a multicultural patchwork of humanity. Diverse in almost every way, from the food they eat to the churches and mosques in which they pray, if one thing unites these global itinerants, it is football.

In the heart of the city stands Stade-Vélodrome, a vast open arena with seating for 60,000 people. The home ground of Olympique Marseilles, one of the leading clubs in France, the stadium had been refitted for the 1998 tournament to allow more people to attend games. The organisers expected this to pay dividends on that mid-June afternoon, when every seat in Stade-Vélodrome would be filled as former champions England took to the pitch for the first match in their World Cup campaign against Group Five opponents Tunisia.

On the streets around the stadium and throughout Marseilles, thousands of other fans would be packing the bars and cafés of the city to watch the spectacle on television, many having travelled considerable distances without tickets. Black, white, Gallic, Arab, this mini-UN of football fans were all driven by the same urge: to experience the World Cup at close quarters, to be near the action as it unfolded on the pitch.

On the evening prior to the big match, a small group of Algerian men gathered unnoticed in a town house not far from the bouillabaisse bistros. Had they wished, they could have joined the football supporters whose singing and laughter they could hear colouring the night from the bars along the waterfront. But in this little corner of Marseilles, darker matters were under consideration than whether the youngster Michael Owen would be given a game by manager Glen Hoddle, or if the England manager had been right to leave the precocious but troubled talent of midfielder Paul Gascoigne at home.

Like the football fans, these five men had several things in common. They shared the same cultural roots and carried the same ideals; they lived and worked in Marseilles, the model of law-abiding citizens. Inconspicuous men meeting in an anonymous house, they were all but invisible. They all had the necessary work permits, paid taxes and went about their lives with an air of normality. One worked nights in an office block as a cleaner. Another drove a bus for a private company, often carrying the schoolchildren of Marseilles to the city's museums. One was attached to the municipality as a translator. Studiously law-abiding, within the large ethnic Algerian community they appeared normal in every way.

The five shared a passion for two things: Islam and football. They often prayed together and spent time in the mosque talking over the issues of everyday life in their native Arabic tongue. They were not unique in this: Arabic is as common as French in parts of Marseilles. Nor were they any different in pursuing their second passion of football. All were season ticket holders at Olympique Marseilles. It is a good side to follow, one of Europe's great football clubs, winners of the French National championship an extraordinary five straight times between 1989 and 1993. Like thousands of others, the five seldom missed a game in Stade-Vélodrome. When the club appealed for volunteers from among their supporters' ranks to act as stewards for the World Cup, they stepped forward and were welcomed with open arms.

But they also had another shared interest that burned every bit as fiercely in their hearts and minds. The five were members of the Group Islamique Armé or Armed Islamic Group (GIA), a disparate Islamic fundamentalist group from Algeria that had been fighting openly since 1992 to overthrow the secular regime in their own country and to export Islamic revolution around the world. Some 100,000 people, mostly innocent civilians, had died during this campaign led by the GIA and extremist groups that were its offshoots.

The leader of the five was a veteran of the Afghanistan campaign, a struggle during which 10,000 ordinary Arabs had fought in a decade-long battle to free the country from occupation by the Soviet Union. He was a Tunisian by birth and was referred to within the tight-knit community as 'Tunis'. He worked as the director of a charity called the Islamic Association, ostensibly aiding Islamic immigrants in the Marseilles area. The association also had offices in other areas of France and was a front for Osama bin Laden and his Al-Qaeda network. Unbeknown to all but a select few, the true purpose of the Islamic Association was to fund and supply 'sleeping' cells of a GIA terror network in France.

The story of how the five men came to be in Marseilles in June 1998 begins some time after 1995. Their leadership in Algiers, acting under the umbrella of the Al-Qaeda organisation, inserted them into the city as sleepers, part of a long-term terror plot that bore all the hallmarks of the leader of Al-Qaeda, the Saudi Arabian-born Bin Laden. In all there were five such GIA cells in France that were activated around this time and a host of support cells spread across Europe.

The cells were supported by money filtered through a network of financial institutions and private individuals. Al-Qaeda used this network to launder funds that were later deposited as clean donations in a variety of bank accounts held by fraudulent Islamic charities around France.

During the spring of 1998, the cells had come alive with activity as preparations were completed. GIA European operations director Ahmed Zaoui had travelled regularly from Switzerland, where his headquarters were established, to oversee the arrival of arms and munitions that would be quietly smuggled into Belgium through Antwerp and across the border into France.

The five cells had different objectives. The main focus was on Marseilles and Paris, the two 'showpiece' events of a series of synchronised attacks planned for 15 June 1998. The objective was brutal, bloody and audacious . . . the targets included the national football teams of England and America.

At 2.30 p.m. that day England would be playing Tunisia in Marseilles, while several hundred miles away in Paris the American squad were scheduled to be watching the match on television in their hotel on the outskirts of the French capital. Outside the Americans' hotel complex the terrorists anticipated a great deal of security, but the Parisian GIA cell had managed to steal hotel staff uniforms and identification passes. With these they would attempt to get past the gendarmes and units of the French army on duty outside and enter the building in disguise, armed with guns and hand grenades. But while this attack would take place behind closed doors, the assault on the English team in Marseilles was calculated to be as public as possible, in front of a global television audience that might reach half a billion.

Osama bin Laden, sometimes called 'The Sheikh' by his followers, was no stranger to football. He had played in his youth and now followed the sport on satellite television either in the Middle East or in the remote mountains of Afghanistan. He knew what he wanted. He had discussed the plot in detail with Zaoui and GIA leader Hassan Hattab when they had met in Afghanistan. Just how well he knew football can be seen in the precision of the instructions that followed this meeting. In a letter dated 24 December 1997 Zaoui gave the following instructions to one of his men:

> Please inform Tunis [head of the cell in Marseilles] that the Sheikh [Bin Laden], may God bless him, has personally prepared a list of those who should be targeted in the operation at the stadium. It is needless for me to remind

you that the Sheikh's support is very important to us and I therefore instruct you to follow these directives carefully. Ensure that Tunis is aware of the requirements, and that he fully understands the identities of the men they are to focus on.

The Sheikh, may God bless him, wishes you to ensure that three men are in position in the stadium. As agreed, they should be free to move around in order to carry out their instructions. He asks that we observe the movements of David Seaman, the goalkeeper of England, Alan Shearer, the most famous player, and the trainer, Hoddle. Also, thanks be to God, his attention has also been drawn to two younger players who are becoming well known, David Beckham and Michael Owen. They are not certain to be playing, but will be visible with the others [reserves] at the side of the field.

(see Figure 1)

These chilling instructions were the blueprint for what was to follow . . .

The morning was clear and sunny on 15 June when three of the five Algerians set off from their safe house for Stade-Vélodrome. Fearful of raising the suspicions of the security forces in any way, they were relieved that elements of England's support were causing trouble that would deflect the gendarmes from their vigilance at the stadium entrances. The first incident occurred outside the gates of Stade-Vélodrome about two hours before the start of the game. As fans emerged from the Métro and made their way toward the stadium, groups of Tunisian and English supporters began hurling bottles and cans at each other and exchanging blows. Running battles ensued. Around a dozen English fans were arrested, and hundreds of police were drafted into the area. Trouble continued and tensions grew between rival fans, drawing practically the undivided attention of the security forces.

This did not bother the three Algerians who had legitimately passed through the flash points and into the ground carrying items other than their yellow stewards' bibs and passes. One had a small amount of TNT and an electrical charge strapped to his body. Another had a .44 Colt pistol. The third man carried two hand grenades. The police were far too involved in handling the English fans to take any notice of them.

Amid the chaos outside the ground, the Algerians had hardly merited a second glance on arrival. They had the necessary identification and official passes, had attended the rehearsals staged for volunteer helpers in preceding weeks and blended in perfectly. While their fellow volunteer stewards were looking forward to the footballing spectacle ahead, however, the three Algerians went to the match in the knowledge that they would die that afternoon at Stade-Vélodrome.

As the world watches, kick-off proceeds on time at 2.30 p.m. At 3.13 p.m., England captain Alan Shearer causes the stadium to erupt, slotting a goal past Tunisian goalkeeper Chockri El Ouaer to put England into a 1–0 lead. A matter of seconds remain before the end of the first half. A worldwide television audience of perhaps 500 million looks on. One minute later, referee Okada looks at his watch and prepares to whistle the end of the first half. Play is in the Tunisian area. Those close to the England goal suddenly notice a new figure on the pitch. A yellow-jacketed steward is making for David Seaman, standing alone in the England goalmouth. Is there something wrong? What has happened to Seaman? Why is this unauthorised man there?

The England goalkeeper catches movement from the corner of his eye, but is intent on following the play of the game and ignores the man until he is almost upon him. By then it is too late. Seaman stiffens and holds out his hands to keep the man from bumping into him, thinking it is some crazed fan attempting to knock him over. Within three metres of the veteran goalkeeper, the Algerian sets off the TNT strapped to his stomach. He and Seaman are blown apart in a horrific blur. The force of the blast hits several photographers behind the goal who are killed outright. Nails packed around the charge spread wildly, almost at the speed of sound, for several hundreds of metres, hitting other photographers, stewards, police and officials on the edge of the pitch. Several are killed by the shrapnel while hundreds more are felled and injured in that one split second.

The ear-splitting explosion and shock holds the stadium momentarily frozen in disbelief. Spectators turn from the football action and stare at a jagged hole in the green field where, moments before, the England goal had stood. Only two people among the 60,000 plus in the stadium make any attempt to move. They were ready for the signal and only have seconds to act.

One of them had positioned himself near the England bench. From his vantage point he could see a tense Glen Hoddle pacing and Beckham and Owen sitting quietly, intent on the action being played out before them. Across the pitch he had also kept an eye on his marker. As his accomplice began his run toward Seaman, he dipped his hands into his pockets. When the first blast goes off, he pulls the pins from the pair of hand grenades he carries, one in each pocket. He has seven seconds before they blow up. He takes one from his pocket and lobs it the 20 metres into the throng of England players and support staff on the margins of the pitch. Then he turns toward the stands packed with English fans. Pulling the second grenade from his pocket, he hurls it into the section of the stand that is most densely packed with painted faces, replica tops and British flags.

Amid the charged atmosphere of the Stade-Vélodrome, the euphoria of the Shearer goal and the commotion at the England goalmouth, no one seems to register these actions, let alone see the grenades, until it is too late. The terrorist's throws are true and his timing perfect: the England dugout is obliterated. Those standing in the area have just enough time to register what has happened to Seaman, but the men sitting on the bench have not had time even to stand when the grenade, lying in their midst, goes off. The entire England bench – Beckham, Owen and England's brightest hopes for the future – are wiped out in the blink of an eye.

A split second later the other grenade goes off, blowing apart dozens of England fans, tearing limbs off others and leaving over a hundred with horrific wounds.

The panic that erupts around Stade-Vélodrome provides cover for the third terrorist. He has drawn his pistol and run onto the pitch shooting, his steward's uniform confusing both his intended targets and the security forces. An Al-Qaeda-trained marksman, shooting a man dead from up to 40 metres away presents no challenge. His targets, the men in the England strips, have stopped, momentarily in shock as they take in what has occurred around them. The gunman heads straight towards Shearer, unloading several shots in the direction of the England captain. Striker

Teddy Sheringham is next and finally he takes aim at midfielder Paul Scholes. In eight seconds, before an armed gendarme pulls out a gun and shoots this third attacker dead, the Algerian has killed or injured three more England stars.

The whole attack has taken no more than 20 seconds. On and off the pitch a dozen England players are dead. In the stands dozens of fans have been massacred. Hundreds around Stade-Vélodrome are lying injured. The television cameras are still rolling. The entire bloody scene has been captured live and relayed to millions of viewers. Osama bin Laden's message has been delivered to the world.

In their suburb of Paris, the US team are watching the England versus Tunisia match on television in their hotel. In this regard they are no different from most people in France who are either watching football on television or listening to it on the radio. Among the latter are three Algerians in position at the US team's hotel. Their signal to go into action is the shocked French commentator on the game in Marseilles suddenly forgetting football to scream into his microphone about the terrible drama unfolding before his eyes.

The US squad are together in a reception room with their attention glued to a large-screen television. Later that day they are due at the Parc des Princes, home to French powerhouse Paris St Germain, to face Germany in their own opening match of the competition. Watching the England match together is useful both as a scouting exercise and a way of relaxing ahead of a big game.

As they witness a game of championship football erupt into carnage, the room goes silent. Players and team officials sit glued to the set in stunned silence. Some jump to their feet as though scalded. Then the room erupts in shouts and cries of disbelief. Seconds later, the door bursts open. A man fills the entrance. He lifts the Kalashnikov automatic rifle that he is carrying and opens fire into the room. Just three of those in the room are Liverpool goalkeeper Brad Friedel and Los Angeles Galaxy star Cobi Jones, both 27, and Leicester City's 29-year-old goalkeeper Kasey Keller.

Elsewhere in the hotel, the second attacker, armed with three hand grenades, searches for part-time musician and football star Alexi Lalas. At 29, Lalas is a veteran of the US side and probably the best known of the

American players. The terrorist deliberately stalks the corridors as gunfire erupts audibly elsewhere in the hotel. Failing to find Lalas, he comes across a lounge in which some of the US coaching staff are relaxing. He pulls the pin and hurls one of his weapons inside, demolishing the room and killing everyone in it.

By now the noise has attracted the attention of the gendarmes stationed outside. As they race into the building, shouting warnings, the terrorist makes one final gesture. He pulls the pin from his second grenade. Before the French police can get to him the device explodes, spreading parts of his body along the length of the corridor. A martyr for the cause, he dies believing that he will go automatically to heaven as a reward for his actions.

Elsewhere, in the centre of Paris, the US embassy is under attack. A man has attempted to drive a small truck towards the embassy at 2 avenue Gabriel. The truck is loaded with TNT. But the instant that news is relayed of the carnage in Marseilles, the streets around the American embassy go into lockdown. The truck is still several hundred metres from its target when the road ahead is blocked by a police car. To the driver of the truck, the leader of the Paris cell, his duty is clear. As two policemen reach the cab in which he sits, he flicks the switch that sets off the bomb. The terrorists, the policemen and dozens of people nearby are killed instantly. Windows up to a kilometre away are blown in.

In Marseilles, a second cell has gone into action. Its members force their way into the offices of the US consulate there and begin shooting. As the authorities close in, the terrorists set off grenades before shooting themselves. They too are now martyrs.

As if all this were not enough, Bin Laden and his co-conspirators have saved their terrifying finale for last. High above the Poitou-Charentes region of France, a different, more sinister drama unfolds. Three Algerian men have boarded a scheduled flight from Aéroport de Poitiers-Biard, taking advantage of the lax security of a provincial airport to smuggle handguns aboard. Soon after take-off the three produce their weapons and take over the plane. The head of this GIA cell knows how to fly. He takes the controls while passengers and crew are herded to the back of the aircraft by his men.

On the ground, air traffic control notes an unscheduled change in the aircraft's direction. A few minutes later, they hear the new pilot praying, moments before he sends the plane into a suicide dive toward the Civaux-1 nuclear power station.

This facility, although not yet fully operational, has a working reactor and is stocked with low-enriched uranium oxide. When the medium-sized passenger jet hits the building that houses the reactor core, it does not matter that the reactor is off line, or that the world's most modern safety system is built into Civaux-1 at all levels. The impact, coupled with a full load of aviation fuel which ignites immediately, causes a chain reaction in the reactor that runs out of control, creating explosions and a fireball which blows off the reactor's lid. It is the nuclear scientists' worst nightmare, a worst-case scenario: it is a complete core meltdown.

Into the air above Civaux-1 swirls a vast cloud of nuclear 'dust'. Nothing short of a miracle can prevent it from being carried across France and Western Europe. The unshielded reactor emits 200 million curies of radiation. The fire set off by the aircraft and its aviation fuel would continue to burn for ten days before finally extinguishing itself.

The French army is called in immediately to evacuate everyone from a 30-kilometre radius. High radiation levels would continue to ensure that this zone continually expanded. But the people of Poitiers, Vivonne, Latille and Journet have already been exposed to radioactivity 100 times greater than that produced by the Hiroshima bomb.

On 15 June, as the Poitou-Charentes region is slowly poisoned, the French army is deployed in major cities throughout the rest of the country. Troops surround government installations, airports, nuclear power plants and railway stations. Instead of the greatest footballing spectacle on earth, television crews now beam to their home countries footage of the bodies of terrorists lying on the streets where they had been felled by security forces, of massacred footballers and the unbelievable events that are afflicting Poitiers.

At a little before 7 p.m. the same day, Sepp Blatter, who a week earlier had been elected as successor to Dr João Havelange as the eighth president of FIFA, and who would take up his duties at the end of the championships, stands before hundreds of reporters from around the world. Tearfully, the 62-year-old Swiss announces that, having discussed the unprecedented disaster with French President Jacques Chirac, US President Bill Clinton and British Prime Minister Tony Blair, FIFA has agreed to abandon the 15th World Cup.

'There can be simply no guarantees that there are not more terrorist cells operating in France at this time,' explains Blatter. 'Without such a certainty, it is impossible for FIFA, the organisers of the World Cup, or the French government to guarantee the safety of participants and spectators, particularly at a time of national disaster and mourning.

'The death of the players and coaching staff from the United States and England puts into perspective that this is a sport. We mourn deeply all the lives that have been lost, and our thoughts are with their families and with those who are in hospitals in Paris and Marseilles, and those murdered in Poitiers.'

With troops on the streets of France, a nuclear cloud spreading over the country and unprecedented security at airports and in most public places, national teams begin leaving the country. Osama bin Laden has turned a sporting fiesta into a battlefield. He has brought the world to a standstill and planted his message of hatred, revenge and Islamic fundamentalism firmly on the global stage.

Two

The Goalkeeper

Football is the world's favourite sport for good reason. Played at its highest level, it is an entertaining and enthralling test of skill, stamina, strength and intelligence – all the attributes that make sport such a compelling metaphor for human achievement. It accomplishes this with a bare minimum of equipment: all it takes to play football is a ball or, failing that, something to kick. This simplicity has ensured its place as the game of the masses on virtually every continent.

Football was the dominant spectator sport in Saudi Arabia in 1957, the year that Osama bin Laden was born. His father, the self-made billionaire businessman Mohammed bin Laden, even gave financial support to local clubs in Jeddah. Given this early connection with the sport, and a well-documented interest in it through the years, it is all the more incredible that four decades later, Osama should be prepared to destroy one of its finer moments for his own evil ends.

Mohammed bin Laden was of Yemeni extraction, the son of a farmer named Awad bin Laden who, during the early 1900s, lived near the town of Tarim in the Hadhramaut, a region situated on the southern tip of the Arabian peninsula. Awad's ancestors had been given a strip of land by the King of Yemen in recognition of the family's support during the nationalist struggle against the occupying Turks. Awad and his family farmed their land and he was also a skilled beekeeper, a valuable accomplishment in a region where bees thrived, and where honey and wax were an important part of the economy.

Though not a wealthy man, in 1928 or 1929, Awad bin Laden was able to afford a visit to Jeddah, the west-coast port of the Kingdom of Saudi Arabia. He went on the Hajj, the annual pilgrimage to Mecca that forms one of the chief tenets of the Islamic faith.

At the time, Jeddah was one of the peninsula's most important seaports and the only major city on the Red Sea. After fulfilling his religious duties, Awad turned his attention to seeking opportunities for work in Jeddah, not for himself but for Mohammed. He was determined that his eldest son should have a better chance to get on in life than he might receive in his homeland. So, before leaving on his return leg to Yemen, Awad sought out a senior Yemeni official at Jeddah and won from him a pledge that Mohammed would have a job if he could get himself to Jeddah. According to family members, several months later – probably late in 1929 or early 1930 – Awad purchased a single passage for his son on a cargo boat travelling from the Yemeni port of Mukalla to Jeddah.

Mohammed was quickly employed on the quayside as a porter, a low-paid job. But he was bright and quick to spot an opportunity. He networked, made contacts for the future and waited. One morning, as he was unloading a vessel, he was approached by a Jordanian who wished to buy a property in Jeddah and needed to find an agent. The young dock porter knew an agent and organised an introduction. The subsequent large purchase led to Mohammed receiving a commission, equivalent to a year's salary for a porter.

By this time Mohammed had made up his mind about the path he wished to follow. Jeddah was going through its most astonishing period of expansion and Mohammed saw his future in the construction industry. He hired some obsolete construction equipment, and used his by now impressive contacts to win a major construction contract for the Jeddah government.

He and his fledgling business went from strength to strength during 1934 and 1935 as Jeddah's boom continued unabated. In less than two years his construction firm employed hundreds of labourers and he had expanded outwards too, taking contracts in Taif, Mecca, Medina and elsewhere. Within a decade of arriving in Saudi Arabia, Mohammed was a millionaire. Such was his importance in Jeddah that he was known to King Abdul Aziz ibn Saud, the founder of the modern Kingdom of Saudi

Arabia, and to Crown Prince Saud. Indeed, it was the Crown Prince who launched him as the anointed contractor for the ruling family and therefore the country as a whole.

In 1948 Prince Saud was planning a grand new palace when Mohammed offered to take on the job for half the price of the lowest quote that he had received. Within 18 months, with Mohammed personally overseeing the work, a breathtaking palace rose up on a patch of barren desert outside Riyadh. Al Nariyah Palace was awe-inspiring, though not built or finished in what outsiders might consider to be the best of taste. The gates of the palace opened onto a half-mile avenue of tamarisk trees, bordered by vast flowerbeds and grass-covered lawns. A 200-room Mediterranean-style palace sat centre stage, filled with an uncompromising mishmash of furniture. Dotted liberally around the palace and its grounds, huge aviaries stocked with songbirds generated a chorus of natural song. Each evening, 25,000 coloured light bulbs illuminated the entire complex. One writer described the scene as a 'vast sparking patchwork mantle . . . the vast compound shimmered magically in the darkened desert as though dropped down by some passing genie . . . '

Mohammed bin Laden's reasoning was shrewd. Although he took a loss on this first job, it was an investment that would pay rich dividends. King Abdul Aziz eventually sired a total of 43 'official' sons and an unknown number of official daughters and illegitimate children from concubines in his harem. Each wanted a palace, and most of them turned to Mohammed bin Laden to design and build it.

In 1955, Mohammed travelled to Damascus, the capital of Syria, on business. It was there that he spotted a beautiful 20-year-old woman. Her name was Hamida. The daughter of a wealthy merchant, she lived a liberal lifestyle with a freedom that had allowed her to develop her own personality and a circle of friends that stimulated her socially and creatively. Without compromising her modesty, as dictated by Islam, she loved dressing in clothes from designer shops and had her own style. In private, she painted in oils; her work was of sufficient quality that her father toyed with the idea of staging an exhibition of her paintings.

Mohammed enquired about her family. He paid a visit to her father to offer his respects and express an interest in her future. Soon afterwards a marriage with Hamida was arranged. It is not known if Hamida herself was happy with the union initially. While the thought of conservative

Jeddah must have been abhorrent to her, Mohammed was a handsome and wealthy man.

Very quickly, however, everything went sour. Hamida found the restrictions of living in Jeddah unbearable and was unprepared for the ill-tempered competition between Mohammed's wives, ex-wives and concubines for his favour. Unable to leave the family compound on her own, she became virtually a prisoner in her own home – anathema to a woman used to a measure of freedom.

Her son Osama was born during the summer of 1957, the 17th male child of a clan that would ultimately number 24 boys and 30 girls. Osama was Hamida's first and last child by Mohammed. Even while she was pregnant her position within the family had deteriorated. So handsome a prize, she was now ostracised by her husband and the many women who also shared his life. Within family circles she was spitefully nicknamed 'Al Abeda' (the slave) and Osama was soon cruelly branded 'Ibn Al Abeda' (son of the slave).

By the time of Osama's birth, Mohammed had forbidden Hamida to come into his sight and, as a result of her estrangement, Osama's mother was forced into a background role in his life. Whenever Mohammed was in residence in the main house, she retreated to an outhouse and remained there. Osama was cared for by nurses and nannies instead of by his mother. A sensitive child, this situation scarred Osama for life. Starved of affection as he grew up, he realised that the attentions of a nanny were not the same as the love of a mother.

Although they might have meant no malice, around the family home Osama's siblings found his Achilles heel and teased him constantly about his parentage and roots. The taunt 'Ibn Al Abeda' was bandied around often in Jeddah. The more his brothers made fun of him, the further he distanced himself from them emotionally. It became one of the roots of his later problems, forcing him to look elsewhere for acceptance.

Due to his difficulties at home, Osama turned in on himself. Those who knew him at the time remember him as an awkward and shy boy, characteristics some interpreted as weakness. Because of this he was ridiculed by his siblings and shunned as a playmate. Only one thing would bring this awkward youngster out his shell. It was a passion for football, shared by most Saudi men and one of the few freedoms they were allowed.

Jeddah, the largest city in Saudi Arabia's Western Province, is the most cosmopolitan in the country. It seems to have experienced a building surge to beat all surges. In 1957 the city spread over no more than one square kilometre, and its population was about 30,000. Today, with a population of approximately one and a half million, Jeddah occupies an area of 560 square kilometres and stretches for 80 kilometres north to south along its coastline.

Life in Saudi Arabia as a whole is a stark contrast to what Westerners would recognise as normal. Religion and conservative thinking dictate the standards of everyday behaviour and life is heavily regulated and controlled by the authorities. Four decades ago it was no different. Due to the country's strict Islamic laws, freedom of expression and association were non-existent rights; political parties and independent local media were not permitted and even peaceful anti-government activities remained virtually unthinkable. Infringements on privacy, institutionalised gender discrimination, harsh restrictions on the exercise of religious freedom, and the use of capital and corporal punishment were also major features of the Kingdom's woeful human rights record.

Capital punishment was applied for crimes including murder, rape, armed robbery, drug smuggling, sodomy and sorcery. In most cases, the condemned were decapitated in public squares after being blindfolded, handcuffed, shackled at the ankles and tranquillised.

Saudi courts continued to impose corporal punishment, including amputations of hands and feet for robbery and floggings for lesser crimes such as 'sexual deviance' and drunkenness. The number of lashes was not clearly prescribed by law and varied according to the discretion of judges. It could range from dozens of lashes to several thousand, usually applied over a period of weeks or months.

The government heavily restricted religious freedom and actively discouraged religious practices other than the Wahhabi interpretation of the Hanbali school of Sunni Islam. Laws were zealously enforced by the Mutawwa'in, the state religious police, known officially as the Committee to Promote Virtue and Prevent Vice.

Saudi women continued to face severe discrimination in all aspects of their lives, including the family, education, employment and the justice system. Religious police enforced a modest code of dress and institutions from schools to ministries were gender-segregated.

During Osama's childhood cinema was banned. Television would not reach the kingdom until the 1970s – when its introduction would cause riots – and children's playgrounds were all but unheard of.

One of the few pleasures open to the masses – or male masses at least – was football. Osama first joined kickabouts with his brothers as a youngster of perhaps eight or nine. The vast, palatial and landscaped compound in which Mohammed bin Laden based his family had ample space for a small impromptu pitch and most afternoons the Bin Laden boys could be found racing around with their long traditional robes hitched up enjoying a game.

Despite his lowly status in the family pecking order, Osama loved the game and was a better player than many of his elder siblings. He was one of those first picked when teams were selected. He loved to play an active role but, as he grew into a tall teenager, Osama found his natural place at the back of the pitch. In addition to his height, he found he was blessed with good hands. He became a goalkeeper.

It was in this role that he first found the attention he so craved. As the anchorman, his contribution was central to the outcome of a match. A good performance brought Osama backslapping and kind words from his peers, a few fleeting moments of acceptance by his teammates and, more to the point, sowed the seeds of a passion that he has carried with him throughout his life.

Despite his emerging talent between the posts, at home in the stifling surrounds of the family's palace in Jeddah, Osama was still generally isolated and friendless. Ten years old in 1967, he was a sad and miserable child. Attending an exclusive private school, Al-Thaghr, near his home, Osama was sulky and, although intelligent, remained on the fringes. He never spoke unless called upon and instinctively attempted to be seated as inconspicuously as possible at the back of the classroom.

An English teacher at the school, Brian Fyfield-Shayler, surfaced in 2001 to tell a British newspaper that Bin Laden was 'quiet, retiring and rather shy'. Fyfield-Shayler described a boy who was courteous – more so than any of the others in his class. Even then he stood out because he was taller than most of his classmates, a height advantage that, out of school, Bin Laden used in his goalkeeping exploits.

'He also stood out because he was singularly gracious and polite . . . he was very neat, very precise and very conscientious. He wasn't pushy at all. In fact he was quite reticent. Many students wanted to show you how clever they were, but if he knew the answer to something he wouldn't parade the fact,' added Fyfield-Shayler.

In 1967 Mohammed bin Laden was travelling home when the helicopter in which he was flying got into mechanical difficulties and crashed in the desert. He died on impact and, in the Islamic way, was buried within 24 hours. The streets of Jeddah were thronged with mourners.

It was an event that shattered Osama. His mother had been absent from his life throughout much of his childhood and now his father had also been taken from him.

The family home in Jeddah in the last years of the 1960s and into the early 1970s was a much quieter place without Mohammed filling it with his big personality. But there were also moments of joy, group holidays and family events. On one memorable occasion the sons and daughters of Mohammed holidayed in Sweden. During the trip the 14-year-old Osama fell foul of his notoriously delicate stomach with a favourite Scandinavian dish, *stekt falukorv med senap och potatis*, dried slices of thick German sausage with mustard and boiled potatoes. He had to take to his bed for a day as a result. Later in Paris, Osama had an attack of vertigo and suffered a furious nosebleed on the viewing deck of the Eiffel Tower. One summer he spent a month in England, joining his elder brothers on a one-month language course in Oxford, while in the Middle East, Osama adored Cairo and had an enduring fascination for the city. He also visited Baghdad and his mother's home city, Damascus.

While the death of Mohammed bin Laden can be seen as something of a watershed in the life of Osama, the year is also notable for another key event in his life. Aged ten, Osama was persuaded to try out for an Under-12s youth team attached to Ittihad Club, the oldest sports club in Jeddah and one of several in the city.

The Saudi Arabian government was almost excessively keen on promoting sport at this time. The point was to keep young people busy in order to protect the grip on power by the House of Saud. It was something that many Communist countries and one-party dictatorships in the late 1960s understood well: that people needed to be kept busy to prevent them thinking too much about politics. The Communist Bloc especially used sport as a means to keep their youth away from any political or intellectual activity. In many Communist countries, state budgets for sport were second only to military expenditure.

This government emphasis on sport also had another devious aim: the creation of a feeling of national 'Saudi' belonging which would supersede and even marginalise the sense among the country's youth of being part of a wider Arab and Islamic nation. For this purpose Saudi Arabia aimed to train a sport-oriented youth which would enable the Kingdom to have a viable and successful presence in international events, especially the Olympic Games.

The Kingdom's commitment to sport ensured not only the provision of a wide range of sporting facilities for the male population as a whole – females up to the age of puberty may only participate in sports behind closed doors – but also improvements in performance in a number of sports. The Saudi Arabian Olympic Committee was established in 1964 and in 1984 Saudi Arabia sent a team to the Olympic Games for the first time, competing in football and rifle shooting. In more recent years, Saudi athletes have distinguished themselves in many sports including athletics, cycling, handball, table tennis, football and volleyball.

But it is in football that the Kingdom has made most inroads as a genuine participant of international standing. In 1984, the same year that the Saudi national team made its first appearance in the Olympic football tournament in Los Angeles, the Saudi football team won the Asian Games Gold Cup. They repeated that success four years later.

In 1994, the Saudi team qualified for the World Cup finals in the United States and latterly went on to qualify for the finals in France in 1998 and Korea/Japan in 2002.

Football was first introduced to the Kingdom in 1928, by the Ittihad Club. In 1959, the Saudi Football Federation was established and later joined the Federation Internationale de Football Association (FIFA), the international governing body of football. The road to becoming a powerful name in Asian football began during the years when Osama bin Laden was playing between the goalposts in Jeddah, when, for the first time, the government began placing political emphasis on sport.

During the 1960s, Mohammed bin Laden, well known as a

philanthropist, especially in his home city, had been a generous patron at Ittihad Club. It is perhaps, therefore, no surprise that Osama quickly made an Under-12s side fielded by the club. But those familiar with the youngster's footballing prowess say that his selection for the team was not nepotism. He had the skills.

Over the ensuing years, as Osama bin Laden went through the trauma of losing his father and the break-up of the family unit that followed, he was increasingly listless and unhappy. He sulked through his early teens. One constant remained in his life, however, and that was his love of football. He was firmly attached to Ittihad Club, a part of their youth programme, and he dreamt of reaching a sufficient standard to join the full squad when he turned 16.

He might even have made it. At the age of 14 he won a regular place in the Under-16s team. A fit and relatively strong boy, his reactions were quick and he could also kick the ball well. In addition to keeping goal, he loved the opportunity to shine in dead-ball situations such as penalties, free kicks and corners. Then, as now, Ittihad Club had a big reputation in Saudi Arabian football and won silverware most seasons. So being number-one goalkeeper for the club's youth team certainly proved that he had some skill.

By the time of Osama's 14th birthday and his elevation to a senior youth squad position in 1971, the game was becoming increasingly important to government policy. Prince Faisal, son of the future King Fahd, a long-time Bin Laden family friend, was installed as Head of the Youth Department with ministerial rank in 1971. Himself keen on football, he went on also to serve as president of the Arab Football Union, Arabian Olympic Committee, Arab Sports Union and Head of the National Committee on Drugs Control. The government gave Prince Faisal all the support he needed. With a massive annual budget for his ministry, he embarked on what amounted to a 30-year programme of construction of sport facilities. He aimed to develop sports villages, centres and stadiums, clubs and fully staffed training facilities of all kinds to meet the nation's needs.

At the same time, Prince Faisal undertook to have the Saudi national team and clubs join international federations in a variety of sports. He hired Western sports coaches at great cost, notably for football. In 1976 he even brought in Jimmy Hill, who was given a special budget with prerogatives to train young people everywhere in the Kingdom. Hill's efforts were commended, but his sojourn in the Kingdom came too late to have an effect on Osama's budding career as by then he had turned his back on football.

Before Hill's arrival, between 1971 and 1973, Osama briefly flourished in Saudi Arabia's footballing revolution. Following a brief period away from Jeddah when he lived with his mother in the Saudi provincial city of Tabuk, Osama won back his place. He now played as a regular in goal for Ittihad Club Under-16s. In 1973, he was 15 years old and just over six feet tall. His progress was marked and Osama was selected as part of a Youth Department coaching programme.

A former Egyptian First Division goalkeeper was based in Jeddah during the 1972–73 season. A handful of senior youths were apprenticed to him for intensive training, and he also travelled around the Western Region of Saudi Arabia giving masterclasses for larger groups. Osama was looked at closely at this time and, while a child from a wealthy and well-connected family would not be apprenticed, he was placed under the personal supervision of the Egyptian.

By all accounts Osama improved further under this tutelage and he might, like so many other youngsters, have dreamt of a career in sport. For Osama, however, it was an all-but-impossible dream. Saudi Arabian football was not professional at the time and most players held down full-time jobs. But young men with Osama's background did not play football after their childhood. Like his brothers, he was expected to complete his education, go on to college and then to university. Eventually he would join the family firm.

Nevertheless, Osama still hoped that Ittihad Club would be forthcoming with a contract to join the senior squad so that he could play as a semi-professional.

Given his emotional state when he was at home, it is not surprising that descriptions of Osama given by his teammates at Ittihad Club contrast sharply with those of family members. They could even be describing different people; in a way, they were. At home Osama was isolated, remote and uncommunicative. Among his footballing friends he was outgoing, popular and given to telling jokes. Between the goalposts Osama was a talented youngster and, as such, he was accepted and respected.

What might have become of Osama had he been able to pursue his dream of joining the seniors and winning a place in the famed Ittihad Club side we can only speculate. They remained one of the most competitive teams in Saudi Arabia, regularly winning trophies and claiming the Saudi Arabia First Division title. The semi-professionals who played for Ittihad Club, while not the millionaire idols of the modern-day English Premiership, had massive followings. In a country where there was little else in the way of popular diversions, club footballers were highly regarded.

Osama completed his secondary level education at the age of 16 in early 1973. Had his family seen the other side of him, as his friends at Ittihad Club did, they might have decided on a different course of action for his future. But, in an effort to salvage a teenager whom they regarded as difficult, introverted and remote, Osama was sent to Beirut to further his studies. It was to prove his undoing in more ways than one.

Three

Sex, Lies and . . . Pelé

In 1973, aged 16, Osama bin Laden had completed his secondary schooling with a set of excellent exam results. He was pleased and was looking forward to moving on to higher education in Saudi Arabia, allowing plenty of spare time to pursue his football.

By this time, Osama believed that he was on the verge of switching from the junior to the senior squad of Ittihad Club. The club itself will not speculate on events of nearly 30 years ago, but in Jeddah a few of those around Ittihad Club at the time, and in a position to recall the junior goalkeeper, remember his enthusiasm. Most days after school, a smart family-sized Mercedes-Benz would arrive at the gates of the club and a driver in uniform would drop the budding goalkeeper off for his training. On weekends and holidays he arrived earlier and trained longer and harder than most at the club. His talents may have been adequate, but his commitment was unquestionable and many in the management were impressed with him.

Of course, it did nothing to hinder his chances that his late father had been a benefactor and that the family continued to support good causes, among them Jeddah's sports clubs. But to suggest that this support was the only reason that Osama progressed in the junior ranks would be to belittle one of the few pure things that he ever focused upon.

As he approached the end of his eligibility to play in the junior ranks, high-level discussions about his future were going on in the boardrooms of Ittihad Club. On a number of occasions he turned out in practice sessions with the senior team, playing alongside and against First

Division stars. Osama did nothing wrong in these informal trials and the club management were seemingly heading towards offering him a contract.

Circumstances intervened, however. The Bin Laden family was apparently not keen that a son of the revered Mohammed bin Laden should be playing football publicly: in their culture, to do so would be an insult to his status in the community, and theirs.

And then there was also the question of his personal attitude. The committed, friendly and happy goalkeeper on the field and at the club was transformed into a pathetic, sulking and unhappy boy when at home. Seeing only this side of him, his family believed he needed a new direction and resolved that the next stage of his education should encompass something of a fresh start. The family reasoned that Osama needed a change in environment. They thought he would be comfortable in Lebanon, so this was where they planned to send him.

Lebanon as a nation has always embraced a cosmopolitan outlook and attitude alongside its Arabic heritage. Most Lebanese are Arabs and the country's official language is Arabic, although French and English are also widely spoken. A member of the Arab League, Lebanon had taken little part in the Arab–Israeli Wars that followed Israel's creation in 1948, but the stage had been set for future problems when many Palestinians fled Palestine and settled in South Lebanon. Its own internal equilibrium had been shaken in 1958 by a rebellion against pro-Western policies when US forces were called in briefly.

The population, then as now, is divided between Muslims, both Sunni and Shiite, and Christians (mainly Maronites). For the most part, the communities lived in peaceful coexistence. Following independence from France in 1943, Lebanon prospered. Its inhabitants embraced both Eastern and Western cultures, creating a unique and attractive society. Lebanon had a service-oriented economy and Beirut, a free port, was the financial and commercial centre of the Middle East. In the early 1970s, Beirut had a sense of life and energy that was almost palpable. It was known as the 'Paris of the Middle East'.

The city was also a thriving educational centre for the Arab world. The American University was considered one of, if not the very best university in the Middle East. Each scholastic year, thousands of students from all over the region flocked to Lebanon and its high-quality schools.

One of the best of these was the prestigious Broumanna High School. It had a pedigree dating back almost exactly a century to a time between 1869 and 1874 when Elijah G. Saleeby opened the first school in Broumanna, a remote village overlooking Beirut. It was called the 'Darlington Station' because it was backed with Quaker subscriptions from Darlington, England. Education at Broumanna High School was based on the Quaker principles of non-violence, equality, the spirit of service and encouragement of the pursuit of higher standards through enlightened methods. The school did not indulge in mission activity, and the students' beliefs in their own religions were never challenged or deprecated.

In 1889, the village was linked by a new road down the mountain to Beirut below and at the turn of the century, the school built the first tennis court in the Middle East. Over the next 50 years, Broumanna High School emerged as arguably the leading school in the country, and one of the best in the Middle East. Taking private students, its reputation allowed it to choose the best teachers and attract a high class of students, extending its reputation further.

At the time of Osama bin Laden's arrival the school was at its zenith. There were so many foreign students clamouring for places in its classes that in 1967 a new boarding house had been opened by HRH the Duke of Edinburgh.

Flying to Beirut International Airport aboard a Middle East Airlines aircraft in late August 1973, Osama was bitter. He did not want to be in Lebanon. His heart lay in Jeddah and at Ittihad Club, with his football career. But in Arab society one followed the family line, and once the elders of the Bin Laden clan had made up their minds there was nothing left but to pack his bags.

For one of such privileged birth, there was no question of boarding and sharing facilities with other boys. Instead, a spacious apartment was rented in the village and a maid and a cook hired to see to Osama's needs. He had a full-time driver and a top-of-the-range silver Mercedes-Benz 350 SE. He now looked the part that his birthright dictated – that of a Saudi aristocrat.

Arriving in the Lebanese capital, he was in for a shock. An innocent

37

young man, wrapped up in football, he was confronted for the first time by an open, liberal society – a considerable contrast to the conservatism of Jeddah where he had lived all his life. For the first time, he found himself in the company of women other than his immediate family, and they were not completely covered in black *abayas*. In Saudi Arabia women were forbidden to wear make-up or perfume. They were veiled in public and even at home wore extremely modest outfits. Lebanon presented an astonishing contrast. In the street he could see women with bare legs and arms, wearing make-up and perfume. It was certainly an eye-opener.

Osama settled well. At Broumanna High School he is recalled as being bright and attentive to his studies. He was polite and well behaved, unusual praise for a child from Saudi high society who were normally spoilt and arrogant.

Glad to be free of the family ties that constricted him in Jeddah, Osama was also able to pursue his dream of playing senior level football. Although he did not join a school football team, contemporaries recall that he had trials with Nejmeh Sporting Club, one of the leading clubs in Lebanon since the sport had been organised properly, and regarded as the Manchester United of Lebanon during the early 1970s, prior to the Civil War.

Having been on the fringes of one of Saudi Arabia's top clubs, Osama believed that he could gain a place in a Lebanese team, and with standards in Lebanon being lower, he set himself the target of breaking into the Nejmeh squad. It was an ambitious undertaking. Nejmeh had joined the Lebanese First Division in 1951 and made a major breakthrough in the 1970s with the rise of one of the greatest teams ever assembled in Lebanese club football, including Mohammad Hatoum, brothers Hassan and Mahmoud Shatila, and Habib Kammouneh. In 1971 the team won the Lebanese Cup and, despite cancelled seasons and competitions, they also claimed the League Championship in 1973 and would go on to achieve a double by retaining the League in 1975.

By the end of 1973, Osama had made contact with the club and, it appears, had begun joining in training sessions. Club officials recall a tall, agile Saudi youngster. A little shy, he still managed to make himself known and seemed to genuinely enjoy the game. However, the club's existing goalkeeper was highly regarded and was part of the Lebanon national squad, so there was little prospect of him warming the bench while Nejmeh used an untried and inexperienced foreigner.

Osama seems to have accepted this and persevered for a time. Later, in 1974, other interests would dim his interest in football but during the spring and early summer he was happy simply to be training and playing informal matches against Nejmeh squad members.

It was his involvement in Nejmeh Sporting Club that brought about one of the strangest twists in Bin Laden's life. In 1974, Lebanon received a visit by no less than the world's greatest player, Pelé. The Brazilian was at the height of his game and arguably the most famous man on the planet at the time. Ever the sporting ambassador, while he was on holiday in Beirut, Pelé arranged a visit to Lebanon's top club. Among a long line of players and officials that lined up to shake his hand was one Osama bin Laden. Years later, visitors to the office Osama bin Laden occupied at the family's corporate headquarters in Jeddah often commented upon the framed picture on his desk that showed a smiling and somewhat awed Osama shaking the hand of Pelé.

Away from football, Osama now found himself settled and coming to grips with his life, perhaps for the first time now that he had escaped the noose that was his home environment in Jeddah. At Broumanna High School his first academic year was an outstanding success. Classmates recall an intelligent boy with an inquiring mind. While the school itself refuses to release details of his time there, it is believed that his grades left him around the top of his classes. His attitude in class was markedly different from that in Al-Thaghr school at home. As he revelled in the freedom of leaving the rest of the clan behind, Osama thrived.

Outside school there were also plenty of new things to explore and, between appearances at Nejmeh Sporting Club training sessions, he fell in with a robust crowd of fellow students who set out to enjoy themselves. Sport was a major focus of their activities. They went swimming in the sea and ice-skating in Beirut. They were frequent visitors to the cinema, which was banned in Saudi Arabia. In the winter they travelled high into the mountains to go skiing.

And there was also something completely new. The cosmopolitan village of Broumanna was crammed with restaurants, bistros, cafés and bars. The village was popular with the upper classes in Lebanese society.

Its mixed Christian–Muslim population was swelled by thousands of students intent on enjoying their non-school time to the limit. In an era of community and tolerance, this made for a lively atmosphere in which there were no outsiders.

For the students of Broumanna High School, the bars lining the main mountain road that threads through the village were a focal point. Many were too young to be drinking legally. But the school itself could only exert minimal control of its students' after-hours activities and there was an understanding that a civil drinking culture would be tolerated as long as it did not get out of hand and did not interfere with studies.

Soon after his arrival in Lebanon, Bin Laden tried alcohol for the first time when he joined his new-found friends for a beer. The tables they occupied would invariably become littered with green Heineken bottles. At 16, Osama quickly became a feature within the student drinking scene and this was to lead to his meeting his first girlfriend. Ironically, 'Rita' was a Christian, the daughter of the owner of one of the bars that Osama and his friends frequented most evenings. The family remains in Broumanna to this day but for obvious reasons does not wish to discuss the relationship.

With his unshaven face, good looks and imposing height, Osama stood out. He was also obviously well bred and showed good manners, which was another unusual trait among the bawdy students of Broumanna and part of his attraction for 'Rita'. They remained close for some time, even joining her family for dinner on occasions. There were no prejudices in Lebanon during those pre-war days and a Saudi Arabian Muslim courting a Lebanese Christian was seen as quite acceptable, even to Rita's parents.

By the early summer of 1974, ensconced in his Lebanese haven, life for Osama bin Laden had never been better. For the first time in his life he had a circle of friends and was accepted as an equal. He had explored most of the popular venues of the drinking scene in Broumanna, had a number of haunts that he frequented and was comfortable with life as a regular, where he knew staff and fellow customers on level terms.

Even Osama's footballing prospects were improving. At Nejmeh Sporting Club, the management was increasingly impressed with his commitment. He had shown himself not in the least bit unsettled by an apparent lack of opportunities. Although he had not gained a contract or squad place within the country's leading club, Osama had benefited from regular training. He was fitter than before and had worked closely with senior goalkeepers at Nejmeh on his technique and vision of the game.

Towards the end of the school year, Osama considered plans that had originally been made for him to return to Saudi Arabia for the summer break. He felt that things were different now and contacted his family requesting permission to stay on through the summer. They readily agreed. With news of this, the organising committee at Nejmeh Sporting Club began to give Osama serious consideration. For a second time, his goal of playing senior level football was almost within his grasp.

Just when things were going well, his life took a sudden change of direction. The catalyst for this was a chance meeting with some older Saudi Arabian men who were on holiday in Beirut and intent upon having a good time. He encountered the men in Lebanon's famed Casino Du Liban, the only casino in the Middle East. On meeting Osama bin Laden, they recognised the family name and, true to the Arabic tradition of networking and earning favours, invited him to accompany them the following evening.

Osama was acquainted with the casino. Roulette he disliked; blackjack was more his game, although he was far from enchanted with gambling and preferred sitting in the bar while his friends lost their money. However, the events of the following evening introduced him to another side of Beirut that he had not bothered with previously, a side that was to captivate him.

Even today, nearly a quarter of a century on, mentioning the Crazy Horse to a Lebanese will elicit a smile, a roll of the eyes or shake of the head. What the Moulin Rouge is to Paris, the Crazy Horse was to Beirut – and more. Even by Beirut's bawdy standards at this time, this was a place that stood out. Hundreds of beautiful, available girls of all colours, all races; all looking to party with a man for the evening and night.

With its raucous atmosphere and plush decor, the Crazy Horse was a magnet for rich Gulf Arabs shuttling into Lebanon. They partook of the pleasures offered at this notorious fleshpot along with government ministers, not a few church ministers and members of the higher end of society who made their way to this extraordinary nightclub each evening.

Osama joined the party for the first time during the summer of 1974. He was just 17 and impressionable, and that night became entranced by a nightlife that he perhaps never knew existed. Quaffing whisky and champagne with his new friends, the young Saudi enjoyed the attentions of a mature woman for the first time. Rita was sweet, but the women who frequented the Crazy Horse were overtly sexual and, what was more, they were available for the right price. From that night onward he was hooked.

When the new school term commenced at Broumanna High School in September, teachers discovered that the calm, presentable and studious Osama bin Laden of the previous year had disappeared. In his place was a man with other things on his mind. He neglected his work and was often absent from classes. Out of school he abandoned the casual look of jeans and a T-shirt in favour of something more fashionable. On the few occasions he was spotted in Broumanna he would be wearing flared suits and kipper ties. His hair was getting longer, as dictated by fashion, and he sometimes had a moustache. A sporty silver Mercedes-Benz 230 coupé now joined his old Mercedes-Benz 350 SE, and the 17 year old thought he looked the part whizzing around the city, despite the need for a driver to take the wheel.

The same sweeping changes shook up Bin Laden's private life. He distanced himself from the student scene and almost disappeared from the bars in the village. Those with whom he had previously skied, bowled, swum and gone to the cinema were now shunned. His new friends were more grown up and had adult entertainment on their mind.

The same fate befell Rita. He dumped her without a word. She was no match for the prostitutes from the Crazy Horse and his generous allowance from Jeddah ensured he was never short of companionship as required.

Unfortunately for Bin Laden, this new direction in his life also interfered with his football, up to now the most important part of his life. Bar-hopping until early morning, he was often drunk and, when returning home, he was usually accompanied by a prostitute. Normally, his partying would only come to an end as the first streaks of dawn were illuminating the sky over Lebanon.

This, of course, hampered his training with Nejmeh Sporting Club. He began to miss training sessions. All the goodwill built up by his consistency and willingness to take the hard route to a place in the club's First Division squad unravelled. The management quickly realised that he had other priorities on his mind.

Although Bin Laden did continue to make occasional appearances at training during the second half of 1974, it was clear that his commitment had waned and his fitness suffered through consistent alcohol abuse. Arriving at Nejmeh the morning after one of his binges, his reactions between the goalposts were noticeably slower.

When Nejmeh Sporting Club lost interest in him as a future prospect, his dreams of becoming a footballer were snuffed out. But in the alcoholic haze that was Beirut for him now, he did not even notice.

Instead of the camaraderie of his student drinking friends or even the banter of his teammates at Nejmeh Sporting Club, Bin Laden now sought the approval of a new set – Lebanese café society. Notoriously snobbish and unwilling to fully accept outsiders, they nevertheless appeared to take this Saudi Arabian to their hearts. The shallowness of the lifestyle or the fickleness of those friendships didn't seem to matter. It was not his flash clothes, sports car or personality that attracted so many, but his wallet, which was always full and always open to sycophants. Bin Laden always picked up the tab and while on the prowl it was he who bought the rounds, growing increasingly extravagant as he became increasingly drunk.

A circle of Lebanese men about his age surrounded him and among them he felt accepted. He was the leader of the pack and he seemed either not to care or not to notice that it was singularly his money that won him this status.

He now often appeared in public with a woman on his arm. They seldom lasted for longer than a couple of evenings and more often than not were professional escorts. Bin Laden is recalled as having a thing for European blondes, but whether the women were Lebanese, Arab, European or American, it seemed to mean little. With money to burn, he cruised the clubs in the seedier parts of the Lebanese capital and indulged to excess.

His table at the Crazy Horse, reserved every night, was stocked with champagne and whisky. As host to assorted hangers-on, Bin Laden drank both with gusto and, normally, to excess. The most outstanding girls in the club would make a beeline for the Saudi when he did arrive: he was a big tipper when drunk and openly paid girls just to sit on his knee while he flirted.

Another of his haunts was the Casbah, which was similar to but less salubrious than the Crazy Horse, while Bin Laden also had a standing reservation at Eve's, a club where the girls were more varied.

But it was the Crazy Horse that remained his clear favourite and as many as three nights a week he and a table of freeloaders would settle down to an evening of binge drinking and womanising. Bin Laden always picked up the tab, and at the end of the night it was rare for him to leave without one or two girls draped over him. Drunk on a potent mixture of Dom Perignon and Black Label, the Saudi might have been worse for wear and heading for a hangover in the morning, but he would rarely miss an evening on the town in Beirut.

Bin Laden's world came crashing down on 13 April 1975, the day that Lebanon began its slide into the morass of a civil war. Gunmen killed four Phalangists during an attempt on leader Pierre Gemayel's life. The Phalangists retaliated by attacking a bus carrying Palestinians through a Christian neighbourhood, killing around 26 of the pasengers. The next day fighting erupted in earnest, with Phalangists pitted against Palestinian militiamen.

The labyrinthine, confessional layout of Beirut's various quarters facilitated random killing. Most Beirutis stayed inside their homes during these early days of battle, and few imagined that the street fighting they were witnessing was the beginning of a war that was to devastate their city and divide the country.

The government was paralysed and the fighting worsened. As various other groups took sides, the fighting spread and the militias became embroiled in a pattern of attack followed by retaliation, including acts against uninvolved civilians. Although the warring factions were often characterised as Christian versus Muslim, their individual composition was far more complex.

In safe, out-of-the-way Broumanna, Bin Laden tried to reassure his family when the inevitable call to return to Jeddah came. But he could not defy them and, with a heavy heart and foreboding about returning to the bosom of the family, he left Beirut in May 1975, never to return.

Four

A New Playing Field

Osama bin Laden returned to his home in Jeddah in May 1975 less than happy to have left behind his hedonistic lifestyle. It is likely that he would have been recalled to Saudi Arabia, war or no war, considering the fact that news of his antics had begun to filter back to his family. A son of Mohammed bin Laden behaving in this way would not be tolerated; indeed, of all Mohammed's offspring, the black sheep Osama was the only one to go off the rails in this manner.

Back in the family fold, Bin Laden discovered his fate. He was to be enrolled in the King Abdul Aziz University in Jeddah, where he would be made to study economics and Islamic economics before joining the family firm.

The rigid school environment was anathema to the free-living new student, and almost instantaneously he rebelled and joined Saudi Arabia's growing faction of disenchanted youth. Young, privileged Saudi Arabians were not slaves to the religious dogma of their parents, and most had at least had a brief taste of freedom abroad. It was a classic recipe for rebellion, the young sharing few common bonds with their old-school parents.

Wahhabiism was conservative by nature and Saudi Arabia was socially backward as a result. Television was stubbornly opposed by the religious right; something as basic as cinema was outlawed. Most archaic was the way in which both sexes were systematically separated. Men and women were segregated in workplaces, schools, restaurants and on public transportation. The law forced women to wear the *abaya*, a black garment covering the head, face, and body. These and many other codes of behaviour were served up as religion when, in fact, the Koran was being twisted as a means to oppress the people. Just as the Koran's message would later be corrupted to support the dogma of Islamic fundamentalism, the Saudi Arabian authorities used the Muslim holy texts as a means of control.

Against this backdrop, Bin Laden entered a world known only to the sons and daughters of the rich and powerful in Saudi Arabia. It was a world of private drinks parties and call girls smuggled into the country. While the rest of the Saudi people lived their lives with the hand of the authorities on their shoulder, the same government turned a blind eye to the children of the Al Sauds, ministers and wealthy families rebelling, as long as this remained a private affair.

Just as he had before, Bin Laden got drunk and slept with prostitutes in abundance. He attended university to keep the family quiet, but his life was built around nightly parties in high-walled villas on the outskirts of Jeddah where he and his fellow 'rebels' could indulge themselves with booze and sex parties.

Around this time Bin Laden also reappeared at Ittihad Club. Before leaving for Lebanon two years earlier, he had almost reached a point when the club was willing to offer him a contract for its First Division squad, but by the latter part of 1975, aged 18, his form had regressed. His excessive lifestyle and lack of exercise had left him carrying a noticeable paunch. He was not the player he had been and, although he was welcomed and encouraged to train at Ittihad Club, there was never any serious chance that he would finally get the contract that he had worked so hard for earlier in his life. Intermittently, he would surface there and pull on the green jersey for a training session or practice game and even to go through the motions of joining in circuit training with the other hopefuls, but he never recaptured his earlier level of commitment.

At university, he was also just going through the motions, although his considerable intellect was able to carry him through and his grades were satisfactory enough not to be a problem.

The morass of booze and paid-for sex that was Osama bin Laden's life finally changed for the better in 1977 thanks to an intervention by his 25-year-old brother Salim. Salim had been one of their father's favourites and he more than any of his siblings had attempted to keep the family together and functioning following the death of Mohammed in 1967. This had included adopting a parental approach to the black sheep of the brood. Salim had seen the destructive path that his younger sibling was on and in 1977 took a proactive approach in attempting to draw him back into the fold. He insisted that his brother join him on the Hajj pilgrimage.

One of the basic tenets of Islam is that a Muslim, if he can afford it and is physically capable, perform Hajj at least once in his lifetime. The Hajj is important because it takes the believer to the place that is the centre of the Islamic world and the site where the divine revelations collected in the Koran were received. But most important, the Hajj is a continuation of what, according to Islam, is one of the oldest religious rituals. During Hajj, a Muslim recalls the events that shaped important persons in Islamic history.

Salim hoped that the time he spent in close proximity with Osama would give him a chance to speak at length on the way his life was going and offer some advice that might lead him to choose a new direction. What happened was much more startling. At some point during the Hajj, the Bin Laden brothers entered caves that were said to be the place where the Prophet Mohammed had received visions of the Angel Gabriel. Here, Osama seems to have had a religious epiphany. He was profoundly moved; the minutes spent there were to influence the course of the rest of his life – and the history of the world – in a way that could never have been imagined.

He returned to Jeddah a different man. The 20 year old gave away his smart Mercedes SL 450 convertible, the most tangible evidence of his former playboy self. He turned his back on his drinking friends, tore up the telephone numbers of the prostitutes and returned to the mosque. He prayed five times a day, threw himself into his studies at King Abdul Aziz University and showed an interest in the family firm. Salim gave him an office and he filled his spare time in religious contemplation or learning the company ropes under the instruction of his elder brother. Osama graduated in late 1977 and joined the company at senior management level. He recalled later: 'I studied economy at Jeddah University, or the so-called King Abdul Aziz University, and then worked at an early age on roads in my father's company.'

For a time this was his life, and he was happy with it. As far as those who knew him then recall, he never drank another drop of alcohol and his sexual excesses were terminated. Over the following two years Bin Laden transformed himself into a model Saudi citizen. He worked hard and attended the mosque. Looking back with the benefit of hindsight, however, those around him can see that Bin Laden had lurched from liberalism to conservatism. His feelings of remorse for his hedonistic lifestyle were like a ticking time bomb. When a strong Islamic cause came along, something was always likely to happen. Enter Afghanistan.

Afghanistan is a large, land-locked Muslim country dominated by spectacular scenery and diehard tribal factional fighting. Backward and seemingly destined always to be so, it breeds a fierce independence and fighting spirit into its population.

The Communist Party of Afghanistan was first formed in 1965. The country's most influential leader at the time was Daoud Khan. Though not a communist, Khan had allied himself with the Soviets in 1954 when he asked for military aid in order to protect the border between Pakistan and Afghanistan. In 1963 Khan was asked to resign because he had increased the country's dependence on the Soviets but in 1973 he was restored to power with the help of pro-Moscow communists. As early as 1975, however, Khan began to change his policies towards the communists. He ousted several from government positions and had himself elected president to legitimise his regime.

When Soviet leader Leonid Brezhnev made a comment that the Soviets were 'controlling' Afghanistan, Khan told him: 'We will never allow you to dictate to us how to run our country and whom to employ in Afghanistan. How and where we employ the foreign experts will remain the exclusive prerogative of the Afghan state. Afghanistan shall remain poor, if necessary, but free in its acts and decisions.' He also attempted a reconciliation with Pakistan which aggravated the Soviets. As a result, in April 1978, the Afghani communists, with the help of the Soviets, assassinated Khan. Left-wing military officers then handed power over to two Marxist-Leninist political parties, the *Khalq* ('Masses') and *Parcham* ('Flag'), who together had formed the PDPA (People's Democratic Party of Afghanistan).

A new socialist government was set up, Nur Mohammad Taraki was named president and the country was renamed the Democratic Republic of Afghanistan. However, uprisings among the middle class and peasants weakened the new government. Having little popular support, the new government forged close ties with the Soviet Union, launched ruthless purges of all domestic opposition and began extensive land and social reforms that were bitterly resented by the devoutly Muslim and largely anti-communist population.

Muslim tribal-based insurgencies arose against the government and these uprisings, along with internal fighting between the Khalq and Parcham governmental factions, prompted an invasion. On the evening of 27 December 1979, an explosion in Kabul crippled the national communications system. After darkness set in, about 5,000 Soviet soldiers, who had been landing during the previous three days at Kabul International Airport, headed towards the presidential palace. At 3 a.m. the news of the formation of a new, Soviet-backed government was broadcast. For the first time since the Second World War, non-Muslim forces had occupied a Muslim country. Within days the revolt of the Muslim rebels, or Mujahideen (literally 'strugglers'), had spread to all parts of the country.

Osama bin Laden has recalled his reaction at the time. 'When the invasion of Afghanistan started, I was enraged and went there at once. I arrived within days, before the end of 1979.'

He flew to Peshawar, in northern Pakistan, the entry point for many foreigners during this period and the place where the Mujahideen could base themselves beyond the reach of the Soviets. The resistance was in a mess and still in the process of being organised, yet Bin Laden, with his money, was spotted immediately by senior Afghan leader Abdul Rasul Sayyaf, a founder of the Islamic movement. Sayyaf introduced him to Dr Sheikh Abdullah Yusuf Azzam, a man that *Time* magazine called 'the reviver of jihad in the 20th century', suggesting that Azzam and Bin Laden organised the foreigners, the so called Arab-Afghans, who wished to offer their services.

Soon after this meeting, Maktab al-Khidamat (MAK) was formed, funded by Osama bin Laden and headed spiritually by Azzam. MAK was a support organisation for Arab volunteers that organised these men into a fighting force that grew and became a highly effective branch of the

Mujahideen. A forerunner of Al-Qaeda, MAK soon had recruitment offices in US cities, London, Paris, Cairo and many other major capitals. Thousands of men travelled to Afghanistan at Bin Laden's expense, to private bootcamps in the mountains of Peshawar and then on to fight against the Soviets. It was a private army that, in terms of numbers, exceeded any other in the world. Driven by Islamic fervour, Bin Laden was also thrilled to find himself the centre of attention, a man who commanded men. He revelled in the attention and the power.

Around half of MAK's recruits, estimated to have numbered between 10,000 and 12,000, came from Saudi Arabia, while others came from Algeria (roughly 3,000) and from Egypt (2,000); the remaining thousands comprised young men mainly from Yemen, Pakistan, Sudan, Lebanon, Kuwait, Turkey, the United Arab Emirates and Tunisia.

Ironically, the USA was also involved with MAK. Soon after the conflict in Afghanistan began, the Central Intelligence Agency (CIA) launched a campaign to arm and train the Mujahideen, supported by a $500 million annual budget offered by President Ronald Reagan to fight a surrogate war against the Soviet Union.

Besides cash, the arms shipped to MAK included advanced Stinger anti-aircraft missiles. In 1986, the CIA helped build an underground camp at Khost. Despite his own wealth, Bin Laden needed the money and arms that the Americans offered him, although he recalls: 'I always hated the Americans because they are against Muslims . . . We didn't want the US support in Afghanistan, but we just happened to be fighting the same enemy.'

With US backing, the Arab-Afghans came to be the backbone of a resistance campaign that confounded the Soviets and caused high levels of human and material losses. Damage was so high that Soviet forces were reluctant to patrol at night, even in tanks, because of armour-piercing rockets that Bin Laden's forces had obtained.

This detail is true, but much of the fable created about Bin Laden's involvement is not. He remained in Peshawar most of the time and rarely entered Afghanistan at all. But he has systematically glorified his exploits in order to capitalise and create for himself the image of a freedom fighter.

In one famous story he eulogises his own invincibility. 'Once I was only 30 metres from the Russians. They were trying to capture me. I was under bombardment but I was so peaceful in my heart that I fell asleep. This experience has been written about in Islam's earliest books. I saw a 120mm mortar shell land in front of me, but it did not blow up. Four more bombs were dropped from a Russian plane on our headquarters but they did not explode. We beat the Soviet Union. The Russians fled.'

Reports from neutrals deny his participation in active duty. Those around him today, including Ayman al-Zawahiri, have succeeded, however, in making him out to be a warrior when in fact he was little more than an effective administrator.

During the second half of the 1980s he admittedly spent more time in Afghanistan and was nominally considered the commanding officer of Al-Ansar, 'the Lions' Den', one of the most important MAK bases in Afghanistan. The Arab-Afghans of Al-Ansar were among the toughest and most battle-hardened, and members of the group came into close contact with their leader. Over long nights by the covert campfire he got to know many of the men and established friendships and alliances that would last a lifetime. He absorbed their Islamic arguments and heard of their hopes that Islam in its fundamentalist form could be introduced to the rest of the Middle East through revolution. These were sentiments that stuck with Bin Laden and, spurred on by Azzam, his partner, mentor and father-figure, he began to think along the same lines. It was no longer enough to save Afghanistan. He absorbed the fundamentalist dogma and swallowed the creed of violence that fellow fighters extolled as the only way.

Afghanistan peace talks had been sporadically going on in Geneva since 1982, under the auspices of the United Nations. As the Soviets' losses grew, so did their interest in peace. On 14 April 1988 a deal was signed by representatives of the governments of Pakistan and Afghanistan. The Soviets undertook to withdraw their troops in nine months, completing the movement on 15 February 1989.

As this process went on and the puppet government crumbled, although resistance continued, MAK began to unwind. Many of Bin Laden's men wished to return home to a peaceful life. They had a true Muslim heart. They had left behind families and jobs to fight a jihad against those who threatened the Islamic world and, having succeeded, they would return to normal existence. If they disliked the system of power in their countries, they would protest, join the peaceful opposition, or even participate in the ruling regime in an attempt to change things from the inside.

Some, however, left Afghanistan burning with the desire to take with them the spirit of revolution and hatred for opponents that they had lived and breathed for so long. Bin Laden had helped them join the jihad; among others, the Americans had helped arm and train them. They were a highly capable and experienced force.

For his part, Bin Laden was unwilling to give up his status. As his brigades of fighters dispersed throughout the Middle East, he hid behind Islam in order to remain a player. 'We deal with the Islamic world as a single state and cooperate with people on a basis of righteousness and piety as far as we can,' he said. 'We are a single nation with one religion.'

The newly emerged Al-Qaeda, he said, aimed to 'unite all Muslims and to establish a government which follows the rule of the Caliphs'.

Proving that he had adopted Dr Abdullah Azzam's creed, Bin Laden now stated that he believed that the Islamic world should be ruled by one caliphate and if necessary a caliphate should be created by force. Al-Qaeda's ultimate goal was to overthrow 'corrupt' Muslim governments. He would then abolish state boundaries and create a super-state.

While the United States had engineered a bloody defeat for the Soviets, it had also set in motion a wave of rabid Islamic fundamentalism that would reverberate around the Middle East, even reaching as far as New York and Washington over the next decade and a half.

Five

An Own Goal in Algeria

Algiers is a thriving port; anyone looking down from the hills on the attractive sweep of its bay might find it hard to think of the capital of Algeria as a 'dangerous place'. Yet Algeria is associated in the minds of many not with its significant slice of the Sahara or with its vast size – at 2.4 million square kilometres it is Africa's second largest country – but with the violence of two brutal wars, one of which still rumbles on. These struggles stretched throughout the better part of the twentieth century and have dragged a nation of high potential towards tragic social and economic ruin.

On the morning of 5 July 1830, Algeria was a sleepy backwater on the fringe of the Ottoman Empire. By the end of that day it had been occupied by a French expeditionary force and one of the most ruthless colonisations of recent history had begun. The French settlers took all the best land, often replacing staple crops with vineyards, and the indigenous population were reduced to a state of dispossession, poverty and cultural disrepair.

Resettlement programmes were implemented by the French government, who used land-owning incentives to draw French citizens to the new colony. The French introduced a wide variety of measures to 'modernise' Algeria, imposing European-style culture, infrastructure, economics, education, industries and government institutions on the country. The colonials exploited the country's agricultural resources for the benefit of France. The concept of French Algeria became ingrained in the French collective mind, while among Algerians, a hatred of the

French became equally fixed. These attitudes were to have grave repercussions.

The period of early French influence over the country saw a huge drop in Algeria's native population, as it fell from around 4 million in 1830 to only 2.5 million in 1890. The French colonials looked upon the Muslim populace as an inferior underclass that had to be tightly controlled. Muslims were not allowed to hold public meetings, bear arms or leave their districts or villages without government permission. Although they were officially French subjects, they could not become French citizens unless they converted to Christianity.

It was a brutal, racist regime, which alienated the vast majority of Algerians. The French attempt at cultivating an Algerian elite backfired badly. The few who were schooled in French academies and infused with French values suffered the inherent racism of their French overlords and became the nucleus of the Algerian nationalist movement.

In the 1920s the tide began to turn. The first Algerian nationalist newspaper appeared in 1924 and the nationalist movement emerged between the two world wars, first simply demanding civil rights for the indigenous peoples of Algeria. The French government proposed making concessions to the nationalists but these were blocked by colonial reactionaries in the National Assembly. The colonials resisted any reform that would give Muslims equal rights until, after 20 years of fruitless non-violent activism, the frustrated nationalists formed a militant anti-French party in 1939 called the Friends of the Manifesto and Liberty, combining Islamic and communist factions.

By the end of the Second World War, Paris had a clear choice: negotiate a settlement or give in to the colonials' demands and suppress nationalism. The French government revived attempts to bring Muslim Algerians into the decision-making process but these were too little and too late to offset deep-rooted colonial attitudes and a growing mutual hatred between the French and their Muslim subjects.

Algerian Muslim attitudes had hardened and an increasing number of nationalists were calling for armed revolution. By the 1950s revolutionaries were being hounded into exile or hiding and the stage was being set for the Algerian War of Independence.

In March 1954 a revolutionary committee was formed in Egypt by Ahmed Ben Bella and eight other Algerian exiles – this became the nucleus of the Front de Libération Nationale or National Liberation Front (FLN).

In the early morning hours of All Saints' Day, 1 November 1954, FLN *maquisards* (guerrillas) launched attacks in various parts of Algeria against military installations, police posts, warehouses, communications facilities, and public utilities. From Cairo, the FLN broadcast a proclamation calling on Muslims in Algeria to join in a national struggle for the 'restoration of the Algerian state, sovereign, democratic, and social, within the framework of the principles of Islam'. The French Minister of the Interior, the socialist François Mitterrand, responded sharply that 'the only possible negotiation is war'.

It was the reaction of Premier Pierre Mendès-France, who only a few months before had completed the liquidation of France's empire in Indochina, which set the tone of French policy for the next five years. On 12 November, he declared in the National Assembly: 'One does not compromise when it comes to defending the internal peace of the nation, the unity and integrity of the Republic. The Algerian departments are part of the French Republic. They have been French for a long time, and they are irrevocably French . . . Between them and metropolitan France there can be no conceivable secession.'

The populist guerrilla war paralysed the country and forced the French government to send more than 400,000 troops in an attempt to put down the uprising. However, the courage and ruthlessness of FLN fighters and their tactical use of terrorism dragged the French into the reactive trap of bloody reprisals against the general population, which served to galvanise the Algerians and strengthen the revolution. This sealed the hatred of the Algerians against France, an enduring hatred that would lead, years later, to a willingness among extremist Algerians to commit terrible atrocities on mainland France.

The cruelty and brutality of French colonial forces and the government's inability to find a political solution turned world opinion against France. Their use of concentration camps, torture, and mass executions of civilians suspected of aiding the rebels isolated France and elicited invidious comparisons with totalitarian regimes and Nazism.

The French government was caught between a colonial policy based upon racism and exploitation and its place as a standard-bearer of democracy. On the one hand, the French colonials were intransigent. On the other, the world community was calling for a cessation of hostilities and a political solution.

In 1958 colonials and French army officers joined forces to bring down the French government and demand the return of General Charles de Gaulle to lead France to victory over the Algerian Nationalists and ensure the preservation of French Algeria. De Gaulle returned to power with the support of the political extreme right but, realising that the war could never be won, announced a referendum allowing Algerians to choose their own destiny, be it independence or remaining part of France.

De Gaulle's move was seen as betrayal by the colonials, the extreme right wing and certain parts of the military. The Organisation Armée Secrète (OAS), a militant terrorist organisation, was formed by an alliance of these groups with the aim of overthrowing the General. The OAS carried out a ruthless terrorist campaign against the FLN and the French government but they were doomed to failure. In March 1962 a ceasefire was negotiated between the government and the FLN, and De Gaulle's referendum was held in July.

The Algerian people spoke with a single voice. They voted for independence. Following the referendum the French departed from Algeria en masse. By the end of the year most colonials had evacuated the country that had once been French Algeria.

The Evian Accords, which were signed in 1962, gave Algeria immediate independence and guaranteed French aid to help reconstruct the country. The French Sahara with its oil resources was also handed over to Algeria. In return, the FLN guaranteed protection and civil rights for the French Algerians choosing to remain in the country and the option of choosing either French or Algerian nationality after three years.

In preparation for independence, the Community Nationnal de la Revolution Algerienne, under Ben Bella, met in Tripoli in May 1962 to work out a plan for the FLN's transition from a liberation movement to a political party. The Tripoli Programme called for land reform, the large-scale nationalisation of industry and services, and a strong commitment to non-alignment and anti-colonialism in foreign relations. The platform also envisioned the FLN as a mass organisation broad enough to encompass all nationalist groups. However, deep personal and ideological divisions surfaced within the FLN as the war drew to a close and the date for independence approached. Competition and confrontation among various factions deprived the FLN of a leadership that spoke with a single voice and showed the cracks that would split the country apart again in the future.

The creation of the Democratic and Popular Republic of Algeria was formally proclaimed at the opening session of the National Assembly on 25 September 1962, but eight years of war had left a terrible legacy. There had been more than one million Algerian casualties and nearly two million Algerians had lost their homes. Having been deprived for over a century by the French of any but the most minimal opportunity to become involved in their country's infrastructure and institutions, Algerians had been turned into a subclass of servants, unskilled labourers and peasants. The departure of the French left the country without the skilled labour needed to keep the country running.

At the same time, the internal conflicts within the FLN deepened and a power struggle between various factions flared up. Ben Bella, with the support of Colonel Houari Boumédienne, the National Liberation Army chief of staff, emerged as the winner and was elected the first president of Algeria in 1962. The country he presided over had been established as an Arab-Islamic socialist state with a single party political system, the FLN being the only legal party. Ben Bella made some attempts to revive Algeria, but eventually succumbed to the vanity of international politics and domestic autocracy. He failed to get to grips with the country's hard-core problems of unemployment and the deficit of technical and administrative skills that prevented the country becoming a modern nation.

In 1965, Houari Boumédienne, now Defence Minister, staged a bloodless coup that removed Ben Bella from power. He formed a 26-member Council of Revolution which became the country's highest government body, with the army displacing the FLN as the overriding political influence.

Although Boumédienne held the reins of power tightly, he also established a more collective form of leadership that finally began to come to grips with building a modern Algeria. The country's oil resources were developed and an industrial sector was established. Education and literacy became a government priority and agricultural land reform continued. In the process, the Boumédienne government developed a socialist political system which was codified in a constitution in 1976. Under the new constitution Boumédienne was elected president of Algeria, a position he held until his death in 1978.

When Boumédienne's chosen successor, Colonel Benjedid Chadli, was elected president, he began to relax the government's authoritarian practices and made a genuine attempt to solve some of the country's problems. Chadli also pardoned Ahmed Ben Bella in 1980 and released him from house arrest. However, for all his liberal tendencies, Benjedid was a product of the FLN-military elite and was re-elected in 1984 because he ran unopposed.

After independence the Algerian government had asserted state control over religious activities for purposes of national consolidation and political calm. Islam became the religion of the state in the new constitution and the religion of its leaders. No laws could be enacted that would be contrary to Islamic tenets or that would in any way undermine Islamic beliefs and principles. The state monopolised the building of mosques and the Ministry of Religious Affairs controlled an estimated 5,000 public mosques by the mid-1980s.

But even these measures were not enough for everyone. As early as 1964 a militant Islamic movement called Al-Qiyam emerged, becoming the precursor of the Islamic Salvation Front of the 1990s and the Islamic fundamentalist groups that later supported Osama bin Laden. Al-Qiyam called for a more dominant role for Islam in Algeria's legal and political systems and opposed what it saw as Western practices in the social and cultural life of Algerians. Although militant Islamism was suppressed at this time, it reappeared in the 1970s under a different name and with a new organisation. The movement began spreading to university campuses, where it was encouraged by the state as a counterbalance to left-wing student movements.

By the 1980s, the movement had become even stronger and bloody clashes erupted at the Ben Aknoun campus of the University of Algiers in November 1982. The violence resulted in the state cracking down on the movement, a confrontation that would intensify throughout the 1980s and early 1990s.

The rise of Islamism had a significant impact on Algerian society. More women began wearing the veil, some because they had become more conservative religiously and others because the veil kept them from being harassed on the streets, on campuses, or at work. Islamists also prevented the enactment of a more liberal family code despite pressure from feminist groups and associations.

The socialist government's move towards secularism and continuing one-party rule fed a fundamentalist backlash that gave rise to widespread rioting in 1985. Islamic leaders branded the government 'a band of atheists' and called for a return to an Islamic government. Islamists gained increasing influence, in part because the government was unable to keep its economic promises.

Chadli responded by initiating a programme of reforms, removing many old-guard Boumédienne partisans from government and making moves toward privatisation and reduction of socialist centralisation. But it was too little and too late.

During the 1980s, despite a worsening political and social crisis, many of the country's Islamists left Algeria for an altogether more urgent struggle – the Soviet invasion of Afghanistan. In the days and weeks following the communist incursion, thousands of men headed for the conflict from all over the Arab region. By the spring of 1980, six months after the Soviets invaded, up to 1,000 Algerians were believed to be circulating in Peshawar. Eventually, Algerians would make up the second-largest contingent in the so-called Arab-Afghani fighting force.

Many were simply good Muslims, outraged at the fate that had befallen an Islamic country and even willing to give up their lives in order to see the Soviet Union ousted. Teachers, students, soldiers, civil servants, labourers and peasant farmers, the volunteers were drawn from all social classes, income groups and ages. United by their anger, hundreds besieged the airport in Algiers to board a handful of Algerian air force flights laid on to take them to airports in Karachi or Islamabad in Pakistan. Others, unable to find passage on government flights, or afford their own passage on scheduled flights to Pakistan, took a longer route, travelling by boat via the Horn of Africa.

Among the throng of Muslim supporters drawn from all over the Middle East, men from Algeria stood out. The independence war against France had created a pool of fighting talent within Algerian Nationalism and especially the National Liberation Front. The socialist government's oppression of its people had driven the freedom fighters of the 1960s from the ranks of nationalists into the more narrow boundaries of the Islamist cause. Silent for decades, the men of this movement and a generation of younger Algerian Islamists found their outlet in answering the rallying call presented by the Soviet occupation of Afghanistan.

The hardliners were a breed apart from the green, inexperienced volunteers, most of whom had never fired a gun, least of all seen action in a war zone. The older Algerian Islamists were battle-hardened and experienced.

Such highly trained individuals were to prove the vanguard of Osama bin Laden's Maktab al-Khidamat (MAK) during its early operations. As MAK grew into a formidable fighting group, it came to be regarded as one of the elite parts of the Afghan Mujahideen throughout the decade-long fight. The Algerians themselves rose through the ranks to lead the Arab-Afghan forces at every level, and their leader surrounded himself with many trusted Algerian advisers and strategists. Men such as Tayeb Messaoudi and Abderrahmane Dahane, who would become known as Tayeb El-Afghani and Dahane El-Afghani respectively due to exploits during the Afghan campaign, established their reputations during the war.

Others such as Abdelkader Hachani, Djamel Zitouni (alias Abou Aberrahmane Amine), Haydar Abu Doha and Mohammad Bensakhria were just a few of the Algerians fighting among the Arab-Afghan legions who would later surface elsewhere, fighting the government in Algeria. The man who would initially lead the bloody Islamist insurgency in Algeria, Mourad Sid Ahmed, alias Djafaar El-Afghani, was another who honed his fighting skills and built a reputation fighting for Osama bin Laden.

When the conflict in Afghanistan ended, the return of well-trained Islamic fundamentalists had an almost immediate destabilising effect on Algeria – as indeed it did on the stability of many Middle Eastern states, including Egypt and Saudi Arabia.

Algeria's economic crisis had also deepened in the mid-1980s, resulting in, among other things, increased unemployment, a lack of consumer goods, and shortages in cooking oil, semolina, coffee and tea. Women waited in long lines for scarce and expensive food; young men unable to find work hung about on street corners in frustration.

An already bad situation was aggravated by the huge drop in world oil prices in 1986. This severely affected Algeria's export revenues. Since most consumer goods, including between two-thirds and three-quarters of the food supply, were imported, the population as a whole suffered a severe decline in living standards when the government decided to compensate for the shortfall in export revenues by reducing imports.

Dismantling Algeria's state capitalist system seemed to Chadli the only way to improve the economy. In 1987 he announced reforms that would return control and profits to private hands, starting with agriculture and continuing to the large state enterprises and banks.

But the government's credibility had fallen dramatically. The manifest failure of world socialism and the government's failure to solve the country's increasing social and economic problems encouraged more and more Algerians to seek solutions in their Islamic traditions.

Notwithstanding the introduction of reform measures, incidents indicating social unrest increased in Algiers and other cities as the economy foundered from 1985 to 1988. The alienation and anger of the population were fanned by the widespread perception that the government had become corrupt and aloof.

The waves of discontent crested in October 1988 when a series of strikes and walkouts by students and workers in Algiers degenerated into rioting. When the violence spread to Annaba, Blida, Oran and other cities and towns, the government declared a state of emergency and began using force to quell the unrest. Throughout the country, thousands of Algerians attacked city halls, police stations, post offices, anything that was seen to represent the regime or the FLN. The disorder and violence were a protest against a corrupt and inefficient government and a discredited party.

The riots raged for six days. By 10 October the security forces had restored a semblance of order. By unofficial estimates, more than 500 people had been killed and more than 3,500 arrested.

The same day, Chadli addressed the nation, accepting blame for the suppression and offering promises of economic and political reform. His hand had been forced. In an effort to regain the political initiative and contain the damage to his regime, Chadli lifted the state of emergency, recalled the tanks, and announced a national referendum on constitutional reform.

The stringent measures used to put down the riots of 'Black October' engendered a ground swell of outrage. Islamists took control of some areas. Unsanctioned independent organisations of lawyers, students, journalists and physicians sprang up to demand justice and change. In response, Chadli conducted a house cleaning of senior officials and drew up a programme of political reform.

In December he was offered the chance to implement the reforms when he was re-elected, albeit by a reduced margin. A new constitution, approved overwhelmingly in February 1989, dropped the word 'socialist' from the official description of the country, guaranteed freedoms of expression, association, and meeting and – at the Islamists insistence – withdrew the guarantees of female rights that appeared in the 1976 constitution.

Though apparently liberal, the 1976 constitution had still been rigged in favour of the FLN, severely limiting the activities of opposition parties. The FLN was not mentioned in the 1989 document at all, however, and the army was discussed only in the context of national defence, reflecting a significant downgrading of its political status. Politics were reinvigorated in 1989 under the new laws. Newspapers became the liveliest and freest in the Arab world, while political parties of nearly every stripe vied for members and a voice. The party which benefited most from this was the Front Islamique du Salut or Islamic Salvation Front (FIS), which came to play a significant role in Algerian politics.

The authorities tried to placate Islamist supporters, appointing officials who were sympathetic to the underground movement and its values to senior positions in government, especially in ministries connected with religious issues, and encouraging the widespread construction of mosques. Their task was complicated by the return of thousands of Islamic fighters from Afghanistan. Ardent and fanatical Muslims, they swelled the ranks of Islamic conservatives in the country, spreading talk of rebellion throughout a population that was tired of its corrupt, elitist administration.

Only one thing prevented open rebellion during the late 1980s: the prospect of free elections and a chance for the people to speak through the ballot box in a multi-party, open election for the first time.

The rising tide of Islamic activism swept the FIS to an overwhelming victory over the FLN in municipal and provincial elections in 1990. The goal of the FIS was nothing less than transforming Algeria into an Islamic state. After decades of socialist incompetence and social and religious repression, the vast majority of Algerians embraced FIS doctrines and handed the party a stunning first-round victory over the FLN in the December 1991 general elections.

With the prospect of the FIS in control of the parliament after the second round of elections, the secular and military elite forced President Chadli's resignation, halted the electoral process and suspended parliament. A High Committee was established with Mohammed Boudiaff named as president. The world community had applauded Algeria's move toward multi-party democracy, but the possibility of an Islamic government taking control had made many Western nations think again.

Thus the stage was set for one of the world's worst-ever civil wars, a situation that was to bring Osama bin Laden closer to the Algerians, an alliance that would see both parties embroiled not only in a struggle for Algeria but actively seeking to ignite a worldwide Islamic revolution.

Six

Corporate Sponsorship, Terror Sponsorship

Osama bin Laden flew home to Saudi Arabia from Afghanistan in the early summer of 1989. As he put it: 'I returned to road construction in Taif and Abha. I brought back the equipment I had used to build tunnels and roads for the Mujahideen in Afghanistan.'

This is the story that he maintains to this day, although it has become clear that his office in the family corporate headquarters was used more for promotion of armed revolution in the Middle East than for building roads. He was consumed by the power he had enjoyed in Afghanistan and while he wished to maintain the network he had built up there partly in order to advance the militant Islamic cause, he also wanted to preserve his power base.

On his return to Jeddah, Bin Laden discovered that he had become a celebrity in his home country. The region's media had for years celebrated the millionaire Mujahideen, a man so committed to jihad that he left behind a lifestyle of luxury to live in caves and fight the Soviets. It was not quite like that, but it was good copy and Bin Laden was only too keen to cooperate with such reporting if it enhanced his image.

The result was star status in Jeddah and around the Kingdom. The attention and adulation that he craved was finally a reality. People recognised him wherever he went. It was better than being a mere footballer. He was a religious hero, a champion of jihad, and this meant more to ordinary Muslims than simply keeping a clean sheet in a league match. Bin Laden found himself the focus of hero worship. Many shops in Jeddah displayed posters of the local idol in their windows and people would stop him in the street to ask for his autograph. He lapped it all up. But gradually the adulation faded. When he walked along the street, people would offer a simple greeting instead of asking for words of wisdom or an anecdote from his time battling the evil Soviets.

For whatever reason – perhaps due to his convictions, or maybe in a desperate bid to remain in the spotlight – from his office in Jeddah, he began developing his network of fundamentalist contacts around the region. One place that was desperate for his support was Algeria and his relationship with the opposition there was to form the cornerstone of his European operations in later times.

Things did not go so well in Saudi Arabia. He clashed with the government, who saw his continuing promotion of jihad as an embarrassment and a source of strain in relations between neighbouring countries and allies. The final straw came when Iraq invaded Kuwait. Bin Laden proposed that he and his Arab-Afghans could defend Saudi Arabia and free Kuwait. When King Fahd ignored his proposal and the government failed to take up the offer, he went on a collision course with the Al Saud family and soon was forced to flee into exile. By 1991 Bin Laden was ensconced in Khartoum, the capital of Sudan, where he had been welcomed with open arms.

In 1989, a military coup had brought General Omar Hassan al-Bashir to power in Africa's largest country. He was backed by the Sudanese spiritual leader Dr Hassan al-Turabi. Sudan was (and still is) in the grip of a terrible civil war – the longest-running internal conflict in history – with a body count that was climbing towards two million. But al-Bashir and al-Turabi had bigger issues on their minds than the plight of their people. Al-Turabi in particular wished not only to create a secular Islamic regime in his own country but also to aggressively export Islamic fundamentalism throughout the world, a project that would see the country placed on the USA's list of state sponsors of terrorism in August 1993.

During the 1990s he turned Sudan into a base for Islamic terrorism, opening the country to dozens of groups, including Hezbollah, Hamas, Palestinian Islamic Jihad and Egyptian Islamic Jihad, among others. It was al-Turabi who encouraged Osama bin Laden – the rising star of Islamic fundamentalism – to settle in his country.

Soon after Bin Laden's arrival he and al-Turabi became engaged in a host of commercial partnerships, carving up government spending for themselves through a handful of plum national infrastructure projects. Al-Hijrah for Construction and Development Ltd was the main commercial front and it took on a handful of contracts that aimed to develop Port Sudan, well placed on the coast of the Red Sea. Al-Hijrah was contracted to build the new airport at Port Sudan and later a four-lane main artery to link Khartoum with Port Sudan.

Bin Laden's construction empire also moved into railways and took contracts on Rosaires Dam. His import–export firms, Wadi al-Aqiq and Ladin International Company, took major government contracts, notably to supply the government army, and he was also involved in banking, aircraft fuel, mining, agriculture and gold prospecting.

The stability and profits of his commercial empire, coupled with support from his hosts for his terrorist activities, offered Bin Laden a secure foundation from where he could now concentrate on his central interest and his old hobby.

By the time that Bin Laden arrived in his new home he had been largely estranged from football for more than a decade. Religion had become his passion and during the intervening period jihad had been an all-consuming drug. If anything from his goalkeeping days remained, it was a faded memory of innocent times in the distant past.

What brought him back to football, for a time, was his sons. By 1991, his eldest son, Abdullah, was ten and keen on the game. While Bin Laden was politicking in Saudi Arabia, his family had remained at home in Jeddah. Like their father before them, during childhood kickabouts they had discovered a taste for the sport. Abdullah was not as precocious as his father during childhood, but nevertheless loved to play the game.

Arriving in Sudan brought a profound change in Bin Laden's life. He had found a place where he could settle, develop his business empire, expand his Al-Qaeda organisation and plot terrorist atrocities without the intrusion of the authorities. Without harassment from the law, he lived the life of a gentleman terrorist. His suite of offices in Khartoum overlooked the Blue Nile, while he resided with his family at one of several farms on the outskirts of the Sudanese capital. Now, with a congenial domestic environment, Bin Laden spent more time at home than circumstances had ever before permitted. Having missed much of Abdullah's early years while fighting in Afghanistan, he resolved to find time in a busy schedule to embrace family life.

Life on the farm suited Abdullah who, like his father several decades before, enjoyed outdoors life. Football was one of the games played regularly in the Bin Laden household.

Even at a such an early age, Abdullah had his own bodyguard. He was watched over by a couple of armed guards at any one time. Naturally he formed attachments to them, and Abdullah often shunned his younger siblings to play ball with his much older companions.

Bin Laden was delighted to discover that Abdullah shared his passion for football. He always had international cable television wherever he lived and Sudan was no exception. Amid the hundreds of pirated channels available to them from networks throughout Asia, Europe and North America, Bin Laden joined Abdullah in following some of the senior leagues around the world. Gradually, his own interest in the sport was rekindled.

In Sudan, football, like most other aspects of normal life, had suffered during the nightmare of a civil war that had raged since 1983, claiming two million lives and bringing famine and disease to large areas of the country. 'Without peace in any place, nothing, especially football, can be properly organised,' said Mohammed Abdallah, head of the technical committee of the Sudanese Football Federation. It was a sad state of affairs for a nation that had been one of the few African states that might have been able to break into the international arena.

Along with Egypt, Ethiopia and South Africa, Sudan was a founding member of the Confederation of African Football (CAF). Influential Sudanese footballing officials Dr Abdel Halim Mohammed, Abdul Rahim Shaddad and Badawi Mohammed were present at the foundation meeting, held in Portugal. At home, the trio helped build one of the most progressive leagues in Africa in the 1950s and a coaching system that looked sure to begin turning out top-class players.

Dr Halim proposed Sudan, which had gained independence in January 1956, as the host of the inaugural tournament of the African Cup of

Nations, as they were constructing a new national stadium. The offer was accepted and on 10 February 1957, just over four months after the new Khartoum Stadium was opened, the inaugural tournament kicked off with three nations competing, South Africa having been refused participation because they would not abide by the condition to send a multi-racial team. Egypt emerged victorious, beating Sudan 2–1 and Ethiopia 4–0.

Thirteen years later, Sudan hosted the tournament a second time and reached the pinnacle of its footballing achievement. After a qualifying programme played in Khartoum and Wad Medani, the hosts met with mighty Ghana in the final. The Ghanaians were the kings of African football at the time and were playing in their fourth consecutive African Cup of Nations final. Dr Mohammed's youth programme in Sudan had paid dividends by this time, however, and the hosts defeated Ghana by a solitary goal in Khartoum Stadium.

With a young national squad and a major tournament victory, hopes were high that Sudan might be that elusive African team that broke the mould and went on to compete with the South American and European powerhouses. It was not to happen.

The last time Sudan competed in a major tournament was in the 1976 Cup of Nations in Ethiopia. After the victory of 1970 the national team management and squad were torn apart with internal division. Part of it was tribalism: there are more than 300 tribes in Sudan. But the real sticking point was religion. The Sudanese people come from numerous different ethnic backgrounds, mainly Arab in the north, and African in the south. About 60 per cent of the population are Muslim, 25 per cent are Animist, and 15 per cent Christian. Petty jealousies and religious divisions surfaced.

By the early 1980s a new management team had been installed. Young talent was still being produced, but then came the civil war. This stunted the development of the country's available talent and, in addition to the sub-standard nature of the league, scouts from overseas clubs found it difficult to visit.

The domestic divisions were ravaged. Sometimes clubs could not fulfil their engagements. At other times they found their players drafted into the armed forces or even senselessly murdered as part of the conflict. But the sport would never die and throughout the war football was still played at grass-roots level. Even in remote villages in the desert, children gathered for a game, often risking their lives and limbs due to the hidden threat of landmines.

By the time that Osama bin Laden arrived in the country in 1991, the sport was doing its best to cope with the crisis. League football was dominated by two clubs, Al-Hilal and El-Merreikh. By 1991 the former had won the league 15 times in 27 years. Only once in those 27 seasons had a club other than Al-Hilal and El-Merreikh won the championship.

In spite of the statistics, Osama and Abdullah adopted the little-known Al-Ahli as their club. Based in Khartoum, the club had never won a major trophy, frozen out by the big two, and had never had the big behind-the-scenes patronage of the armed forces and senior politicians that sustained Al-Hilal or El-Merreikh. But they were, nevertheless, an above-average side and usually won more games than they lost.

Observers at the time recall that a Bin Laden entourage would occasionally visit Al-Ahli Stadium, a small, untidy affair that had seen better days. More often, however, it was just Abdullah and his armed escorts, with perhaps some of his smaller brothers in tow, who were there.

By 1992, Bin Laden had extended some support to Al-Ahli via sponsorship. His Al-Hijrah for Construction and Development Ltd, now one of the country's major contractors due to government patronage, became involved in the club, sponsoring many advertising hoardings around the ground.

Undoubtedly it was partly vanity which spurred Bin Laden to become involved and splash his presence so publicly. The few thousand working-class Sudanese who followed Al-Ahli for the love of the game had little to do with his grand scheme.

For Osama bin Laden had other things on his mind than building a winning football club. He wanted to build the most comprehensive and powerful Islamic fundamentalist group in the history of modern Islam – Al-Qaeda. With millions of dollars at his disposal, he maintained training camps in both Afghanistan and Sudan. His loyal Arab-Afghan fighters trained and based themselves at these, awaiting his orders and the opportunity to fight. Many would be dispatched to Bosnia and Chechnya. Several thousand Arab-Afghans also worked within his commercial empire, as labourers.

But the bases and the men, with their battle experience and expertise in areas such as explosives, arms and guerrilla warfare, were also central to Al-Qaeda's wider interests. Like his hosts, who threw open their borders to like-minded terrorist groups from other countries, Bin Laden sought to bring organisations with a similar identity under his influence. Few could come close to his financial muscle; none had access to such substantial amounts of technically advanced weaponry as Al-Qaeda, nor the expertise. His overtures were almost impossible to resist and gradually a handful of groups came under Al-Qaeda's umbrella – which by definition was Bin Laden's umbrella.

One of these groups was Egyptian Islamic Jihad, headed by Dr Ayman al-Zawahiri, an alleged paedophile who would later come to serve as number two within Al-Qaeda and be one of Bin Laden's most trusted advisers.

Then there were the Algerians. Civil war was now claiming lives in the country, thanks in no small part to the support of Al-Qaeda. During 1991 most senior Algerian opposition leaders visited Khartoum to sit with Bin Laden. These included men who already had a relationship and a history with him. Of these, the most prominent was Mourad Sid Ahmed, alias Djafaar El-Afghani, one of the men who had been closest to their leader in Afghanistan, and the first acknowledged leader of the Armed Islamic Group (GIA). Another welcome in Sudan was Abdelhak Layada, leader of the GIA's Arab-Afghans, who had won himself a fierce reputation while battling the Soviets.

Mansuri Messaoudi, a founding member of the Algerian opposition, was noted as being close to Bin Laden, while another man, Djamel Zitouni, was prominent but only emerged as a leader in 1994 after the death of several of his predecessors. Another future head, Sherif Ghousmi, was observed in Bin Laden's presence on many occasions.

But one of the most interesting of the Al-Qaeda chief's Algerian associates was Abou Khalil Mahfoud. He was another who would go on to be leader of the GIA. But what is most interesting about Mahfoud is that he was a paid informer for French intelligence. His treachery to the Islamist cause would come to play a major role in the life of Osama bin Laden.

Egyptian Islamic Jihad and the GIA were not the only groups brought under the Al-Qaeda umbrella, but almost from the beginning they were the pair closest to Bin Laden's heart. They could not have been more different. While Egyptian Islamic Jihad was a remote group, on the fringes of the country and with little popular support, reduced to limited operations; at the beginning of the 1990s the GIA was at the forefront of a bloody civil war in which Bin Laden revelled. It was the closest that Islamic fundamentalism came to replicating the active thrust and struggle of a war zone. Bin Laden delighted in being a patron and major supporter of the Islamists in Algeria; the slide into anarchy and towards a death toll that would eventually come close to 100,000 was in no small part a result of this liaison.

In response to growing social unrest during the late 1980s, the Algerian government had passed a new constitution reducing the role of the ruling FLN and allowing limited political opposition for the first time since independence. This legislation had formally legalised political parties and established a system of proportional representation in preparation for the country's first multi-party elections.

Proportional representation was intended to benefit the FLN, but the new electoral code did the exact opposite, magnifying the plurality of the Islamic Salvation Front (FIS) in the local and regional elections of 12 June 1990. The FIS, competing with more than 12 political parties and numerous independent candidates in the country's first multi-party elections, captured the greatest share of the anti-FLN/anti-regime protest vote and won a crushing victory.

Despite the devastating defeat dealt to the ruling party, the June 1990 results went undisputed by the government and the new council members assumed their positions. The date for national legislative elections was advanced to the following June and the country appeared well on its way towards achieving the region's first peaceful transition of power to an opposition party in a multi-party system.

In March 1991, the government passed a bill increasing the number of parliamentary seats while altering their distribution to achieve over-representation in rural areas where the FLN's base of support rested. The bill also created a two-round voting system – if no party received an absolute majority in the first round, only the top two candidates would participate in a second-round run-off. The likely candidates in such a run-off would be the FIS and the FLN. The FLN anticipated that the general public, faced with a straight choice, would favour the FLN's more traditional and secular platform over a party that represented a radical Islamist view.

Most parties responded angrily to this distortion of the electoral process. The FIS decried the targeting of the Islamist party by laws prohibiting the use of mosques and schools for political purposes and laws severely restricting proxy voting by husbands for their wives. Many secular opposition parties denounced the electoral changes as leaving only 'a choice between a police state and a fundamentalist state'.

In June 1991, when campaigning for the country's first national multi-party elections deteriorated into public demonstrations against the electoral reforms, the president called in the army to restore order, declared martial law, dismissed the government, and postponed the parliamentary elections.

Specifically targeting Islamists, the military arrested thousands of protesters, among them FIS leaders Abbassi Madani and Ali Belhadj, who were later tried and sentenced to 12 years in prison. The military also took advantage of the situation to reassert its influence in politics, calling for the resignation of the prime minister and his cabinet. A new caretaker government was named, consisting largely of technocrats – a conservative elite drawn from the top ranks of the civil service and former state-owned enterprises.

Two months before the rescheduled elections, in October 1991 the government issued a new electoral law, the bias in which was hardly better disguised than that of the March reforms. The law increased the number of seats in the assembly, redistributed them to favour FLN strongholds and omitted earlier provisions facilitating the participation of independent candidates. Moreover, most of the FIS political leadership was in prison and all newspapers were banned. Once again the government sought to ensure that the results of the elections would be to its, and the military's, liking.

In November 1991, even before the first round of elections, armed Islamic resistance to the government and its electoral games had emerged. Two of Osama bin Laden's Arab-Afghans, Tayeb Messaoudi (Tayeb El-Afghani) and Abderrahmane Dahane (Dahane El-Afghani), led an attack on a military post at Guémar in south-eastern Algeria. They butchered some 15 young conscripts guarding the post and got away with large quantities of arms and ammunition.

Dahane was killed in an operation outside Biskra in December 1991, just a week before the election. Tayeb was arrested in the course of a military operation in February 1992 at El-Oued and was executed in 1993.

What is clear from this is that, even before the election, the Islamists were under no illusions that the Algerian government would play by its own biased rules. With Bin Laden's help they were already preparing for war.

Nearly 50 political parties participated in the first round of the elections on 26 December 1991. The FIS won 188 of the available 232 seats in the National Assembly outright in the first stage of a two-stage election and was expected to win eventual control of the Assembly. Its popular support was 25 per cent, well down on the 55 per cent of the municipal elections, but it was clear that the FIS would be able to form a government. Much to the anxiety of the ruling regime, it threatened to call for an Islamic state in Algeria. This immediately brought it into head-on collision with the fundamental tenets on which the Algerian state had been based and revived fears among the country's military leadership that Algeria's revolutionary ideals and their vested interests in the status quo would be threatened.

The result was another clear victory for the FIS and an equally clear humiliation for the FLN, which once again performed poorly. The FIS appeared certain of achieving the two-thirds parliamentary majority necessary for constitutional reform.

The military, however, quickly affirmed its unwillingness to see power transferred to a political party it regarded as a threat to the security and stability of the state. Calling the government's position toward the Islamists 'accommodating', the army called for the president's resignation and the suspension of the scheduled second round of elections.

The situation was extremely tense and troops were put on alert throughout the country, tanks and armoured cars were deployed throughout Algiers and military checkpoints were set up.

President Chadli resigned on 11 January, citing 'widespread election irregularities' and a risk of 'grave civil instability'. An executive body appointed by the military immediately assumed full political authority, suspending all other political institutions, voiding the December 1991 election results and postponing future elections.

This coup initially went virtually unchallenged because even the FIS leadership discouraged its followers from provoking clashes with the military. A period of relative calm, however, was as deceptive as it was brief. Within a month Islamists struck back against the military crackdown. At the time these were fleeting attacks, staged by small groups of Arab-Afghans and outraged but inexperienced radical FIS members, supplied from Sudan. But quickly the government's opponents began to get better organised.

The new government reimposed a state of emergency, banned the FIS in March and dissolved the communal and municipal assemblies, most of which had been controlled by FIS members since the June 1990 elections. The government also banned all political activity in and around mosques and arrested Islamist activists on charges ranging from possession of firearms to promoting terrorism and conspiracy against the state. Military courts tried and sentenced the activists to lengthy imprisonment or death, without right of appeal or full awareness of the charges brought against them.

Thousands of demonstrators were taken to makeshift prison camps in the Sahara Desert, while hundreds of others were detained for questioning and often tortured. Most of the remaining top FIS leadership were arrested and thousands of rank-and-file party members were forced underground. Other reversals of the democratisation process followed. The press, which had slowly gained freedom, was quickly reined in, the National People's Assembly was indefinitely suspended and the omnipresent and ubiquitous *mukhabarat* (state security service) resurfaced.

The repressive military actions taken by the government against the Islamists were reminiscent of the military force used by the French colonial authorities against the nationalists during the War of Independence. Thousands of troops were mobilised and assigned to cities and all major urban centres. Curfews were imposed, removed and reimposed. Entire neighbourhoods were sealed off because of police sweeps and other searches for accused 'terrorists'.

Islamists retaliated by killing military personnel, government officials and police officers by the hundreds. Some 600 members of the security forces and hundreds more civilians and Islamist demonstrators were killed in the first 12 months following the coup. The majority of

Algerians, meanwhile, were caught in the middle, distrusting the army as much as the Islamists.

The government, citing a need to 'focus its full attention' on Algeria's economic problems, warned that it would not tolerate opposition. In reply, FIS leaders warned that the popular anger aroused by the political suppression was out of their control. Hardliners in the FIS split from the more moderate pragmatists, criticising the FIS leadership for cooperating with the government. As a result, radical factions replaced the relatively moderate FIS leadership, now long imprisoned. Meanwhile, other independent and radical armed Islamist groups arose, impatient not only with the government but with the FIS itself. The new radicals, FIS officials acknowledged, were beyond FIS control.

Out of this political morass emerged an organised armed Islamic resistance. The foundations of several armed groups already existed, dormant, waiting for the right time to surface. The government's mishandling of this electoral process was just the catalyst that the Islamists needed to gain wider support.

The most radical and violent of the organisations claiming to be Islamists was the Armed Islamic Group (GIA). Osama bin Laden had been funding and supplying arms to disparate elements of what would become the GIA for over a year at this point. The GIA officially came into being a couple of months before the Algerian parliamentary elections of December 1991, although elements had existed throughout the 1980s.

A GIA spokesman, speaking to the media in the mid-1990s, offers this populist version of history:

> Contacts were made between people who saw jihad as a legal-religious duty imposed on every Muslim, when God's law is not implemented, when the land of Muslims has been usurped, and when the women and families of Muslims are being disgraced. Many youth joined Sheikh Mansouri Meliani. They set up cells in villages and towns, and played a large part in the launching jihad. The Mujahideen who fought in Afghanistan joined the group. From this base the GIA was formed, and a *bayan al-wahdah* [statement of intent] was issued . . . The GIA was much different from the FIS, especially in their non-

acceptance of elections and democracy, and rejection of the idea of a national reconciliation with the current regime in Algeria.

After the election, the Islamists had the excuse they needed. The GIA believed in the need for armed struggle to establish an Islamic republic in Algeria and, after the interruption of the electoral process in January 1992, declared total war on the government. They had been making preparations to wage war and the time had come.

Al-Qaeda had quietly been smuggling arms into Algeria to support Bin Laden's former Afghanistan comrades. Shipments of thousands of Kalashnikov rifles, explosive materials and ammunition came by sea, land and air. From his arms dumps in Afghanistan – in part the residue of CIA largesse during the war on the Red Army – truckloads of munitions were smuggled through Pakistan and then sent by boat to be dropped at remote beaches on Algeria's Mediterranean coastline. Other shipments were made via the remoteness of the Sahara Desert, unloaded in terrorist-friendly Sudan and often shipped by camel train through Libya, Chad or Niger to the south of Algeria. At other times heavier equipment reached the GIA by small planes from Sudan.

'Blood and martyrdom are the only way to seize power by force and establish an Islamist state,' said Ali Belhadj, the fiery second-in-command who represented the radical fringe within the FIS. 'Democracy is a stranger in the house of God.'

Opposed to any ceasefire or dialogue with the government in power, the GIA also claimed responsibility for most of the assassinations of journalists, intellectuals, political activists opposed to its point of view and foreigners living in Algeria.

It is difficult to evaluate precisely the structure and size of the GIA (estimated at about 10,000 men) because it is composed of so many more or less autonomous groups controlled by as many 'emirs', although a single command unit does exist.

The GIA mainly recruited from former Algerian volunteers trained in guerrilla tactics by Bin Laden's Arab-Afghan freedom fighters, as well as among young men from the most disadvantaged social groups. Many members of the dissolved FIS joined its ranks, while local gangs of petty criminals and drug dealers were also said to be mixed up in its activities.

A large part of its membership was said to be of ethnic Kabyle or Berber origin.

Although their objectives were identical and their methods similar for the greater part, relations between the GIA and the other major Islamic resistance group, the Army of Islamic Salvation (AIS, the armed branch of the FIS) were characterised by personal animosity and rivalry between leaders and regions.

Experts believed that the GIA was led, at least initially, by Mourad Sid Ahmed, a notorious Arab-Afghan and a close friend of Osama bin Laden. Ahmed was a noted commander within the elite Al-Ansar (Lion's Den) group that Bin Laden took personal charge over during the second half of the 1980s. Ahmed had joined Bin Laden during 1979 and eventually became a trusted aide de camp, often escorting him as a bodyguard when he was in northern Pakistan on non-combative business. In the field he was a fearless fighter and an excellent military tactician.

He returned to Algeria from Afghanistan in 1989, having secured from his leader a promise for support in his new mission: to create an Algeria under his control that was extreme Islamic. But Ahmed was a wily operator and did not launch an all-out campaign right away. He bided his time, quietly receiving arms from Al-Qaeda, recruiting disaffected youth and training them.

Several thousand Arab-Afghans were now based in Algeria. A majority remained within the fledgling GIA network while some were affiliated to other similar groups, including the FIS. Around him, Ahmed had the cream of the Algerians who had served alongside Bin Laden in the struggle against the Soviets, including Zitouni, Messaoudi, and Dahane. Estimates of the combined strength of the Islamic fighting groups in Algeria during the early 1990s range from Algerian government figures of 6,000 to the 40,000 claimed by French intelligence.

The GIA quickly gained a reputation for being by far the most violent of Algeria's Islamic fundamentalist groups, engaging in a campaign of attacks on urban targets and intimidating the population as a whole. Their rationale for this was that those who voted in the election – a majority of the population – were considered to have broken strict Islamic fundamentalist laws. 'If people vote against God's law, that is nothing less than blasphemy,' declared one statement. 'In that case, the miscreants must be killed, for the simple reason that they want to substitute God's authority with their own.'

With this mantra and a contorted version of Islam behind them, the GIA and similar groups believed they had carte blanche to wage a war and begin an indiscriminate killing spree. Their manifesto was a frightening indictment of everything that Islamic fundamentalism stands for.

The areas the GIA controlled were concentrated in the Boumerdes–Blida region, Sidi Bel Abbès, Tiaret and Tlemcen, where 60–65 per cent of their cadres operated. But boundaries were ill-defined and the GIA, at any time, controlled swathes of the country. Only Algiers remained free from overall control, although the city was subjected to terrorist attacks, assassinations and random shootings.

In the areas the GIA controlled, any deviation from its own brand of conservative Islam public morality was ruthlessly punished. The GIA seemed particularly concerned with the oppression of women. Women who appeared unveiled in public were beaten. Any pregnant women not sufficiently covered were killed 'to prevent them from giving birth to new Muslims with similar poor values'. One GIA splinter group calling itself 'The Rebels Against God', on catching women not covered, cut off the index finger of their right hand (that being the one with which devout Muslims make their profession of faith), their eyelashes and eyebrows.

The mainstream GIA was no better. At Bentahla, just outside Algiers, some 40 gunmen cut the throats of 200 women and children, or burned them to death. The crime of the 200 victims was living peacefully in a government-controlled area and not rebelling.

In May 1994, the GIA issued an edict, signed by Abu Abdallah Ahmed, head of the judicial branch of the GIA. Abu Abdallah Ahmed was a regular visitor to Khartoum during 1992 and 1993, where he conferred not only with Osama bin Laden but also Ayman al-Zawahiri, who was by now one of those closest to the Al-Qaeda head and an adviser to him on Islamic policy matters. It is doubtful that the radical new contents of Ahmed's statement would not have been rubber-stamped by the Al-Qaeda leadership.

Abu Abdallah Ahmed's statement announced that any woman married to an 'atheist' must leave him or be killed. Any woman who married any government official was sentenced to death. Any woman who refused the GIA's practice of 'marriage of pleasure' was sentenced to death.

The latter was a particularly insidious invention. It is temporary marriage, to which only the man need consent, which enabled GIA fighters to rape women indiscriminately but avoid charges of sexual assault in the eyes of God. Abu Abdallah Ahmed justified this using a passage of the Koran, twisted out of context and interpreted for his own devices; an interpretation – false and deviant though it might be – that met the approval of the GIA's paymaster, Osama bin Laden, and his cronies in Khartoum.

For a time, the political FIS continued to believe that it could mediate with the Algerian military to stop the civil war before it evolved into 'total war'. The assassination of President Mohammed Boudiaff on 29 June 1992 ended any such hopes.

Through 1992 and 1993, the GIA embarked upon a campaign that grew ever wider in scope and brutality. But while the GIA terrorists were inhuman in their treatment of civilians, so were the authorities and the military government and this only served to attract greater numbers of people to the Islamist cause.

The assassination on 21 August 1993 in Algiers of Kasdi Merbah, former prime minister and ex-chief of military security, who was trying to mediate contact between Islamists and government, was a bold move by the GIA and showed that it had the government on the back foot. The group had no intention of abandoning its goals.

In late 1993, the GIA announced that its priority targets would be foreigners, non-Islamic journalists and intellectuals, civil servants and members of the security forces. The first foreigners slaughtered were a pair of hapless French geologists on 21 September 1993. During the initial years of the conflict 120 foreigners were murdered, as well as innumerable soldiers and policemen on leave or on duty and over 100 intellectuals and media professionals. In addition 69 journalists were killed and, since a campaign to close down the school system began in 1994, hundreds of teachers have died.

In the areas it controlled, GIA members regularly mounted checkpoints on roads and simply killed any passers-by or passengers on buses carrying identity cards that showed them to be security personnel or members of other condemned groups. Terrorist leader Mourad Sid Ahmed also decreed that his men adopt trademark 'signatures' to mark the dead as victims of the GIA. Individual murders were usually carried out by throat slitting or beheading. Often the victims' heads and bodies were found in different locations.

Despite its wanton cruelty, the GIA remained powerful and even popular in urban areas, particularly in central Algeria. Regular claims by the regime that the security situation had improved belied the fact that the government rarely managed to take control in the face of a committed, well-equipped and well-trained GIA. The regime's ability to control the capital was not repeated elsewhere in the country. Much of the security operation was, in effect, 'privatised' into a series of paramilitary groups – the local militias, *gardes communales d'auto-défense*, and the privately controlled and armed autonomous patriots who were suspected of behaving as brutally as the GIA towards the population.

In the ensuing stalemate, both sides held their ground and terrorised civilians. The Algerian military was strong, but the Islamists were growing in numbers and expertise. Their volunteers were trained in Al-Qaeda camps in Sudan and later Afghanistan, returning to their country having been drilled in handling weapons, tactics of guerrilla warfare, close-combat fighting and techniques in using explosives.

Algeria had become Bin Laden's pet project, the country most likely to fall to his Islamic fundamentalist revolution. He hoped that the fall of Algeria would start a domino effect, encouraging Muslims in other countries to rise up and replace their governments with conservative regimes.

Seven

Football and Fatwas

The streets of north London are typically row upon row of nondescript red-brick Victorian terraced houses. It's not the sort of place where you would expect to find a football stadium, let alone one as imposing as Highbury. Approached on foot through these old streets, it is suddenly right there in front of you: one of the most elegant and recognisable football grounds in England.

This is the view that greeted Osama bin Laden in 1994 when he used the opportunity of a trip to the UK to witness the only live top-class football matches he had ever seen. It is a telling insight to anti-terrorist cooperation between states prior to 11 September 2001 that he was even able to enter the country in 1994. Less than 18 months after the first bombing of the World Trade Center in New York, with the Saudi Arabian authorities seeking his arrest and Yemen reportedly requesting Interpol's assistance to apprehend him, Bin Laden was nevertheless able to fly into Heathrow Airport undetected.

Evidence suggests that he was using a Bosnian passport, allegedly furnished by the Bosnian government as the terror chief was supporting the Bosnian Muslims while they fought to defend themselves from the ethnic cleansing of the Serbs and Slobodan Milosevic.

The intelligence community believes that the Bosnian embassy in Vienna issued a passport to Bin Laden in 1993. This was also suggested in reports that appeared in the Yugoslav press during this period. The Bosnian government denies this; however, they have admitted that 'some passport records have been lost' relating to their embassy in the Austrian capital.

The specific reason for his trip to London remains a mystery, but it must have been important for Bin Laden to risk it. What has emerged is that he used his time in London to strengthen ties with a plethora of Saudi exiles and Islamic fundamentalist fugitives living there. With its easy visa laws and liberal policies on political refugees, London was – and still is – probably the main base of Islamic fundamentalism in the West.

No other country in the West has harboured so many terrorists linked to Bin Laden; the apparent porosity of British laws has long led the French to refer to the capital as 'Londonistan'. At the conclusion of the Afghan conflict many Arab-Afghans – notably Libyans, Tunisians and Egyptians – arrived in London, having found themselves unwelcome in their home countries. As many as 2,000 Middle East dissidents a year were arriving in Britain at that time.

Over the course of several months, Bin Laden used his time to boost Al-Qaeda's ties with like-minded exiles in Britain and to set up a propaganda information service for Al-Qaeda under the guise of an Islamic charitable mission – the Advisory and Reformation Committee.

His primary contact was allegedly an old friend, Mustafa Kamel, known as Sheikh Abu Hamza Al-Masri, or Abu Hamza, a firebrand cleric based at the Finsbury Park Mosque in London.

Born in Egypt, Abu Hamza has lived in London since the early 1970s and holds a United Kingdom passport. Considering his open hostility to America and the country he now calls home, the people of Britain may consider it an affront that their country's asylum laws have allowed him 30 years of residency among them and, worse still, that he is officially British.

After losing a hand and an eye during his time fighting in Afghanistan, he returned home and reportedly enjoyed the ongoing support of Bin Laden, running a group called Ansar Al-Shari, or Supporters of Shariah, an organisation that he described as a pressure group for oppressed Muslims. Others describe the organisation as a broad church for fundamentalists of all nationalities.

Ansar Al-Shari also provides another link between Bin Laden and Algeria's GIA. The British authorities and others in Europe consider that Ansar Al-Shari is the GIA's primary propaganda outlet in Europe.

Abu Hamza himself is a controversial cleric who has reportedly used his position to promote religious tensions. According to Agence France-

Presse, Abu Hamza delivers 'incendiary' sermons from the Finsbury mosque, denouncing the 'Great Satan' (America) and all who help it.

During his career as an imam he has issued a fatwa praising assassinations that included those of prominent Middle East figures and a two-year-old Algerian child. He has also called for US planes to be blown up in mid-air using 'flying mines hanging from balloons'. In a television interview in January 1999, he supported violent actions if they were carried out 'for the sake of God' and would 'stop state terrorism by Britain and the United States'.

'It was when the Americans took the knife out of the Russians and stabbed it in our back . . . In the meantime, they were bombarding Iraq and occupying the Arabian Peninsula, and then with the witch-hunt against the mujahideen, everything cleared up: it was a full-scale war. The Americans wanted to fight the Russians with Muslim blood, and they could only justify that to the Muslims by triggering the word jihad. Unfortunately for everyone except the Muslims, when the button of jihad is pushed, it does not come back that easy. It keeps going on and on until the Muslim empire swallows every existing empire.'

In addition to his sermons, Abu Hamza is accused of running weekend military training camps for Islamic youth in Britain. Allegedly staffed by former British army officers, these camps are reported to have instructed young Muslims in the ways of jihad and encouraged them to travel overseas to fight.

Credible intelligence has allegedly linked him with the Islamic Army of Aden, a Yemen-based fundamentalist organisation credited with taking 16 tourists hostage in 1998. The Yemeni government called fafor his deportation to Aden after members of this group were arrested in June 2001 and found with explosives, small arms and a map of the US embassy in Yemen's capital, San'a. The Islamic Army of Aden has also been implicated in the attack on the USS *Cole* in October 2000.

In January 2002, Abu Hamza's son, Mohammed Mustafa Kamel, flew into Heathrow airport having been extradited from Yemen after serving three years' imprisonment for plotting sabotage. Kamel was accused of masterminding a plot by Islamic fundamentalists to bomb British targets in the Yemeni port of Aden. Eight British passport holders were originally convicted of involvement, including Kamel.

For Bin Laden, London was also important as a global financial market and he spent time with a number of supporters putting in place mechanisms that would keep laundered money flowing through the City. The Albanian-Arab Islamic Bank, now defunct but at one time shifting tens of millions of dollars around the world to support Islamic fundamentalism, was just one of the organisations using London as a hub.

There were also a great many people to see. The Muslim Brotherhood was active in Britain. Bin Laden circulated in this Islamist underworld and over the course of his visit extended help to other groups with aims similar to his own. From the north London suburb of Cricklewood, Hamas published *al-Filastin al-Muslima* (Muslim Palestine) and it was around this time Jordanian militant Abu Qurtada began to circulate *al-Ansar*, a pamphlet championing the slaughter of Algerian policemen and civilians. Both were established and run with money provided via the Albanian-Arab Islamic Bank and other Al-Qaeda fronts.

Throughout the 1990s such activities continued unabated and ignored by successive British governments, with most ordinary people unaware of the Islamic underworld that thrived among them. Only brief glimpses offered an indication. After Abu Hamza praised the 1997 massacre of 58 European tourists at Luxor for example, Egypt attacked Britain for providing a haven for radicals. The Egyptian authorities said that seven of their fourteen most-wanted terrorists were based in Britain. Foremost among them was Yasser al-Sirri, sentenced to death *in absentia* for plotting the failed assassination of an Egyptian prime minister and still active at the Islamic Observation Centre in London, a mouthpiece for Egyptian rebels.

In February 1998, Saudi dissident Mohammed al-Massari and Omar Bakri, leader of al-Muhajiroun, signed a statement calling for attacks on American targets. Sixty UK groups added their names. Two weeks later, Bin Laden echoed the call in a statement issued by the Advisory and Reformation Committee. 'In compliance with God's order,' this said, 'we issue the following fatwa to all Muslims to kill the Americans.'

Bin Laden also went house-hunting and purchased a property on, or near, Harrow Road in the Wembley area of London. He paid cash and used an intermediary as the named owner. This small and anonymous residence in the suburbs of the British capital was home throughout his stay. It later became the London offices of the Advisory and Reformation Committee.

One of those reportedly drawn into the Al-Qaeda inner circle in London was Khaled al-Fawwaz, a businessman from the Saudi heartland of Nejd, who has been accused by the FBI of being linked by telephone records and bank statements to the embassy bombings in East Africa. He is also alleged to have acted as Al-Qaeda's UK spokesman. For a time he was based in a flat in the Dollis Hill area of London.

But while there was a serious purpose to Bin Laden's time in Britain, there was also some down time to engage in some quite out-of-character sightseeing. He even indulged in the tourist practice of sending postcards home. From these it is known that he visited the British Natural History Museum and the British Museum. Several of London's museums had Islamic exhibits and he toured these. He may also have visited Scotland as one of his postcards depicted Edinburgh Castle.

But Bin Laden's most audacious undertaking during his sojourn to England was joining the crowds at Highbury, the home of Arsenal Football Club, not once but four times.

In the way that many foreign football fans do, for no apparent reason other than a liking for the colours in a strip, or the charisma of a leading player, the Bin Laden family had plumped upon Arsenal as 'their club'. In Khartoum, Bin Laden and his eldest son, Abdullah, had often settled down in front of their satellite television to see 'the Gunners' in action.

The club they chose has a long and illustrious history. It began life in 1886 as Dial Square, then changed its name to Royal Arsenal, Woolwich Arsenal, and finally just Arsenal. The club came to prominence thanks to Henry Norris, a property developer and mayor of the London borough of Fulham who had a vision of a football club based in the capital that could take on and beat the massive teams from the north of England. The club was in a bad way when Norris took over in 1910. He renamed them 'The Arsenal' and shifted them to a new site in north London at Highbury, where they first played in September 1913. By the 1919 season, Arsenal were in the top division and have stayed there ever since. Since 1927 the club has officially been simply 'Arsenal'. Highbury stadium, opened in 1932, has held crowds of up to 70,000 at some of the greatest games of football played in Britain.

Bin Laden had followed the sport since childhood. He likely saw First Division matches in both Saudi Arabia and Lebanon when attached to clubs himself. What finally persuaded him to make the pilgrimage to

Highbury for the first time was the glamour of a European fixture. He probably joined the Gunners faithful in Clock End – so named for the 12-foot clock in the centre of its roof. With his long beard, streaked with a sweep of grey, he must have made quite a contrast to the rank-and-file Arsenal supporters.

Arsenal was enjoying a run in the European Cup-Winners' cup. Club star Ian Wright – Abdullah bin Laden's favourite player – had helped spur the team on to successes over Odense BK of Denmark and Standard Liege of Belgium in the first two rounds of the competition. On 15 March, Osama bin Laden was one of a 34,678 crowd at Highbury for the second leg of the tie that saw a single Tony Adams goal separate Arsenal from Torino of Italy and propel the Gunners into the semi-finals of the competition.

Attending the match was an eye-opener. Bin Laden had become involved in Sudanese football as a sponsor for unknown reasons but at Highbury, he recaptured the past, his youthful passion for the game itself, reawakening memories of his days standing in the same position as Arsenal's goalkeeper, the England international David Seaman.

The atmosphere at Highbury during the match against Torino was electric and those close to Bin Laden believe that – as in most things – there were no half measures with him. He was hooked and began to take a close interest in Arsenal, in between organising his British terrorist network.

Ahead of Arsenal that year lay one of the most challenging periods of their season. They were not having a good domestic campaign, especially considering the perennially high expectations attached to the Gunners. A Cup double the previous season – FA Cup and League Cup – had led many to believe that the squad could go on to mount a serious bid for the Premiership title.

Their Premiership challenge had fizzled out, however, under the weight of too many draws early in the season and an over-reliance on Ian Wright for goals. Manchester United and Blackburn had pulled away and were set to fight out the championship between them. Arsenal would eventually go on to finish fourth. Manager George Graham's side also failed to defend their two trophies from the previous campaign with fourth-round exits to Aston Villa and Bolton.

The die-hard faithful of Arsenal were buoyed up by the chance of a good run in Europe. English sides were again starting to make a mark in continental competitions following the six-year UEFA ban, the first success coming courtesy of Manchester United's Cup-Winners' cup win over Barcelona in 1991.

A wealthy friend of Bin Laden's managed to procure tickets for the sell-out game at Highbury on 22 March, when Arsenal hosted Manchester United. If the match against Torino had been a gripping affair, then the game against the Red Devils was a roller-coaster. Two sides with a deep-seated rivalry fought out a classic game of football that ended in a 2–2 draw. Players such as Tony Adams, Ryan Giggs, Roy Keane, Ian Wright and the indomitable Eric Cantona were on the field, offering Bin Laden an on-the-spot insight into sport at this level that he had only previously been able to watch on television.

Just four days later he was back for a third visit, this time to see Arsenal defeat Liverpool by a solitary Paul Merson goal. Although it was a Liverpool side far removed from the club's great era, the presence of the likes of Ian Rush, Robbie Fowler and Steve McManaman meant that it was, nevertheless, a game of the utmost class.

Between the Liverpool game and his final visit to Clock End, Bin Laden received news that should have affected him, but he appears to have continued, unruffled, with his trip. On 7 April, the Saudi Arabian government revoked his citizenship for behaviour that 'contradicts the Kingdom's interests and risks harming its relations with fraternal countries'. About this time, Bin Laden began to hear whispers that people were looking for him. London was no longer safe – if it had ever been. He knew that Saudi Arabian intelligence was using its sources to pinpoint his whereabouts, and knew that he had been sighted in London. The British government might have been informed.

Incredibly, he went ahead with his final flirtation with English football. On 12 April he was back in the Highbury stands again to see French side Paris St Germain dispatched by a Kevin Campbell goal, putting Arsenal in the final of the European Cup-Winners' cup. With his work completed, and his tourism finished, he again used his Bosnian passport to slip out of the country and travel home to Sudan.

In May, Arsenal faced Parma in the final, a team which included the likes of Tomas Brolin, Gianfranco Zola and Faustino Asprilla. Graham picked veteran Alan Smith up front as he thought that Smith's height would cause Parma problems. But it was his foot that did the damage, launching a fierce shot early in the first half that beat the keeper and thudded in off the post. It was surely a moment that Bin Laden and a wide-eyed and excitable Abdullah would not have missed on their wide-screen television in Khartoum.

Strangely enough, Bin Laden had attended four games at Highbury and never seen Arsenal hitman Ian Wright score a goal. But this does not seem to have dented Bin Laden's enthusiasm for the star – or indeed that of 13-year-old Abdullah. Flying home to Sudan, Bin Laden carried gifts for all his family, but the finest present was reserved for his eldest son. It was a replica Ian Wright shirt that Abdullah wore almost religiously for months.

In all, Bin Laden had been in Europe for three months and had accomplished much. But perhaps more importantly, the germ of an idea had been planted in his head: he had started thinking of a sinister plan involving the sport he loved, which would bring his name to prominence on a world stage. The English fascination with football had shown him a way.

Eight

All the World's a Stage

For hundreds of millions of people around the world, everyday life almost came to a standstill for one month in the summer of 1994. The reason? The 15th football World Cup, a festival of the world's most popular sport held every four years. The tournament matches, staged in the United States, were played in front of a record number of spectators – 3,587,538 – while a combined global television audience was estimated at 30 billion.

The biggest surprise had been the decision to award the event to the USA, a country where 'football' means American gridiron football, and where 'soccer', as the game is called there, lags far behind baseball and basketball in popularity.

The disappointment in Morocco, America's biggest rival to host the tournament, at being passed over was enormous. An African nation had still never organised a finals tournament since the World Cup was founded in 1930. In choosing the United States and quietly lobbying against the Moroccans, FIFA president João Havelange followed the scent of sponsorship and television money. 'The Baron' claimed he was opening the door to a new frontier. But it was the opening of new bank accounts that appealed to FIFA, a juggernaut that was changing the game immeasurably, overseeing a metamorphosis from a sport rooted firmly in the working-class masses to one that belonged to corporate backers – 'the prawn sandwich supporters' to which Manchester United captain Roy Keane would so famously allude.

Havelange had been called a dictator and an autocrat. However, he had built FIFA into a corporate giant with an estimated $4 billion in the bank. No one on his gravy train was complaining. If Havelange decided to send the championships to the United States, it was a decision that simply needed to be rubber-stamped within FIFA. Few voices were raised in support of Morocco, for fear of earning the Baron's anger. 'I will have the joy to leave my successor $4 billion to live on for the next ten years,' Havelange said, using every interview and every television appearance to showcase his legacy. 'I feel very happy about that.'

Safely back in Sudan, Osama bin Laden, his eldest son Abdullah and other family members watched one of the most remarkable World Cup tournaments in recent memory unfold, game after game, on their TV screen. Even the qualifying rounds had thrown up some startling results. A record 147 countries had entered, among them South Africa, back after a lengthy exclusion. Many premier footballing nations, however, had not made it to the finals: England, Denmark, the 1992 European champions, Portugal, Poland, and once again France, knocked out by a Bulgarian goal in the last second of their last qualifying game.

And results in the United States were equally shocking. Bulgaria, who had never won a World Cup match in 16 previous attempts, created the biggest upsets, beating Germany en route to the semi-finals. There was drama when Diego Maradona, Argentina's hero of 1986, tested positive for drugs and was expelled from the tournament, and there was tragedy too when Colombian Andres Escobar was murdered days after returning home from scoring an own goal against the United States. The hosts and Saudi Arabia – whose striker Saeed Owairan scored the best goal of the tournament – shocked many by making it into the quarter-final draw.

The final, on 17 July, was a clash between footballing giants, Brazil and Italy, two nations that had already won the World Cup three times each. But what in theory should have been the ultimate match proved to be the ultimate disappointment: a dour, physical game that had to be settled on penalties. When the dust settled Brazil emerged victorious, the first nation to win the World Cup four times.

More remarkable to Bin Laden than the result were the pictures of the crowd at the final. Around 100,000 spectators crammed into the Rose Bowl stadium in Pasadena, California. This was roughly three times the crowd he had experienced at Arsenal's Highbury stadium. Even via satellite television, in the remoteness of Sudan, he could understand and feel something of the unique aura of the event.

By the time that Bin Laden was following the events of the 1994 World Cup, his operations in Sudan were expanding apace. Al-Qaeda had increased its activity and was already the powerhouse of Islamic fundamentalism, dominating the 'industry', by far the leading terrorist organisation in the world.

Before the World Cup, on 26 February 1993, an explosion in the World Trade Center parking garage in New York resulted in six deaths, 1,042 injuries and damage of over $500 million. The blast was caused by a 1,200lb bomb. In Manila, an Al-Qaeda cell came close to assassinating Pope John Paul II. When the cell was broken, agents uncovered plans to assassinate US President Bill Clinton and to orchestrate a series of simultaneous US aircraft hijacks from airports all over Asia, involving up to a dozen planes.

All over the world, there was a surge in troubles during the early 1990s, and most of the shadowy groups involved had roots deep in Al-Qaeda. Its training camps continued to turn out fighters. Bin Laden deployed hundreds of men in Bosnia. At one point, 2,000 of his men were serving in Chechnya, fighting the Russians.

But Al-Qaeda's biggest 'success' had been in Somalia. The country had imploded, hundreds of thousands of Somalis had been killed in civil war or died through famine. More faced the same fate if the international community did not act. In December 1992, US Marines went ashore in the Somali capital Mogadishu aiming to establish an expeditionary infrastructure to facilitate security and the delivery of food to the starving Somalis.

Humanitarian aid was not uppermost in all minds, however. One of Somalia's most prominent warlords, General Mohammed Farrah Aidid, appealed to Sudan for military help and during October and November 1992 Al-Qaeda worked like Bin Laden had envisaged, shipping arms, exporting its own fighters and helping train Aidid's men. With this support, Aidid was emboldened. Soon after the United Nations-organised UNOSOM II got into its stride, gunmen ambushed Pakistani troops attached to the international effort, killing 24 soldiers.

An attempt was made to capture General Aidid but it ended in tragedy.

During operations in a neighbourhood near the Olympic Hotel in Mogadishu, a US Blackhawk helicopter was downed. Soldiers from both sides were slaughtered, as were civilians who poured into the streets to see what was going on. When the bodies of two US soldiers were later paraded around the city by rebel soldiers, television cameras were there to capture the scene and to underline to global audiences the callous and evil nature of the forces that the United Nations was dealing with.

By March 1993, mass starvation had been prevented and security was much improved. But under international pressure critical of its operations, the UN force was withdrawn. In mid-1994, the last US troops left Somalia, having failed in their task. Somalia slid back into anarchy, factional fighting and wanton killing of citizens.

Somehow, putting aside the massive loss of life and destruction wreaked on Somalia, this was seen as a major success for Islamic fundamentalists and Bin Laden was given much credit for bloodying the nose of the Americans. The Islamists appeared not to notice or to care that significant numbers of Muslims had been sacrificed en route to this 'victory'.

In the wake of these 'successes', Bin Laden and his group were already creating cells of operatives in European states and planning far into the future. The 1998 bombings of the US Embassies in Tanzania and Kenya had already passed the planning stage and men were slowly infiltrating East Africa, sleepers who would spend years living normal lives before being called into action.

It is impossible to determine exactly when Bin Laden and his cohorts within Al-Qaeda first turned their attention to an operation centred on football. It may be that even as he stood on the terraces at Highbury stadium in London, Bin Laden had already begun to think about the scheme. It is more likely that the possibilities afforded by the biggest of all stages first became apparent during the summer of 1994 while the World Cup was played out in the United States.

As much as it had been a success, Bin Laden's operations in Somalia were remote and a long way away from hitting the heart of his enemy. The Western world – and America in particular – was bloodied but had hardly been dealt the blow of which he dreamt.

The more he looked at it, the more the 1998 World Cup, scheduled to be held in France, presented an ideal opportunity. For so many reasons, the country and tournament seemed the perfect theatre of operations and target. The country's borders were porous and easily penetrated. Al-Qaeda already had cells firmly established on mainland Europe and a network of supporters. What was more, the former French colony of Algeria had a vast community living in France: as many as 600,000 of a total of 3,000,000 Muslims in the country, 7 per cent of the entire population.

With Bin Laden supporting an Islamic insurgency inside Algeria, he had close ties with a number of fundamentalist groups and was confident of their operational ability, Al-Qaeda having trained many of its people in Sudan and Afghanistan.

The idea was mooted within Al-Qaeda's command structure during the latter months of 1994. Bin Laden became ever more convinced of the validity of the concept. The United States had automatically reached the finals of the competition as the previous hosts, were improving in leaps and bounds and looked likely to qualify for France. Other nations, such as England and Scotland, represented close allies of Washington, France was no friend to the Islamists and any one of the major European footballing powers would be likely targets.

Bin Laden went on to note that the qualifying countries for the finals were likely to include the emerging Asian football power, Saudi Arabia, and usually included one or two North African Arab nations. The presence of any Arab teams in the finals presented further operational cover for a plot that he hoped would include a direct assault on the tournament itself, coupled with a major strike on French and US targets in the country. The championships provided a backdrop that would grab global attention, allowing the Islamic fundamentalists' message to be driven home in no uncertain terms.

Within Al-Qaeda's Khartoum headquarters, opinion was divided. Several influential members of the 'board of directors' were opposed. The deciding factor was the GIA, which proved itself a capable operational partner during late 1994 and the following year. During early 1994, Bin Laden had hosted several senior GIA leaders in his base in Khartoum. Most of the men he had first dealt with in helping establish the Algerian group were now dead or jailed: Mourad Sid Ahmed, alias Djafaar el-Afghani, had been shot by Algerian security; Abdelhak Layada had been captured and condemned to death; El-Wed, alias 'The

Pakistan', a co-founder of GIA, was supposedly killed in the Serkadji prison massacre of January 1995, although he would later apparently surface in 1998 in Paris prior to the World Cup.

The Khartoum meeting led to an extraordinary challenge for the GIA. Al-Qaeda wished to sponsor a major assault on the 1998 World Cup but the Algerians had to prove themselves capable partners for Osama bin Laden.

Analysts have pondered over a sudden change of GIA policy in the mid-1990s. Until that time the group had never embarked upon attacks on mainland Europe but suddenly there was a spate of bombings and other terror operations. It is now possible to outline the likely reason.

The events of late 1994 and 1995 were ordered by a triumvirate of planners. From the Algerian side two men were most prominent. The first was Djamel Zitouni, alias Abou Abderrahmane Amine, who became head of GIA in 1994 and was another Arab-Afghan who was personally close to the Al-Qaeda head. The other was Ahmed Zaoui, the GIA's chief in Belgium and overall commander of GIA operations in Europe. Together, these two men quickly took the Algerian civil war to mainland Europe. Zitouni and Zaoui worked to develop a full-blown campaign against France, amid a period of evolution for the GIA as a whole. With Al-Qaeda's financial and logistical support the group changed from a ragtag militia into a well-functioning organisation.

In early 1994, the GIA published a document outlining its policy and evolution. *The Strategy Plan of the GIA Command Council in January 1994* was recorded in an article that appeared in *al-Wasat* newspaper on 30 January 1994.

This concentrated upon the following points:

- A comprehensive national strategy from the GIA for the military field operations;
- Formation of a comprehensive strategy to break the barrier of the internal and external media black-out thrown over Algeria by the government;
- Provision of a more effective resistance framework for the masses;
- Streamlining of arms smuggling networks and evolution of new networks;

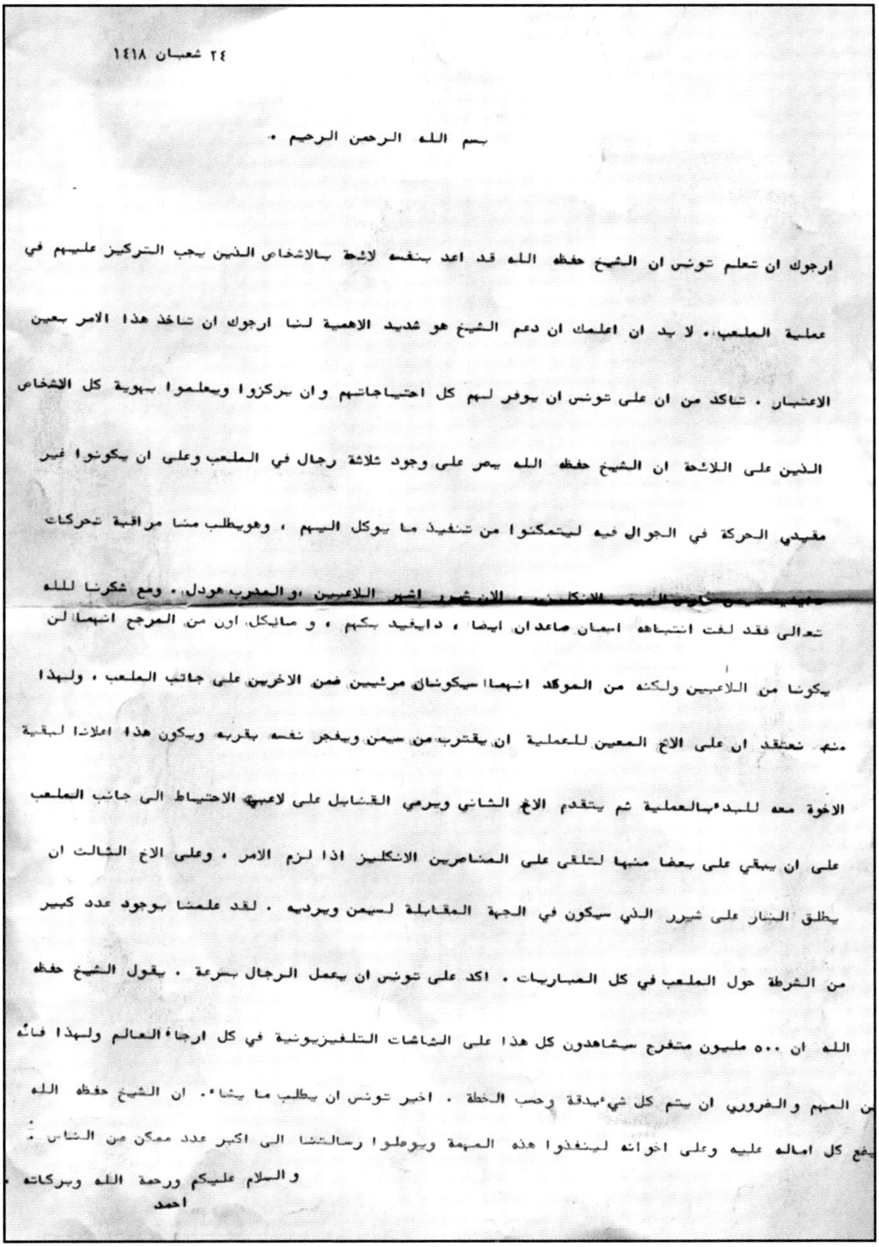

٢٤ شعبان ١٤١٨

بسم الله الرحمن الرحيم .

ارجوك ان تعلم تونس ان الشيخ حفظه الله قد اعد بنفسه لائحة بالاشخاص الذين يجب التركيز عليهم في

عملية الملعب . لا بد ان اعلمك ان دعم الشيخ هو شديد الاهمية لنا ارجوك ان تأخذ هذا الامر بعين

الاعتبار . تأكد من ان على تونس ان يوفر لهم كل احتياجاتهم وان يركزوا ويعلموا بهوية كل الاشخاص

الذين على اللائحة ان الشيخ حفظه الله يصر على وجود ثلاثة رجال في الملعب وعلى ان يكونوا غير

مقيدي الحركة في الجوال فيه ليتمكنوا من تنفيذ ما يوكل اليهم ، وهويطلب منا مراقبة تحركات

حتى يتمكن الاخوة المكلفين بالانتحار اشهر اللاعبين (والمدرب هودل) . ومع شكرنا لله

تعالى فقد لفت انتباهه ايمان صاعدان ايضا ، دايفيد بكهم ، و مايكل اون من المرجح انهما لن

يكونا من اللاعبين ولكنه من المؤكد انهما سيكونان مرئيين ضمن الاخرين على جانب الملعب ، ولهذا

منه نعتقد ان على الاخ المعين للعملية ان يقترب من سيمن ويفجر نفسه بقربه ويكون هذا اعلانا لبقية

الاخوة معه للبدء بالعملية ثم يتقدم الاخ الثاني ويرمي القنابل على لاعبي الاحتياط الى جانب الملعب

على ان يبقي على بعضا منها لتلقى على العناصرين الانكليز اذا لزم الامر ، وعلى الاخ الثالث ان

يطلق النبار على شيرر الذي سيكون في الجهة المقابلة لسيمن وبردسه . لقد علمنا بوجود عدد كبير

من الشرطة حول الملعب في كل المباريات . اكد على تونس ان يعمل الرجال بسرعة . يقول الشيخ حفظه

الله ان ٥٠٠ مليون متفرج سيشاهدون كل هذا على الشاشات التلفيزيونية في كل ارجاءالعالم ولهذا فانه

من المهم والضروري ان يتم كل شيءبدقة وحسب الخطة . اخبر تونس ان يطلب ما يشاء . ان الشيخ حفظه الله

يضع كل امله عليه وعلى اخوانه لينفذوا هذه المهمة ويوصلوا رسالتنا الى اكبر عدد ممكن من الناس .

والسلام عليكم ورحمة الله وبركاته .

احمد

Figure 1: GIA Communication dated 24 December 1997

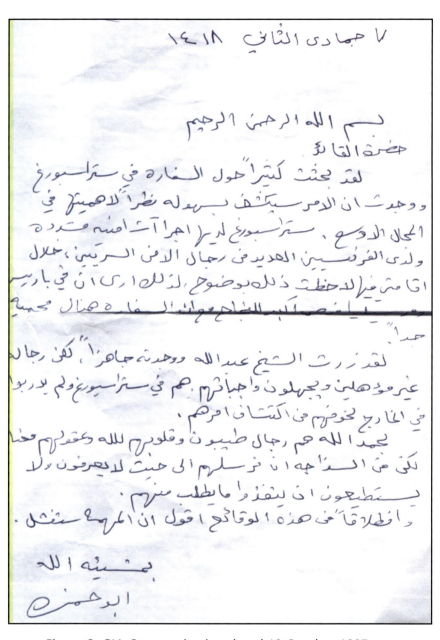

٧ جمادى الثاني ١٤١٨

بسم الله الرحمن الرحيم

حضرة القائد

لقد بحثت كثيراً حول الغارة في ستراسبورغ
ووجدت ان الامر سيكشف بسرعة نظراً لاهميتها في
المجال الاوسع . ستراسبورغ لدير اجرا أثارامنه متعددة
ولدى الفرنسيين العديد من رجال الامن السريين ، خلال
ايا مشهر [لاحظت ذلك بوضوح ، لذلك ارى ان في باريس

ــ

جيداً

لقد زرت الشيخ عبد الله ووجدته جاهزاً ، لكن رجاله
غير مؤهلين ويجهلون واجباتهم .هم في ستراسبورغ ولم يدربوا
في الخارج لخوضهم في اكتشاف امرهم ،
نحمد الله هم رجال طيبون وقلوبهم لله وعقولهم حض
لكن من الصعب اجهه ان نرسلهم الى حيث لايعرفون ولا
يستطيعون ان ينفذوا ما يطلب منهم .
وانطلاقاً من هذه الوقائع اقول ان الامر سيفشل .

بمشيئة الله

ابو الرحمن

١٥ شعبان ١٤١٧

بسم الله الرحمن الرحيم.

حضرة القائد

هاريمان هي هدف مهم وكبير، وهو الآن متقدمة في
السن فانه من المتوقع ألا تكون في محيط السفارة خلال
العملية. كذلك فانه من المؤكد أنها ستحضر المباراة اذا
تأهل الفريق الامريكي في فرنسا فمن الممكن أن تستغل
هناك ؟؟

بمشيئة الله

ابو حمزة

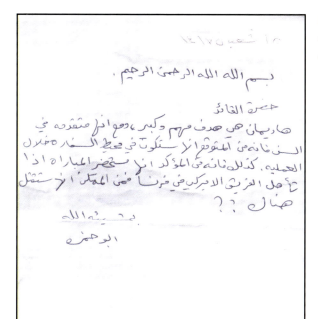

Figure 3:
GIA Communication
dated 26 December 1996

٩ شعبان ١٤١٨

بسم الله الرحمن الرحيم،

حضرة القائد.

لقد وصلتني تعليماتك وتكلمت مع تونس سوف يذهب لجلب الاغراض بنفسه
مع اني طلبت منه ان لا يفعل لان المخاطر كثيرة وليرسل احد معاونيه.
لقد كان سعيداً جداً لمعرفته بوفرة ما سيرسل اليه فلديه مهمتين وهو يؤمن
بان ذلك سيجلب كثيراً من السعادة لك وللشيخ حفظه الله.
بعون الله لقد تم اختيار سفير جديد لامريكا في باريس وهو بالتأكيد
سيحضر مباريات الفريق الامريكي على الاقل المباراة الاولى في باريس،
ولذلك فمن المؤكد انه سيكون في السفارة قبل انتقاله الى الملعب. مكتبه
يقع في واجهة المبنى وهنا سيكون مركز الهجوم. ان مقتل السفير سيكون له قيمة
معنوية كبيرة.

بمشيئة الله

ابو حمزة

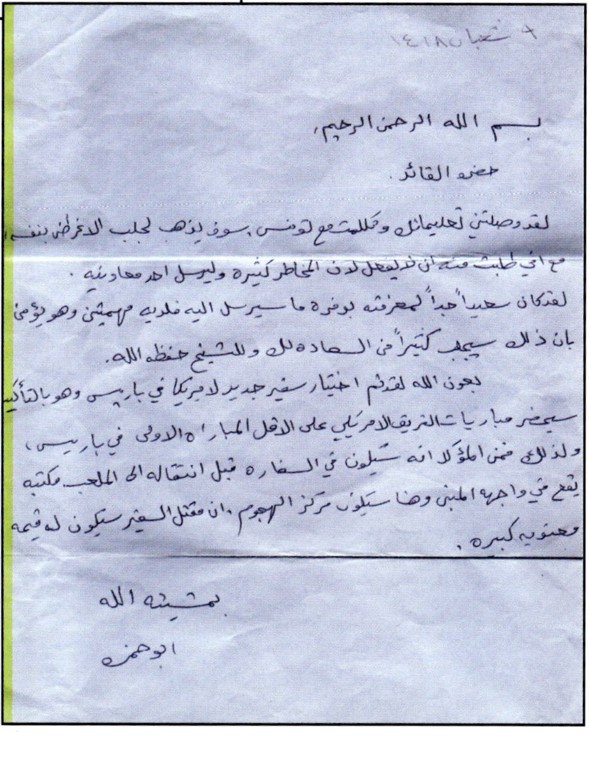

Figure 4:
GIA Communication
dated 10 December 1997

LEFT: Pelé holding aloft the Jules Rimet Trophy. For many years Bin Laden kept a framed photograph of his 1974 meeting with Pelé on his desk at the Bin Laden family corporate headquarters in Jeddah. © Allsport

BELOW: Arsenal's famed Highbury stadium was where Osama bin Laden gained his first intoxicating taste of football at the highest level during the early months of 1994.

© PA Photos

ABOVE: Sheikh Abu Hamza Al-Masri, a prominent Islamic cleric
based in London with alleged links to both Osama bin Laden and
the Armed Islamic Group.
© PA Photos

BELOW: (Left to right) David Beckham, Alan Shearer and
Michael Owen, three of England's elite players targeted by
Osama bin Laden during his planned assault on the
1998 World Cup finals in France.

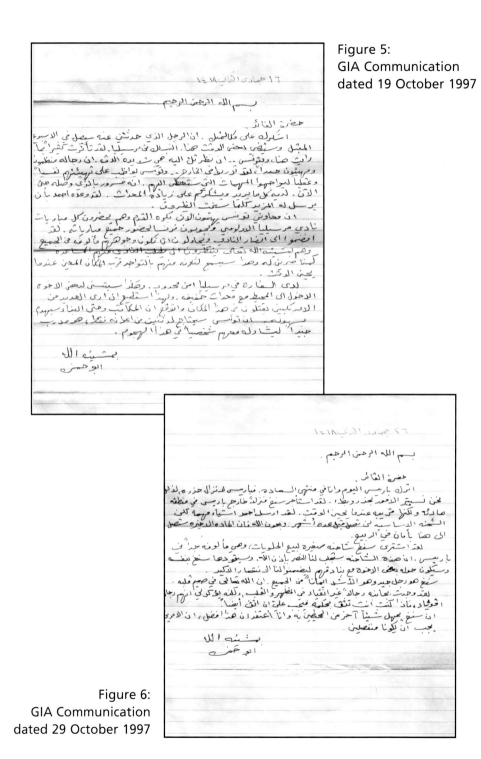

Figure 5:
GIA Communication
dated 19 October 1997

Figure 6:
GIA Communication
dated 29 October 1997

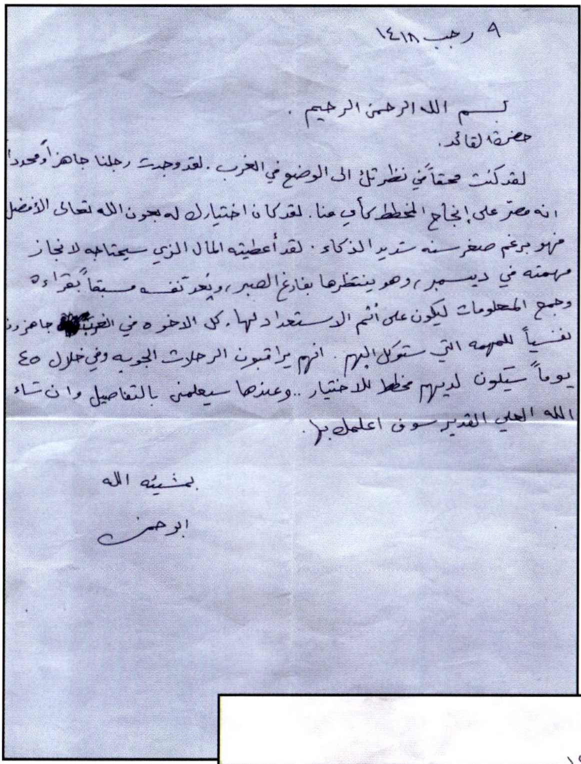

٩ رجب ١٤١٨

بسم الله الرحمن الرحيم.

حضرة القائد.

لقد كنت محقاً في نظرتك الى الوضع في الغرب. لقد وجدت رجلنا جاهزاً ومحدداً
انه مصر على إنجاح المخطط كأي منا. لقد كان اختياري له بعون الله تعالى الأفضل
فهو برغم صغر سنه شديد الذكاء. لقد أعطيته المال الذي سيحتاجه لانجاز
مهمته في ديسمبر، وهو ينتظرها بفارغ الصبر، ويعد نفسه مسبقاً بقراءة
وجمع المعلومات ليكون على أتم الاستعداد لها. كل الاخوة في الغرب جاهزون
نفسياً للمهمة التي ستوكل اليهم. انهم يراقبون الرحلات الجوية وفي خلال ٤٥
يوماً سيكون لديهم مخطط للاختيار.. وعندها سيعلمني بالتفاصيل وان شاء
الله العلي القدير سوف اعلمك بها.

بمشيئة الله

ابو حمزة

Figure 7:
GIA Communication
dated 10 November 1997

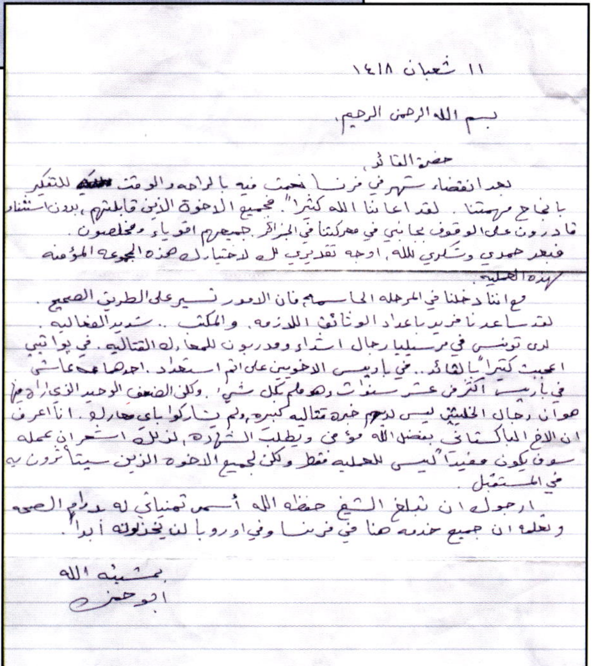

١١ شعبان ١٤١٨

بسم الله الرحمن الرحيم،

حضرة القائد،

بعد انقضاء شهر في فرنسا نحمث فيه بالراحة والوقت للتفكير
بانجاح مهمتنا. لقد اعاننا الله كثيراً". فجميع الاخوة الذين قابلتهم، بدون استثناء
قادرون على الوقوف بجانبي في معركتنا في الجزائر. جميعهم اقوياء ومخلصون.
فبعد حمدي وشكري لله، اوجه تقديري لك لاختيارك هذه المجموعة المؤمنة
لهذه العملية.
مع اننا دخلنا في المرحلة الحاسمة فان الامور تسير على الطريق الصحيح.
لقد ساعدنا فريد باعداد الوثائق اللازمة والمكتب.. شديد الفعالية.
لدى تونس في مرسيليا رجال اشداء ومدربون للمعارك القتالية. في بواتيي
اعجبت كثيراً يا القائد.. في باريس الاخوين على اتم استعداد. احدهما عاش
في باريس اكثر من عشر سنوات وهو ملم بكل شيء. ولكن الضعف الوحيد الذي ارى هو
ان رجال الخليج ليس لديهم خبرة قتالية كبيرة، ولم يشاركوا باي معارك. انا اعرف
ان الاخ الباكستاني بفضل الله مؤمن ويطلب الشهادة، لذلك استشعر ان عمله
سوف يكون مفيداً ليس للعملية فقط ولكن لجميع الاخوة الذين سيتأثرون به
في المستقبل.
ارجوك ان تبلغ الشيخ حفظه الله أسمى تمنياتي له بدوام الصحة
وتعلمه ان جميع جنوده هنا في فرنسا وفي اوروبا لن يخذلوه أبداً.

بمشيئة الله

ابو حمزة

Figure 8:
GIA Communication
dated
11 December 1997

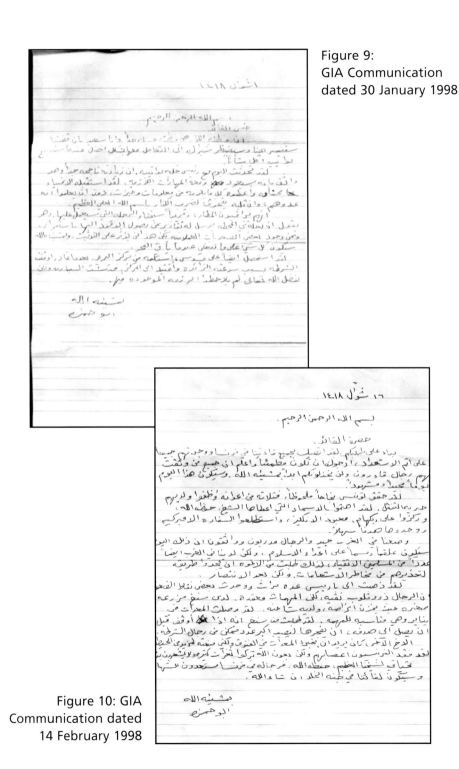

Figure 9:
GIA Communication
dated 30 January 1998

Figure 10: GIA
Communication dated
14 February 1998

- Development of fund-raising activities;
- Provision of greater financial and social services cover for the families of martyrs;
- Killing of activist traitors, hypocrites and spies.

During the 1990s, thanks to the ingenuity of Zaoui, who at one point was charged by the Belgian authorities with smuggling, fund-raising and forming cells in Europe, the GIA grew on the continent. A few incidents have offered the rest of the world a small insight into the scope of Zaoui's activities.

In 1992, French convert to the cause Didier Guyon was arrested in Algeria, together with four other residents of the French town of Sartrouville. They had left France ten days earlier. Their car was full of arms and explosives destined for the GIA. Investigations showed that the GIA usually acquired weapons in Belgium, Germany or Slovakia, and smuggled them to Algeria via France and Spain.

Two years later, in 1994, Abdelhakim Boutrif was arrested on a motorway east of Paris. A search of his car uncovered large quantities of explosives and detonators, as well as heavy weapons, ammunition and radio transmitters. A year later an Algerian was arrested at a railway station in Barcelona while carrying a suitcase full of weapons and forged French identity papers.

Zaoui boosted his support structure in Europe with thuggery of the worst kind. Many unwilling Algerians living abroad were forced to support the GIA with money, transportation and other services, when Zaoui's men threatened to kill family members in Algeria if they did not cooperate.

Whether action against France was ordered by Bin Laden, or simply a result of increasing GIA frustrations remains uncertain. However, by 1995 there was a noticeable increase in the group's threats against France. Several GIA statements referred to the country as 'the mother of Evil', because of economic and military support extended to the Algerian government. One GIA communiqué in January 1995 focused upon the issue and stated that 'France has now become a full partner in genocide by paying mercenaries and rewarding its agents and financing arms deals.'

Other GIA statements and newsletters highlighted that the struggle was being exacerbated by foreign support that propped up the government. These statements fumed over the Algerian military's use of foreign helicopters and newly imported combat aircraft – the Russian-built MiG-25 – 'which were never seen before'.

A January 1995 communiqué stated bluntly that: 'The mujahideen consider anyone aiding the oppressive regime an enemy of Allah . . . as a result he/she becomes a military target.' The GIA's definition of human targets was very broad, encompassing writers, journalists, and simply people using the French language.

During this period the GIA accused the military of using napalm on villages in its territory, although this charge has never been proven.

Without doubt, France retains a special interest in Algeria and its well-being: its national security depends on the health of its former colony. France's aid to the military dictatorship had not caused any decrease in the killings and might even have aggravated the situation, however, a policy of laissez-faire only opened the way for more innocent deaths. As the left-wing *Libération* newspaper put it, 'when the question of "what to do" is asked, the answer is all too often, nothing'.

The first salvo against France came in December 1994 when the GIA came within a whisker of completing the first use of a civil airliner as a flying bomb. Operatives for the group hijacked Air France Airbus A-300 Flight 8969 while it was still on the ground in Algiers on 24 December. Of the 227 passengers, 40 were French nationals.

Four terrorists posing as Air Algeria employees boarded the plane, ordered the female passengers to cover themselves and prohibited anyone from smoking or drinking. After they had released some 60 women and children, they killed a French diplomat and, as armed police and troops looked on, dumped his body on the tarmac. They then killed an Algerian police officer, after shaking his hand as a sign of farewell, and a Vietnamese diplomat, after making him believe he would be liberated. A freed hostage later described how one passenger pleaded for his life before he was shot in the head. 'He screamed "Don't kill me, I am married, I have a child."'

French Prime Minister Edouard Balladur, chairing a crisis cabinet meeting in Paris, held Algeria responsible for the safety of French hostages after the Algerian government declined a French offer of anti-terrorist specialists to deal with the hijacking. Algerian President Liamine

Zeroual gave permission for the plane to leave Algeria shortly after the third killing.

The intention of the GIA cell, led by 25-year-old Abdul Abdallah Yahia, was to crash a fully fuelled plane into the Eiffel Tower in the heart of Paris. The French consulate in Oran, meanwhile, had received an anonymous warning that the ultimate aim was to blow the aircraft up in mid-air over Paris. Further debriefing of the passengers released in Algiers revealed that the four hijackers were carrying explosives on board, had requested and received a wristwatch from a passenger and had discussed martyrdom.

Early on 25 December, the jet, with hostages and crew still on board, took off from Algiers and landed in France an hour later. The plane landed at Marseilles-Marignane airport only because there was not enough fuel for it to fly to Paris.

Terrified passengers spent Christmas Day in captivity. The plane, parked in a remote area of the airport, was surrounded by security forces and French anti-terrorist police who had flown in shortly before the plane arrived. Negotiators established direct contact with the hijackers and were trying to secure the release of more passengers in exchange for the refuelling. But it was immediately clear that this was probably a suicide mission. The hijackers ordered a much larger amount of fuel than would be necessary to fly to Paris, enough to fulfil their ultimate objective to blow up the plane and maximise the death toll on the ground.

When the Algerians grew angry at what they saw as the obstinacy of negotiators, they killed a fourth passenger and fired shots at the control tower. With these actions they effectively signed their own death warrants and ended the mission. As darkness fell, elite Groupe d'intervention de la Gendarmerie Nationale (GIGN) troops blew out the plane's doors with explosives and threw stun grenades. With gunfire ringing out, passengers began escaping from the plane by emergency chutes. All four hijackers were killed. Two passengers, the pilot, and a member of the GIGN elite force were injured in the operation which lasted 15 minutes.

Watching from Khartoum, Bin Laden might have been impressed with the failed hijacking as a show of force by the GIA, but he required more – a sustained campaign.

France and Europe were already key areas of operation for the GIA in terms of raising finance. In mosques throughout Europe, money was collected for charity. A percentage was channelled to the GIA and other radical Islamist groups. Extortion of 'war taxes' from businesses was also a major source of income. Some contributed voluntarily. Others were coerced with intimidation and, where necessary, actual physical assault. Rarely did this become public knowledge. However, in the mid-1990s several Algerian shop owners in suburbs of France brought charges against GIA activists for subjecting them to a strong 'moral pressure' by implying that they would lose clients and get into 'trouble' if they refused to pay. The GIA was also involved in drug smuggling, petty crime and larger schemes such as bank robbery.

The sustained terror campaign in France began with the GIA eliminating an opponent in its battle for the hearts and minds of the Islamist population in France. On 10 July, the GIA issued a death list of authority figures, police and military officials in Algeria and vocal clerics around the world who opposed armed struggle in Algeria or belonged to rival terror groups in the country. A day later, Sheikh Abd al-Baqi Sahraoui, a senior voice in the Islamic Salvation Front (FIS), was murdered in a Paris mosque.

During the spring and early summer of 1995, the GIA, with strategic support from Al-Qaeda, which had its own cells and supply lines into France, prepared a full-blown bombing campaign against Paris. For the purposes of the overall action in France, Ahmed Zaoui had appointed senior aide Boualem Bensaïd as the point man for the entire project. Using specially infiltrated Algerian operatives, or men recruited from the mosques in France, three central cells were formed, based in Chasse-sur-Rhône, Lille and Vaulx-en-Velin.

The Vaulx-en-Velin cell was key to the project. This was led by an ethnic Algerian with a French passport, Khaled Kelkal, who, after being killed by gendarmes on 29 September 1995, was linked by forensics to a handful of terror operations in France. The gun that killed Sheikh Sahraoui was discovered in his apartment in Paris.

On 25 July 1995, seven people were killed and another eighty wounded in an afternoon terror attack that took place in the Paris Saint-Michel underground station, near the Latin quarter. Several people were trapped by the blast that ripped through the station. It was necessary to amputate the limbs of at least one passenger in order to extricate him from the wreckage. The explosion was timed to claim maximum casualties, occurring during afternoon rush hour.

Paris braced itself. It had been the target of an evil campaign before. In a September 1986 wave of terrorism, 11 people had been killed and 160 injured in five separate bombings by an Iranian-backed Lebanese group.

Then on 17 August, another strike at the centre of Paris went for the heart of the lucrative tourism industry when a bomb exploded near the Arc de Triomphe. The device, described as an 'anti-personnel device' by explosive experts, injured 16 people. Three of those injured were described as being in critical condition in the immediate aftermath, but all ultimately survived.

After the blast, the entire area near the Champs-Elysées and the Arc de Triomphe was evacuated and cordoned off as police and explosives-detecting dogs searched rubbish bins and other likely hiding places for additional devices. Sources close to the Paris police said that the device was particularly troubling because it was designed to cause maximum injuries or deaths among those in the vicinity. They pointed to the use of nails and other metal objects that would become shrapnel as the device detonated.

French Prime Minister Alain Juppe visited the site shortly after the explosion and attempted to reassure Parisians and to rally their spirits by asking them not to 'give in to the psychosis' of terrorism.

On 6 October, a major disaster was narrowly averted in another bombing near a subway station in south-east Paris. The blast occurred at a little after 4 p.m. outside the Maison Blanche station on the Avenue d'Italie. Terrorists had placed a time-delayed device in a rubbish bin. A passer-by noticed the device and called the police and fire brigade. It exploded as emergency officials were preparing to defuse it, but by this time people had already voluntarily evacuated the area, thus preventing a massive number of injuries.

In the wake of this GIA operation, the French government instigated a joint gendarmerie and military operation known as 'Vigipirate' designed to counter the security threat. In groups of three, one gendarme and two soldiers armed with machine guns patrolled major public areas such as Gare de Lyon, Gare Montparnasse, Charles de Gaulle airport and Orly airport, and checked at random the papers of individuals who appeared suspicious. The effect on terrorism was difficult to measure but there was a drop in crime during that period.

On the other side of the Mediterranean, there was satisfaction at the outcome of the terror campaign despite the loss of its two chief architects. Djamel Zitouni had been killed in Ain Defla in a battle with Algerian forces during the spring of 1995, while European GIA chief Ahmed Zaoui had been arrested in Belgium in March the same year. Zaoui, however, would remain a player in the 1998 plot.

Now Al-Qaeda and the Sudanese leadership received Antar Zouabri, the new head of the GIA and another Arab-Afghan who had trained and fought under Bin Laden in Afghanistan. Zouabri can only be described as a psychopath who would send GIA policy into its most bloody phase. Not the clever tactician that his predecessors had been, he reached his leadership position with a reputation earned from the culling of innocent civilians.

Bin Laden, the millionaire Mujahideen who rarely got his own hands dirty, was not an obvious bedfellow of Zouabri, whose personal body count was in the hundreds. But Zouabri was pliable and willing to obey Al-Qaeda orders while his organisation was being sharpened through Bin Laden's money, arms supplies and access to training camps in Sudan.

Towards the end of 1995, Zouabri was in Khartoum when Bin Laden felt sufficiently confident in the abilities of the GIA to finalise his plans for the 1998 World Cup. It was an ambitious project. Bin Laden pressed upon his ally that he needed the GIA who, as Algerian operatives, would easily get lost among the 600,000 Algerians already in France. Zouabri was not in a position to decline, had he so wished, as he would have risked the displeasure of his most generous sponsor. But even to a man of his limited intellect, the prestige of an attack on France, on the largest international stage possible, needed little explanation.

Bin Laden offered the GIA funding to rebuild its European headquarters in Brussels, which had been breached and shattered following the arrest of Zaoui. It was agreed that the Brussels command would be energised and provided with a network of safe houses. Funding would be supplied via Bin Laden's charitable network that ran throughout Europe and had proved so successful while sustaining Al-Qaeda's operations in Bosnia.

Zouabri would also be responsible for inserting several dozen sleepers into France. These operatives would be completely legitimate, going about everyday lives. They would be average members of the community, until such time as they were woken in advance of the championships.

Cells of sleepers would be left out to pasture in major footballing cities of France, such as Bordeaux, Lyon, Marseille and Nantes, cities that were most likely to host games during the World Cup. Others would be centred in Paris, awaiting targets that not only had a sporting theme but could include US targets such as the American embassy.

Patience is a virtue in terrorism and Bin Laden had three years to wait until this project matured. A great deal would change for him during the intervening period, but throughout that time he would never take his eye off the ball.

Nine

The Baron

On 2 July 1992, the executive committee of the Federation Internationale de Football Association (FIFA) held a general meeting in Zurich, Switzerland, to award the 1998 World Cup to France, Morocco losing out by twelve votes to seven.

Just as he had seen Morocco defeated and the United States awarded the 1994 championships, FIFA president João Havelange had decided against Morocco again and had made it known that the North African state was not his choice. Like sheep, a majority in the executive committee followed his directive.

This was an extraordinary triumph for the French after a grubby campaign. Tens of millions of dollars had been invested in lobbying FIFA officials in an effort to convince them that France was the ideal host country.

The 1998 World Cup was branded well in advance as the biggest event in sporting history. Public relations gurus were building up the sporting angle, projected record television figures and were talking up the prospect of several million football-supporting tourists visiting France.

But behind the scenes, in football's corridors of power, the actual game had been superseded. Television figures equate to sponsorship money; packed grandstands equal high gate receipts and advertising revenue. Successful tournaments generate billions of dollars in turnover and hundreds of millions of dollars in profits. Interest in goals and games is left to fans and players. It is the bottom line, not the goal line, that football's administrators concentrate on.

Ironically, it was the bastion of amateur sporting ethics, the Olympic movement, which led the way in showing what can be achieved when marketing minds take to the field. Members of the governing body of the International Olympic Committee (IOC) are rich, and the political clout they now carry ensures that they are appropriately fêted as they travel the world. IOC president Juan Antonio Samaranch became an international power broker, all but transforming sport into politics through his ability to influence the IOC committee to award the Olympic Games to a nation or to withdraw a country's Olympic status for crimes that are completely outwith his jurisdiction.

It was much the same in football. Havelange, a former Olympian, a swimmer at the 1936 Olympics and water polo team member in the 1952 games, became president of FIFA in 1974. The job carries no salary but the *Financial Times* once estimated that its perks could add up to $500,000 a year.

The FIFA he inherited was a provincial organisation, a collection of European soccer officials who met to update the rules and organise the World Cup. The election of Havelange, a South American, ended a 70-year monopoly of European rule and he immediately set about making football the world's number one sport. One profile captured his attitude succinctly. 'The man who has done more than anyone else to turn the beautiful game into a pressure cooker of financial aspirations insists that "football is power".'

By the time of his retirement, Havelange could claim that he had racked up an average of 800 hours flying time every year pursuing the cause and had visited 186 countries while in office. Havelange drilled FIFA's executive committee into a smooth-running machine where dissent rarely left the meeting room or spilled over into official releases. Despite contentious issues such as marketing and television rights featuring high on the agenda, all decisions were typically unanimously approved by the 24 members of the executive committee.

'There was no vote because there was unanimity,' FIFA secretary general Sepp Blatter often informed the media, trying to explain the fact that 24 men and women all thought exactly the same way. People on the outside may have been critical but it was nevertheless a remarkable achievement on the part of Havelange: using diplomacy, strong-arm tactics and methods bordering on blackmail to bully those under him into conformity. One prominent writer memorably called the FIFA executive 'a motley bunch of ex-politicians and bureaucrats, well heeled and well steeled in the art of big business and diplomacy . . .'

From among the footballing elite, only a handful of men dared to challenge him. Havelange had publicly feuded with Lennart Johansson, the Swedish head of UEFA, who was often quoted in the media as saying Havelange's style was too autocratic. Pelé, a Brazilian like Havelange and football's greatest star, called him a 'dictator', the highlight of several years of acrimonious relations. Elsewhere he was known simply as 'The Baron'.

Under Havelange, FIFA became rich and powerful. A gold rush of modern corporate sports sponsorship was inspired by his leadership. He struck rich commercial deals and founded lucrative new tournaments for all age groups and both sexes. It was on his watch, for example, that the Women's World Cup was created, opening up big-time team sports to half the world's population.

Every World Cup over which he had presided was more successful than the last. His bold decision to champion an American bid for the 1994 tournament paid off with the biggest World Cup ever. But that was the very least of his priorities. The World Cup decision in turn sparked the creation of Major League Soccer in the United States. At a single stroke, America won entry into the world game and FIFA won entry into American boardrooms. Both have profited handsomely.

Havelange also made FIFA a force for political change in the Third World. In 1967 he orchestrated the expulsion of South Africa from world football and thereby put FIFA at the forefront of the anti-apartheid movement. It is up to historians to determine precisely to what extent the South African triumph in the 1996 African Cup of Nations contributed to the smooth transition to majority rule, but no one disputes that it was considerable.

But the Baron became increasingly deluded about his powers, claiming that football could succeed where politics had failed. 'Only football has the power to solve the problems of international conflicts,' he said. 'In Asia and the East, we have had football matches between countries in conflict.'

There is no doubt that Havelange became one of the most powerful men in international sport. But while the Baron did good things for football, his relentless desire for commercialisation changed it irrevocably along the way, and it lost much of its original identity and appeal. Football has become a global business that has a turnover approaching $300 billion a year. The World Cup in particular is a licence to print money, and as such is fiercely fought over not only by the competing teams but by hopeful host nations and multinational sponsors.

As an indication of the extent to which nations and companies are prepared to go, Japan and Korea between them spent upwards of $100 million on their bids to host the tournament in 2002. In 1996 Nike signed a ten-year $300-million deal with the reigning champions Brazil. The terms of the contract remain secret but are widely believed to allow Nike to influence both team selection and the choice of opponents for friendly matches, thus placing their marketing interests before the technical needs of the squad.

Havelange had ensured that his swansong, the 1998 World Cup in France, would be a mammoth competition. Throughout 591 days of preliminaries, 168 participants played 643 matches and scored 1,922 goals. For the first time, the championship finals would be a 32-team affair. Sixty-four matches in ten different cities around France were scheduled and all were sold out well in advance, guaranteeing a total of 2.5 million spectators attending at an average of about 39,000 per game.

Television rights netted a premium. FIFA as usual kept most figures secret but a few details were leaked. In the United States, ABC, ESPN and ESPN2 planned more than 230 hours of coverage, including live broadcasts of every match. The Disney units paid a reported $24 million for US rights to the games, double the outlay for USA 1994. Despite this cost, Disney was already heading to the bank itself. All of the advertising time had been sold years in advance to key sponsors including Nike, Canon, FedEx, National Car Rental, Honda and the US Army.

For the French Coup du Monde, FIFA also had its big corporates signed up. A dozen multinational giants paid hundreds of millions each for a right to be associated with the championships. These included Adidas, Budweiser, Canon, Coca-Cola, Gillette, McDonald's and MasterCard, all of which would also pump additional millions into global advertising promoting their involvement as one of FIFA's Official Sponsors.

France spent upwards of $50 million courting FIFA to secure the right to host the 1998 World Cup. They had staged it first in 1938; 60 years was too long to wait to host the event for a second time, they said. The French connection with the World Cup was too great to ignore, they claimed, stretching back to the first goal in the 1930 World Cup. The highest-scoring player ever in the World Cup finals was also a Frenchman, Just Fontaine in 1958. Above all it was another Frenchman, Jules Rimet, who had pioneered the concept to establish the World Cup. On 19 June 1938, in the old Olympic stadium of Colombes, near Paris, 50,000 spectators had witnessed the triumph of Piola's Italy over Sarosi's Hungary in the final of football's third World Cup. The French could wait no longer for a second chance to be hosts and were prepared to go to almost any lengths to seize the opportunity.

The idea to hold the World Cup in France was first tabled officially on 21 July 1983. Fernand Sastre, then president of the French Football Federation, sent a letter to FIFA to inform the body that his association was willing to stand as a 'candidate for the 1990 World Cup', specifying, however, that should Italy run as candidate the same year, France would postpone its application to 1998. Italy did go on to stage the 1990 event and France set its sights on the 1998 event, the last World Cup of the twentieth century.

Aiming to attract FIFA to Paris, over $50 million was spent directly on high-profile presentations and promotional materials spread around the footballing world and on high-powered French delegations visiting other nations in order to convince them that their votes would be best used in support of the French bid. But much of this extraordinary sum was also spent on wining, dining and entertaining hundreds of officials from other countries who visited France in order to assess their bid.

For two French presidents, the late François Mitterrand and his successor Jacques Chirac, securing the event and then putting on a remarkable, acclaimed tournament was central to their personal legacies. For the French government, it was a rare opportunity to show, on the very widest and highest world stage, a modern France, confident, robust and healthy.

In the early part of 1992, the French government was active through various sporting bodies such as its Olympic Committee and Football Association in handing out sizeable development grants to sports associations in countries seen as 'waverers' ahead of the vote. Such grants were common in the bidding for major sports events such the Olympics and World Cup. The French were doing nothing illegal or that nominees for event hosts had not done for a generation.

To outsiders, such activity might seem to be nothing short of outright bribery, but during the years where Juan Antonio Samaranch and João Havelange ruled the twin pinnacles of international sport, achieving host status became a free-for-all that denigrated the principles on which the IOC and FIFA were founded.

Nine years on from that initial letter, on 2 July 1992, FIFA's executive committee convened in Zurich to award the 1998 World Cup to France. The French government formed the most extensive and professional management team ever assembled to preside over the championships. This became FRANCE 98, and was given legal status on 10 November 1992 under the aegis of the French Football Federation.

At its head was a high-profile executive committee that included, as co-president, Michel Platini, one of the greatest players France had produced; Jacques Georges, the FIFA delegate to FRANCE 98; Claude Simonet, president of the French Football Federation; Noël Le Graet, president of the France National Football League and André Delelis, the Mayor of Lens, who represented the host cities.

The committee had a general budget of $311 million, to be financed by two main sources of income: ticket sales and the commercial marketing of the World Cup itself. The estimated general budget covered the costs of the actual organisation, as well as investments for the installation of infrastructure such as the media centres, hospitality villages and accreditation units.

Ten towns and cities were selected as hosts: Paris (Parc des Princes), Saint-Denis (Grand Stade), Bordeaux, Lens, Lyons, Marseilles, Montpellier, Nantes, Saint-Etienne and Toulouse. Since the stadiums in most of these cities had been renovated when France organised – and won – the European Championships in 1984, only limited work was needed to equip them for the world event. An exception was Stade-Vélodrome in Marseilles which was to have a significant facelift, upgrading capacity from 45,000 to 60,000.

The committee promised a national pageant on an international stage, providing a package of additional entertainment that would dazzle the world. The Three Tenors – Jose Carreras, Placido Domingo and Luciano Pavarotti – were quickly booked to perform with the Orchestre de Paris in the Champ de Mars Park next to the Eiffel Tower – a mass concert in the French capital. In the ten World Cup cities in France, 32 folk groups from the qualifying countries were to perform, and there would also be other music, dance, theatre and art exhibitions. Big screens in major cities would entertain those who could not obtain tickets for major matches. In Paris, amid concerns of scalping, the local government introduced price controls. 'It is imperative that Paris not be labelled an expensive town,' said Mayor Jean Tiberi, adding that World Cup crowds would swell the normal June influx of tourists visiting Paris. 'Based on experiences in Spain and Italy we foresee about 300,000 to 400,000 extra tourists coming in,' he predicted.

The French government also began looking at its security arrangements. After the GIA bombing campaign three years later, this work took on a new urgency and was given a higher priority.

It is not clear exactly how early Islamic fundamentalist groups, led by Al-Qaeda, began staking out plans to attack the 1998 World Cup. Sometime during late 1994, Bin Laden had raised the possibility, while the relative success of the GIA in planning and executing a bombing campaign in Paris during the summer of 1995 was a coup for the Islamic fundamentalists.

The number of French civilians killed had been low, but the effect of the campaign had cut into French receipts from tourism as many American and European holidaymakers had stayed away. This economic success was seen as an added bonus. A mild rift developed between Paris and Algiers when a high-profile French–Algerian summit was cancelled because the French president, keen not to provoke the Islamists further, announced that he would not shake the Algerian president's hand. Insulted, the Algerians quickly cancelled.

That said, France continued to offer economic aid to Algeria. It also promoted IMF and World Bank support for its faltering economy. In the United Nations, France keenly supported the Algerian regime as it refused to accept international interference in its civil war. France also headed a European-wide crackdown on Algerian Islamic fundamentalists, especially the GIA.

111

Terrorist planning for 1998 received a setback with the death of Djamel Zitouni and the capture and imprisonment in Belgium of Ahmed Zaoui, along with Bin Laden they were the key masterminds behind the plot.

Belgian authorities had been watching Zaoui for some time as a result of information sold to the French Intelligence Services by Abou Khalil Mahfoud, a senior GIA figure who would play a significant role in the unfolding story of 1998.

Zaoui was tracked while meeting with known militants and becoming involved in some dubious activities. He was followed throughout Europe by Belgian detectives in 1993 and 1994. He had been a leading member of the FIS, Algeria's banned political opposition and had served on the organisation's consultative council. In Algeria's general election of December 1991, which was later quashed by the military, he had been elected as a Member of Parliament.

A lecturer in the Islamic Institute of Algiers, for a time Zaoui had remained in the country in the hope that the situation would be resolved. But soon after the forced dissolution of the AIS, the military wing of the FIS, by the government on 4 March 1992, he had to leave the country in fear of arrest. He travelled via Saudi Arabia to Belgium, where his transformation from an ardent but peaceful pro-Islamic politician into the GIA's man in Europe was widely noted. The authorities in Brussels considered him the leader of the GIA in Belgium, while Interpol suspected that he masterminded the Algerian group's insurgency throughout the continent.

Belgium had finally moved in March 1995 when a surveillance operation threw up sufficient evidence against Zaoui and those around him. He and seven of his accomplices were arrested and sent to trial. Among those was Abdel Nasr, who was also known to liaise between Zaoui, his leadership in Algeria and their paymaster in Khartoum.

Building the case against them took 18 months. During that time, so well organised were Zaoui's men in France that they continued their bombing project regardless.

Astonishingly, in court in Brussels, Zaoui's expensive legal team presented a reasonable platform of defence that cast doubt on the state's case. While the seven Islamists arrested with him were found guilty, charges against Zaoui were dismissed in October 1995 for what the court felt to be insufficient evidence. Zaoui had claimed that the forged passports discovered in his possession were for humanitarian use, ultimately to be given to political refugees from Algeria, helping them escape from a regime intent upon killing them. It was an extraordinary defence that moved the court and won Zaoui his freedom in October 1996.

The release of Ahmed Zaoui was a triumph for Islamic fundamentalism in Europe as he had proven himself a highly effective organiser and built an organisation in Europe that was unparalleled. He also ensured that many of his sleepers, already in place, were virtually uncontactable by anyone but himself, a hedge against the possibility that his masters in Algiers might sacrifice him in favour of an untarnished and unsuspected replacement.

After his release, Zaoui remained under a cloud. Gendarmerie General Commander Derrider, a competent and widely respected policeman in Belgium, continued surveillance operations on his target. But Zaoui was aware that this was happening and went about his activities with significantly more care. On several occasions he flew from Belgium to a 'clean' African or Middle Eastern state, slipped through a number of safe houses in order to lose any observers who had followed him and later made his way to a provincial airport. Using fake passports, he then flew to Algeria to see his masters, or to Khartoum to see his ally Osama bin Laden.

By the end of 1996, the plot to disrupt the 1998 World Cup was still in its infancy. The French had announced where the games would be played, but only the general outline of targets had been discussed. Documents subsequently leaked indicate that Bin Laden had focused on the United States and England squads as footballing targets. Zaoui, or those within his organisation, had focused upon the US embassy in Paris and a nuclear power station in the west of the country as strategic targets. All were to be attacked simultaneously by a number of cells.

During most of 1997 Zaoui led a double life. In Belgium he portrayed himself as a political activist, meeting visibly with those seeking a legitimate political solution to the civil war in Algeria. But even these gatherings were used to aid behind-the-scenes meetings with GIA men from around Europe.

More urgently, when outside Belgium, Zaoui began rebuilding his operation in Brussels, sending in others to establish safe houses, restart arms smuggling operations and set up a number of Islamic charities to front a financial platform that could sustain GIA cells throughout Europe.

The GIA had almost recovered in Europe during this one-year period. Dozens of Algerians and some sympathetic Moroccans, most of them with credentials that showed them to be gainfully employed in their own country and with records that showed no association with Islamic militants, moved into Europe as economic refugees, mainly to France. Their papers were legitimate and they found jobs. Some moved with their families, their children going to school and growing up alongside non-Muslims. From every possible angle, the authorities could have no cause to suspect these men, part of a Europe-wide population of Muslims estimated at well over ten million as early as 1991. They simply looked like men who had been driven from their homelands by civil war and were seeking a better way of life.

They were classic sleepers.

Ten

Hoddle's Italian Job

By the summer of 1997, with the World Cup in France just one year away, the GIA had largely recovered in Europe, rebuilding with support from Osama bin Laden. Intelligence services were at least partly aware of this revitalisation, as a segment that appeared on ABC News on 18 October 2000 revealed. This report highlighted how British intelligence had tracked 'wire transfers from Bin Laden's then-headquarters in Khartoum to a London cell of the GIA'. What they did about it, if anything, remains a secret. However, this activity continued apace during the latter part of the 1990s, after Bin Laden shifted to Afghanistan and after he finally made a definite decision to proceed with his project built around the World Cup.

While the tournament remained months and years in the future there had been little forward planning that could be done other than to map out a strategy and begin infiltrating men as sleepers into the continent, primarily into France.

Meanwhile, the footballing world continued its carefully orchestrated build-up to the main event through the programme of qualifying matches that would lead 31 teams to France, where they would join the hosts.

All was not well, however, in the home of perennial contenders England. In 1993, English football had been in disarray after manager Graham Taylor's blundering team failed to qualify for the 1994 finals in the United States. After months of cruel mockery from the media, including ongoing comparisons with a turnip, Taylor quit. Everyone looked to his successor, Terry Venables, to put a smile back on the face of English fans.

Venables, a former Barcelona and Tottenham coach, quickly restored pride and took England to the semi-finals of the 1996 European Championships, where they lost in a penalty shoot-out to the eventual tournament winners, Germany. Ahead of 1998, England was aiming to qualify for the World Cup for the tenth time and, as always, to prove that their 1966 victory in the tournament on home turf had not been a fluke. Venables, however, made a somewhat acrimonious exit from the top job, and was replaced by Glenn Hoddle, a former England midfield star.

England went into the qualifying stages of the competition in a Group Two that included former champions Italy and the highly capable Poland, in addition to outsiders Georgia and Moldova. Cup qualifying was a sporadic affair drawn out over one year between September 1996 and October 1997. Hoddle maintained Venables' upward trend and created a team that pundits said performed with imagination, a far cry from the hit-and-hope style under Taylor.

Predictably, England and Italy dominated the group. When they finally met at Wembley on 12 February 1997, both had a perfect unbeaten record. Injuries forced two key Arsenal players, David Seaman and Tony Adams, out of the match, and Italy used the home side's defensive weakness to stun the partisan crowd with a solitary goal from their most dangerous forward, Gianfranco Zola. This was enough to win them the game and they became the first team to beat England at Wembley in a World Cup match.

England were sent reeling, facing the danger of missing football's greatest showcase for the second time in a row, as only the winner of the group was guaranteed an automatic place in the finals.

Neither Italy nor England lost a game during the remaining group matches, but two disappointing draws on the part of the Italians in Poland and Georgia meant that England's visit to Rome in October would decide which of the two nations progressed directly to France the next summer. Italy were in a must-win situation.

On 11 October 1997, the spectre of hooliganism returned to haunt English football. What happened in Rome was as bad as anything that had gone before. Millions of television viewers tuning in for the crunch match got more than they bargained for: a sideshow of riot police belting the English fans with batons and running battles in the streets. Hundreds of English fans in the 81,200 crowd in the Olympic stadium clashed repeatedly with baton-wielding police. About a dozen fans, some from each side, were sent to hospital. English and Italian fans hurled coins, bottles and even seats at each other.

Police headquarters in Rome announced that 69 people had been injured at the game. That included 33 English, one of whom was hospitalised with a stab wound to the abdomen, and 19 police officers. Rome Police Chief Rino Monaco attributed the incidents to 'repeated attempts of English hooligans, all under the influence of alcohol, to push toward the south section and past their cordons of the security forces'. English authorities and fans blamed the police.

British Prime Minister Tony Blair in part blamed Italian authorities for failing to keep rival English and Italian fans separated. He wrote in a British tabloid newspaper: 'I will never excuse violence by England fans but there was a breakdown which meant rival fans mixed where they should have been kept apart. The Italians, like us, will want to learn the lessons. Nobody can fault the efforts of the British government, the British police, the Football Association and the organisers of official travel groups in trying to ensure the match was trouble-free.'

A total of 23 English fans were arrested. None of them were among the 7,000 supporters who had obtained tickets through the English Football Association's official membership. The trouble came from those who had arrived in Italy without tickets and bought tickets originally intended for Italians, thus grouping rival fans close to each other.

Football Association chief executive Graham Kelly said the Italian authorities had sold tickets to English spectators on the day of the game, making a shambles of the English ticketing arrangements. 'We are responsible for the tickets to the England fans but the way the Italians handled it made it impossible for us to fulfil our responsibilities,' Kelly said, while David Mellor, head of a new soccer task force set up by Britain's Labour government, told the BBC: 'That was not the behaviour of a civilised police force . . . The Italians should be ashamed of themselves for the manner in which they reacted.'

On the pitch the English need only a draw to win their group and qualify automatically. Italy, the 1994 runners-up, had to win or else face a tricky play-off. Defender Tony Adams summed up the feeling among the players. 'You don't get too many opportunities to play in the World Cup, so it intensifies things,' he said. 'This is the biggest game. We've got to grab the occasion with both hands. If this game doesn't motivate you then it's time to get out of the sport.'

Hoddle had the advantage of taking to Rome seven players from the Manchester United team that had downed Italian champions Juventus 3–2 in the Champions League the previous week, although he was missing several important players. England captain Alan Shearer had broken his ankle in a pre-season game and was sidelined, while Les Ferdinand and Robert Lee pulled out with injuries. In their absence, two 33 year olds, Manchester United's Teddy Sheringham and Arsenal's Ian Wright, joined the squad, along with Paul Gascoigne, then 31.

Meanwhile, the Italians were weakened by the absence of Roberto Di Matteo, who was suspended, and had to rely heavily on AC Milan's Demetrio Albertini to link up with the forwards and create chances.

In the event, England stayed back and held off Italy's attacks just enough to earn a goalless draw. Hoddle's side played slowly and patiently through the midfield, with most of the play fed through the former Lazio star Gascoigne. Rarely coming out of a defensive shell, England did well to hold off the home side, who also suffered from the 76th-minute expulsion of Juventus midfielder Angelo Di Livio. During injury time, Wright hit the post with the Italian goalkeeper and defence trailing behind him, while at the other end, from an Italian breakaway, Christian Vieri shaved the England post with a powerful header. 'We went from one emotion to another,' said England coach Glenn Hoddle, 'I thought the header was going in.' The game ended in a goalless draw.

It was the tactical sort of match, with few risks taken, that Italy has been known for through the years and it put an end to the Italian's streak of 13 straight World Cup wins at the Olympic Stadium. England topped Group Two with nineteen points from six wins, one loss and one draw, with unbeaten three-time title-holders Italy coming second with 18 points from five wins and three draws. Italian coach Cesare Maldini called it 'an injustice' that his team would have to face a play-off, despite going through qualifying play undefeated.

The United States entered the preliminary stages of the 1998 World Cup with high hopes of making their fourth successive finals appearance. Despite their lowly reputation in the footballing world, the US team had an excellent record in reaching the finals, better indeed than many of the world's long-established footballing nations, especially England. As hosts in the 1994 event, they had surprised many by reaching the quarter-finals, and on the back of this success the US had seen the introduction of Major League Soccer.

High-class competition created an environment which produced players that were fitter, possessed improved ball skills and were able to compete at a higher level.

The US went into its qualifying group with an obvious chance of booking tickets to France. Against the unheralded likes of Canada, Costa Rica, El Salvador and Jamaica, only Mexico in their group had a better reputation and were perennial qualifiers in what was considered one of the world's weaker entry points to the finals.

As the qualifiers progressed, group rankings materialised largely to form, with Mexico dominating. With one round of games remaining in the CONCACAF zone, Mexico had qualified with 17 points. The United States led the pack to claim second spot and entry into France with 14 points, while Jamaica had 13, El Salvador 10, Costa Rica 9 and Canada 6. Having hammered Canada 3–0 earlier in the competition at home, the USA were favourites to claim that runners-up position as they travelled to Canada for their penultimate qualifying match on 9 November 1997.

American star Claudio Reyna's opening goal set the tone. He fired into an empty net after Roy Wegerle had broken free and drawn the Canadian goalkeeper to the side before passing to the wide-open Reyna. Roy Wegerle added two late goals to seal a conclusive victory. It was all the more impressive for the fact that the US side was missing some key players, including midfielder John Harkes and Jeff Agoos, who were suspended, and midfielder Tab Ramos and goalkeeper Kasey Keller, both of whom were injured.

American striker Eric Wynalda commented later: 'In the last couple of years, the United States has established itself as a team that should be at or near the top of the group. We've done extremely well because we're the first team to beat Canada here. That says a lot.'

After American players paraded around Swangard Stadium in celebration, the excited US coach Steve Sampson joined in the celebrations with fans. 'This means we can continue our growth,' Sampson said. 'We can try and bring in those fans who are sitting on the fence, try and embrace them and make soccer a major sport in the States.'

Between the 11 October qualification of England and the 9 November qualification of the United States – which had already appeared inevitable before the game in Canada – there was a sudden, inexplicable change in the GIA's European network. Ahmed Zaoui seemingly stepped aside. For one year after his acquittal by a Belgian court on charges of subversive activities, the GIA chief of operations in Europe had remained resident in Brussels. He knew he was being watched more closely than ever by the Belgian security services and Interpol and for all intents and purposes he remained 'in character' while in Belgium, posing as a charitable figure trying to peaceably keep a legitimate Algerian political opposition together.

He held meetings with 'legitimate' members of the Algerian political opposition in exile and worked for several charities that supported displaced Algerians in several states in Europe. Both presented him with opportunities, that from the outside looked legitimate, to mix with fellow members of the GIA. The charity umbrella was a key way in which the GIA could legally, though surreptitiously, fund its operatives while they awaited orders, and the Bin Laden web of finance was so tangled and complicated that these funds were virtually impossible to trace.

But in the wake of his close shave with Belgian law, Zaoui was no longer able to operate efficiently. He had to take care when meeting anyone for fear of drawing attention to any GIA operatives in the field. It was clear that, while he could boost the GIA's quasi-legal network of charity fronts and engage in political work, any active operations could not be masterminded by someone who was under such close surveillance.

During 1997, Zaoui had left Belgium on a handful of occasions en route to destinations in the Middle East or North Africa. Usually he would be seen arriving in low-risk nations such as Morocco or one of the Gulf States, after which he would simply disappear, losing the European surveillance officers who inevitably tailed him. During these moments of free movement, Zaoui often headed for either GIA-held areas in Algeria or to Afghanistan.

Afghanistan was by now once more the home of Al-Qaeda and Osama bin Laden, and any consultations on the master plan to sabotage the World Cup had to be carried out there. Plotters knew that Bin Laden wanted simultaneous attacks on key football teams as well as American targets to carry his message to the global audience that the tournament would guarantee. It was 'work in progress' until the latter stages of 1997 when the qualified nations, their groups and playing arrangements were finalised.

It was also clear that Zaoui, whose operational experience in Europe was vital to carrying out a plan of this size, could not do so in Belgium where there were just too many people watching him. He himself complained that his home was routinely searched, his office bugged and his telephones tapped. In order for him to successfully oversee operations in France, manage the smuggling of arms and explosives into Europe and bring in the technical expertise needed, Zaoui needed a fresh start.

During 1997, Bin Laden quietly used sympathisers to purchase a number of safe houses in Switzerland, a country without a history of allowing Islamic fundamentalists to create bases there. Using Swiss banking secrecy laws, a well-trodden route in Al-Qaeda's money laundering network, accounts were opened in Geneva and men inserted into legitimate jobs there. These individuals would run a management cell in Geneva that would be operated from a distance by Zaoui.

After England's success in Italy, on 2 November, Zaoui packed his bags, built a small fire in the garden of his home to burn any files he considered might be incriminating or capable of rousing suspicion and then drove out of Brussels. Knowing that his conversations were being listened to, on the telephone he told an associate that he was planning to spend a weekend in the southern city of Arlon, near the border with Luxembourg.

After managing to give his ever-present police tail the slip, Zaoui made straight for the French border. He drove through France to the Swiss border and, using forged papers and a new, false identity, gained easy access to the country. Unimpeded, he drove to Basle.

A few days later, Zaoui made himself known to the Swiss authorities and applied for political asylum. This guaranteed him a judicial review, the beauty of which was that its drawn-out system of hearings and appeals could take years to complete. During this intervening period, Zaoui would be free to do as he pleased as long as he was not breaking Swiss law.

He was assigned by the Swiss government to live in Sion, the capital of Valais province, until his case could be heard. By this time, the Swiss security services had identified him as a potential troublemaker, acting on a tip-off by their Belgian counterparts. They mounted 24-hour surveillance.

This time, however, Al-Qaeda and the GIA were prepared. They had built a joint management cell of safe houses and operatives that could function within the confines imposed upon them. On numerous occasions Zaoui would leave his home and inexplicably disappear, leaving those trailing him without a clear idea of where he was going. He was adept at this and would change his coat and hat to alter appearance while on the move and out of sight of the men in his wake. Not once was Zaoui's new network in Switzerland compromised, such was the sophistication of these Islamist groups in the modern era.

Safe houses were located in Geneva, Lausanne and Bern. As part of the terms of political asylum, Zaoui was required to report once a week to the office in Sion which was handling his case. This schedule gave him ample opportunity to slip out of the city and to one of his safe houses for several days at a time.

To give himself legitimacy, on 21 April 1998 he announced the creation of a provisional office of the council on the co-ordination of the Islamic Salvation Front (FIS) abroad, over which he would himself preside.

Swiss law gives foreigners the same rights of freedom of expression and association as Swiss nationals. Although the Swiss government also had the constitutional right to expel any foreigner who posed a threat to the internal or external security of Switzerland, with no proof of Zaoui's underground activities there was never support at the Switzerland Federal Department of Foreigners to take this measure.

Zaoui went to great lengths to protect himself. He issued a statement claiming he was the subject of a 'lynching campaign' and that the Belgians were attempting to associate him wrongly with the GIA. It would be wrong, he reasoned, for the Swiss to deny him refuge on the basis of this 'propaganda'. Zaoui claimed he was but a simple teacher from the Islamic Institute of Algiers who had been condemned to death by the self-same GIA for supporting a political solution to the crisis in Algeria.

While Zaoui, ensconced in safe houses dotted around Switzerland, was now able to begin acting on Bin Laden's ideas, events elsewhere on the football pitch were providing a further boost. On 12 November, Saudi Arabia qualified for the finals for the second successive time, beating Qatar 1–0 in the last match of Asia's Group A. The Saudis had become the first Arab Gulf country ever to reach the second round of the competition when they had qualified for the 1994 World Cup finals in the United States.

In Group B of the Asian qualifiers, South Korea was the other automatic qualifier, while Iran and Japan met in a play-off in Malaysia on 16 November to decide the continent's third team in the finals. Iran, the losers of that tie, went on to defeat Australia – winners of the Oceania qualifying group – over a two-leg play-off for a final spot. This was another boost for Bin Laden: a plethora of Saudi Arabian and Iranian fans in France would offer excellent cover for his operatives.

Meanwhile, in North Africa, Tunisia was providing more reasons for celebration among the terrorists – perhaps the best news short of the qualification of Algeria. With Algerian football stunted due to its civil war, no country in the world better suited the plans of Bin Laden than Tunisia.

Tunisians and Algerians have much in common, not least that French is spoken commonly as a second language after Arabic. The two countries share a long, porous border; Algerian operatives could slip into the neighbouring country with ease, and use forged passports to pass themselves off as Tunisian fans.

The same applied in France. To a casual observer, Algerians and Tunisians were identical. Both also had large ethnic communities living in the country and the French authorities were far less likely to look twice at a Tunisian, the latter having no history of civil war and no groups capable of perpetrating terrorist acts in Europe. In short, the Tunisians presented ideal cover.

Once the doormats of African soccer, Tunisia had improved considerably. In Group Two of the Africa qualifiers, they were paired with the strong Egyptian side and the lower-tier sides of Liberia and Namibia. Predictably, for the most part the big two steamrollered over the others, but when it counted Tunisia more than matched Egypt, winning against them at home by a solitary goal and playing an excellent goalless draw in the powder-keg atmosphere of Cairo. Egypt also stumbled to a shock 1–0 defeat in Liberia.

In their final game in Tunis, the home side cruised to an easy 4–0 success over Namibia to claim a place in France. The capital erupted in celebration. It was only Tunisia's second time in the finals, the previous being an appearance in Argentina in 1978. On that occasion, Polish stalwart Henry Kasperczak had helped his country eliminate the North Africans. In 1994, however, Kasperczak had been named Tunisian coach and, with delicious irony, was now a national hero in Tunisia. With the enthusiasm he injected into the team, plus technical know-how, he had led them to a second-place finish at the African Cup of Nations and into the 1996 Olympics. For a team made up of amateurs and semi-professionals, it was no mean achievement.

Almost too fortuitously for Al-Qaeda, Morocco – another of Algeria's neighbours with easy-to-infiltrate borders – also won a trip to France. Morocco had been the first African country to win a group when they took Group F in 1986. They were handed a relatively easy route to France in African qualifying Group Five when they were paired with war-torn Sierra Leone, a disappointing Ghana and Gabon.

Led by the supremely talented Mustapha Hadji, who played his league football in Spain with Deportivo Coruna, aside from a 2–2 draw in Accra against Ghana, Morocco never dropped another point. Through the group stage, they scored 14 goals. Henri Michel coached the Moroccans, heading up his third World Cup team. He previously coached France and Cameroon; he had also guided the 1984 French Olympic team to a gold medal.

On 7 December came another milestone for the plotters. Afghanistan may be a footballing backwater, but this day the sport took centre stage, at least for the very limited audience with access to television. It was the draw for the 1998 World Cup finals in France and it was watched with such anticipation in that untamed corner of Asia that one would almost think they themselves had entered a team. In a sinister sense, they had.

Osama bin Laden had been ensconced in Afghanistan since being asked to leave Sudan by his erstwhile governmental sponsors there. He had received a red carpet welcome in Afghanistan from Mullah Mohammed Omar, spiritual leader of the Taleban, an extreme religious group that had swept through Afghanistan in 1996 thanks, in no small part, to Al-Qaeda bankrolling their military efforts. Mullah Omar had banned television as an instrument of evil. But Bin Laden, his friend, was not subject to such religious edicts. He was strangely somehow above what Mullah Omar declared was God's law.

Bin Laden loved television. He owned several portable satellite receivers that could be used in the field to tap into the cream of American and world television. Throughout the remote Hindu Kush mountain range, he maintained command centres, caves that had been secretly excavated and fitted with living quarters, an armoury and a communications centre that gave him access to satellite television and the Internet. It was likely to have been in one of these that Bin Laden watched the draw for the 1998 World Cup finals in December 1997, televised live from Marseilles.

The event was a slick affair, staged before 38,000 fans in Stade-Vélodrome, and broadcast on networks all over the world. It also threw up some intriguing matches, none more so than in Group F. This group brought together Germany, Yugoslavia and political foes the USA and Iran. This was the match that the world's media chose to highlight: 'One end of the stadium will have fans in Uncle Sam suits shouting "U-S-A!" The other will have spectators jeering "the Great Satan",' speculated one reputable and normally staid wire service.

Others in the footballing world immediately saw an opportunity to help relations between the two countries. Both teams' representatives said that they would attempt to avoid the political distractions. 'This is going to be a great opportunity to show that soccer and the World Cup can do what politicians and diplomats can't,' said US Soccer Federation president Alan Rothenberg. 'Maybe we can have soccer diplomacy like we had ping-pong diplomacy with China.'

Iran Football Federation president Darius Mustafavi hit the same note of *entente*. 'The meaning of FIFA is peace and unity,' he said. 'We are thinking only of soccer, not politics. We are friends of the people of the USA.'

Elsewhere, away from such distractions, events threw up more golden opportunities for Bin Laden and his allies. Morocco were drawn in Group A alongside Brazil, Norway and Scotland. Saudi Arabia joined the hosts, Denmark and South Africa in Group C. Neither appeared to be of any strategic value, aside from offering a reason for many Islamic fundamentalist operatives to enter France by passing themselves off as Saudi or Moroccan fans. It was the pairing in Group G of England and Tunisia that most interested him, especially the fact that they were scheduled to meet in Marseilles, the home of a vast immigrant population of North Africans, including Algerians.

Fate was smiling upon Osama bin Laden as he put the wheels in motion to attempt the most audacious terrorist attack ever planned.

Eleven

The Road to France

In mid-December 1997, Ahmed Zaoui slipped out of Switzerland using a false passport and entered Austria. In Vienna he caught a Pakistan International Airlines flight to Karachi. From there he chartered a small private plane to make the short hop to a remote dirt airstrip in the Kandahar province of Afghanistan.

He was joined in Afghanistan by several of the leadership elite of the GIA. Documents that have surfaced recently suggest one of them might even have been the infamous El-Wed, also known as 'The Pakistani'. El-Wed was a hardened Algerian Islamist who, as his alias suggests, was not even Algerian. He had fought with Osama bin Laden during the struggle against the Soviet occupation of Afghanistan and, at the conclusion of the conflict, had opted to remain within 'the struggle'. With nothing to fight for in his native Pakistan, he moved where the action was. During the early 1990s, Islamic fundamentalism's most prominent war front was in Algeria.

El-Wed had been one of the founders of the GIA and had become a notable component of the group. He had no ties in the local community and had little time for those who differentiated between Algeria's ruling military regime and the people who lived peacefully under it. El-Wed argued that living peacefully under the military-backed government equated to supporting it. All who resided in government-controlled areas – men, women and children – were therefore legitimate targets. In an organisation which was known for its brutality, El-Wed became notorious for his bloodlust.

A trail of massacred peasants attributed to El-Wed ended in 1994 when he was detained by the military and placed in the supposedly secure Serkadji Prison. However, in January 1995 the facility erupted into chaos and weeks of rioting. Conflicting reports circulated, one was that El-Wed had been murdered by guards during the crisis, and another that he had been one of a number of prisoners who had escaped. No body was ever presented to the public despite government claims that he was dead.

Throughout the next few years, reports persisted of sightings in Algeria and of his participation in various terrorist activities. The Pakistani, it seemed, might still be alive. As late as 1997, in documents relating to the World Cup plot, his name was mentioned as an active participant.

Within the circle of plotters was a new face. He was Hassan Hattab, a product of the fall-out surrounding a recently failed attempt at organising an election in Algeria where the unrest had entered a new and increasingly bloody phase.

The year 1997 was a watershed in the struggle within Algeria. Allies of President Zeroual formed a political party in March to contest seats in the June elections. This party, the Rassemblement National pour la Démocratie or National Democratic Rally (RND) – took 155 of the 380 seats in the Algerian Popular Assembly, with the pro-government FLN winning a further 64 seats. Moderate Islamist parties Hamas and al-Nahdah won 25 per cent of the seats between them. Local councils, a third tier of government, were elected on 25 October. The turnout was as low as the 1991 elections and the RND only managed the slight majority that the FIS had received in December 1991. This may have been because the election process in reality meant little, as constitutional changes in late 1996 had rendered the Popular Assembly largely powerless and gave the power of veto to non-elected (i.e. military) offices.

Protests ensued from all sides. Voting irregularities and widespread fraud were alleged. Street protests took place. Opposition parties called for US diplomatic intervention and for enlisted men and lower-ranking officers within the Algerian military to turn on their commanders.

Allegations continued to appear in the media charging that the military was implicated in the slaughter of villagers which had previously been blamed on the GIA. In addition, army and police deserters reported widespread human rights abuses by the security forces.

The election and attitudes towards it caused caused a partial break-up of the Islamic opposition into smaller entities. These were led by two competing Armed Islamic Groups, one led by Antar Zouabri and another smaller entity which competed for the same name, led by Mouloud Hebbi. Later the larger group would again absorb the smaller. Also embarking upon a terrorist campaign in Algeria during this period were the Army of Islamic Salvation and the Islamic Movement for Preaching and Jihad, led by Mustapha Kertali. At least five additional groups were either associated with or splintered from these four and of these, arguably the highest profile was Hassan Hattab's Salafist Preaching and Combat Group (GSPC).

Born on 14 December 1967 at Touiba, 30 kilometres south of Algiers, Hattab emerged within the ranks of Islamists in 1984 when joining forces with Mustapha Bouyali and Abdelkader Chebbouti. The three of them are recognised by some as the founders of Algeria's jihad.

Bouyali was a wild operator. Dubbed the 'Robin Hood of Algeria', he organised spectacular operations, raiding banks and blowing up food stores, then distributing his booty to the poor, but he was killed in the spring of 1987.

Hattab, meanwhile, was more astute. During his military service in 1988 he persuaded a group of paratroopers to turn against the armed forces, aiming to trigger an uprising. He went on to join the paramilitary opposition under noted commander Mohamed Allal, joined the GIA and became leader of the Al-Fath brigade. When Djamel Zitouni became leader of the GIA in 1994, he appointed Hattab as chief of the three active brigades in the Algiers area, Al-Ansar, Al-Quds and Al-Fath.

In June 1995, Hattab became emir of the GIA's second region. As commander of an area covering Algiers and Blida, he was believed to have 3,000 men under his command. He proved to be a highly effective leader, and the men in his units were considered the finest in the Islamic opposition. So loyal were they to him personally, that when he announced a partial separation from the GIA, to form the Salafist Preaching and Combat Group, all but a handful went with him.

Hattab had encountered Bin Laden when the latter was still in Sudan. As a close aide of early GIA leader Mourad Sid Ahmed, an Arab-Afghan who had secured support from the Al-Qaeda leader for his civil war effort, Hattab had been one of those who shuttled to and from Khartoum for meetings with Bin Laden. After the death of Ahmed, Hattab had remained among the group's hierarchy under Zitouni, during which time he graduated to being one of the GIA's decision-makers and had come into close contact with 'The Sheikh', Bin Laden.

But he was an ambitious man and wanted to be his own boss. Al-Ansar, Al-Quds and Al-Fath all maintained a presence in Sudan when Bin Laden was there, utilising Al-Qaeda bases for training. Al-Qaeda had also supplied all three brigades with arms.

The 1997 election presented a pretext for Hattab to pursue his own agenda. During the period of division, as the Islamists decided how to respond, the GSPC issued a statement that it was now a separate entity from the GIA, although in reality Hattab and his men remained within the sphere of the GIA.

While he had now established his own fiefdom, Hattab and his GSPC continued to cooperate actively within the GIA as before. It is no surprise, therefore, that he was involved in the World Cup plot, working alongside the GIA's European chief Ahmed Zaoui and the mysterious GIA figure El-Wed.

These three joined Bin Laden in Afghanistan in mid-December 1997, representing the Algerian side of the proposed operation. It is probable that Hattab was there as leader, with Ahmed Zaoui below him in the GIA pecking order. El-Wed, who is only named as a peripheral player in later events, may have been an observer for the GIA high command. From Al-Qaeda there was Bin Laden, influential Egyptian Ayman al-Zawahiri and Kishk Samir.

Al-Zawahiri was by now considered Bin Laden's chief henchman, the man who filled Bin Laden's sometimes troubling need for a dominant male figure in his life. Following the assassination of Osama's first 'father figure' in Islamist circles, Dr Abdullah Azzam, with whom he founded the Maktab al-Khidamat to organise Arab-Afghan fighters in Afghanistan, the impressionable Saudi had lurched towards Dr Hassan al-Turabi, the power behind the throne in Sudan. When he was let down by al-Turabi on being expelled from Sudan, Bin Laden turned to al-Zawahiri.

A bloodthirsty man, al-Zawahiri had pushed the Al-Qaeda head toward an anarchic vision of Islamic fundamentalism, using his protégé's strange fixation upon him to gain a voice. He had a key role in determining the direction in which Al-Qaeda would develop and its strategies, and played up to the affection he received.

Like Bin Laden, al-Zawahiri is a strange character to be at the head of Islamic fundamentalism. He grew up in an upper-class neighbourhood in Cairo. Both his grandfathers were renowned scholars. An uncle was the first Secretary-General of the Arab League. After graduating from medical school he had begun working as a paediatrician.

While a student in the 1960s, al-Zawahiri became involved in the fundamentalist movement rolling through Egypt. In October 1981, President Anwar Sadat of Egypt was assassinated and Islamic extremists were tried and convicted in a military court. Al-Zawahiri was one of 302 suspected activists charged as being co-conspirators in the plot. Although acquitted, he was convicted on an unrelated weapons charge and spent three years in prison.

His middle-class background had given him an advantage over many of those sharing the dock with him, especially his ability to speak English. He was promoted as a spokesman for the group. 'We want to speak to the whole world. We are Muslims who believe in our religion. We are here, the real Islamic front and the real Islamic opposition,' he said on one occasion.

After serving his time, al-Zawahiri had moved into the top ranks of the Islamic activists. He attempted to promote religion, bizarrely while also maintaining a decidedly suburban medical practice as a paediatrician. He allegedly abused this position by molesting children. This allegation has never been backed up by solid evidence, but nevertheless a scandal was brewing in Cairo during the early years of the 1980s. As a result of a police investigation into allegations by several parents, he was accused of molesting small children while they were under anaesthetic and using his position to gain the trust of other youngsters. For a time this police investigation was kept low-key due to the wide respect for al-Zawahiri's family. However, when a decision was made to pursue the allegations on an official footing, family members stepped in behind the scenes to make sure a highly embarrassing enquiry did not get off the ground. The issue quietly went away.

In 1985 he appeared in Afghanistan to join the resistance against the Soviets. But his interest in children appears to have remained, judging by the persistent clouds that surrounded him later when based in Sudan, Switzerland and Afghanistan.

Al-Zawahiri's post-Afghanistan career began with Egyptian Islamic Jihad, the group that was responsible for the 1981 assassination of President Sadat and the attempt to murder his successor, Hosni Mubarak. This latter action was the incident that forced Bin Laden to switch his base from Sudan to Afghanistan, Sudan having come under international pressure and sanctions for sheltering known terrorists.

During the Khartoum years, Bin Laden and al-Zawahiri had got to know each other well, working on a variety of projects which had resulted in both gaining stature in the eyes of international Islamic fundamentalists. Al-Zawahiri had been operational commander in the Somalia operation, for example.

He would also play a key role within the World Cup project. During the summer of 1995 he had run an office in Geneva from where Bin Laden and the main states sponsoring terrorism, Iran and Sudan, hoped to launch jihad directly into the USA. The project was largely a white elephant, but one useful spin-off had been that Al-Qaeda's roots had begun to spread into Europe. Al-Zawahiri had travelled widely on the continent and had his own people on the ground in several countries.

During the summer of 1997, he also undertook what is considered by experts to be a working holiday in Europe. Arriving via Spain, at first he was untroubled by being tracked by the authorities. For two weeks he visited the mosque to pray, drank coffee in public coffee shops and visited museums. At times, he cheerfully nodded to those tailing him, making it obvious that he knew they were there. On the telephone in his Valencia hotel room, he would speak to friends who called and then thank the security services for listening.

But the showboating could not go on indefinitely as there was serious work to be done. One night, al-Zawahiri left his hotel under cover of darkness and gave the slip to those who were supposed to be monitoring his activities. It was a serious blunder on the part of the security services.

During late September and into early October 1997, al-Zawahiri had five surveillance-free weeks in Europe. Travelling on false passports, he shuttled between Islamists in Britain, France, Belgium, Italy and possibly elsewhere. According to reliable intelligence sources, in London he met, among others, with senior Islamist Sheikh Abu Hamza Al-Masri.

Strangely the name 'Abu Hamza' appears in documentation linked directly to the World Cup plot. Whether this is the same Abu Hamza is open to speculation.

Al-Zawahiri also spent time in France and it is likely that he used this time to review and report back to Bin Laden on the status of the cells already established in the country. Within two months of the al-Zawahiri trip, a clearer picture of the World Cup qualifying teams, groups and fixtures would emerge. Only at that time would the GIA's sleepers come to life and begin preparing for the project.

One of those who had been moulded to be a key European operative for Bin Laden was Kishk Samir, a former member of Egyptian Islamic Jihad under al-Zawahiri. Samir had a reputation as a smart operative. While al-Zawahiri could never be permanently based in Switzerland, Samir remained in Europe to become one of the senior managers of Al-Qaeda cells in half a dozen countries. The plot against the 1998 World Cup would have his fingerprints all over it.

Bin Laden had called the meeting at Kandahar in December 1997 to review progress on his pet project. Assembled before him was the effective leadership of the GIA and his own Al-Qaeda in Europe. Hassan Hattab, although the leader of a GIA faction, was Bin Laden's preferred Algerian partner in this project, perhaps with the support of the GIA's shadowy high command at home who, at the time, were split and struggling to prevent moves toward establishing peace in Algeria on government terms. The GIA's bombing campaign in the 1990s had shown that it had a operational network of cells already in France. Through 1996 and 1997, with Al-Qaeda's patronage, the group laid ever-deeper roots. Furthermore, and perhaps most valuable to the cause, the GIA had recruited disaffected youth of North African extraction in France as well as inserting some of their own operatives into the country.

In the wake of the draw for the championships, a clear picture was now available as to the movements of Bin Laden's footballing targets. He had already decided on 15 June, the day of the England versus Tunisia match, as the date of his operation. This was also the day that the United States team was scheduled to play their first group match in Paris, meaning that they would be exposed either travelling to the ground or staying in an unfamiliar temporary hotel ahead of the match. Either way they would be surrounded by new faces and the security operation around them would inevitably be at its weakest.

The other elements of the Bin Laden plan – attacks on the US embassy in Paris and on a nuclear power station that had been monitored in the west of France – could easily be fitted in around a footballing schedule. With Bin Laden dictating the date and timing of the attack, the meeting in Afghanistan had been called in order that the European leadership of both Al-Qaeda and the GIA could flesh out the operation. They had six months to go to turn this deadly vision into a reality.

Twelve

Bin Laden's $4.1 Billion Bomb

The city of Poitiers is the capital of France's Poitou-Charentes province on the Atlantic coast. Heart of the cognac region, it is an unremarkable if picturesque city, a 'chocolate-box town' with its timber-framed buildings and skyline dominated by church spires.

Founded in pre-Roman times, Poitiers maintains a medieval aspect with many churches and old streets, but it is also the home of the famous Parc de Futuroscope, a mind-boggling range of virtual reality rides just eight kilometres north of the old city.

The region attracts millions of tourists each year who come to enjoy the golden glow of the vineyards, the River Charente, the castles, house façades and Romanesque churches. Away from the city, they are enchanted by ocean views, farmlands criss-crossed by hedges and trees, marshes and vineyards – a veritable geographical mosaic.

Poitiers University, one of the oldest in Europe, exerts a strong influence on the city. Its 12 faculties boast an annual intake of around 28,000 students, including some 2,000 foreign students from over 90 countries. The student population keeps more than just the bars busy, the economy of the region as a whole benefits considerably from having such a large student body in its midst.

The one blot on an otherwise idyllic landscape is the Civaux power station. The peace of the region was punctured and its picturesque, untouched image gravely dented by the trauma of a bad-tempered fight over nuclear power in the late 1980s and early 1990s. When the dust settled, nuclear power became another thing that Poitiers and Poitou-

Charentes was most notable for throughout France. The residents were far from happy.

Electricité de France (EDF) began seeking authorisation to build its Civaux power plant in 1986 and received final government authorisation to begin construction in 1993 after an extended period of enquiry. Civaux-1 was to be France's 57th operating nuclear power reactor. Situated on the River Vienne, just south of Poitiers, it was planned as the third unit of France's advanced 1,450 MW N4 reactor series. Almost from inception this was a controversial project with strong local resistance and a series of operational problems in the later stages of its development.

EDF launched their project in 1986 against a background of significant anger, especially as this was also the year that the nuclear industry – already suspect in the public's eyes – suddenly became almost demonised in the wake of the worst accident in the history of nuclear power. As early as the late 1950s the unpredictable nature of the industry had been clear. As nuclear power spread and became fashionable among governments, the catalogue of errors and glaring problems escalated. Then came Chernobyl.

In 1986 – the year the Civaux project was announced in France – an explosion ripped through Reactor Four of the Chernobyl nuclear power plant in Ukraine. It was the world's worst nuclear accident.

At 1.23 a.m. on 26 April 1986, staff conducting an unauthorised experiment lost control of the reactor and it exploded, blowing the unit's roof into the air and sending a cloud of radioactivity over most of Europe. Poorly trained and managed workers made it worse with an improper shutdown that nearly triggered a meltdown.

As the radiation spread throughout Ukraine, Belarus and Russia, scientists in Scandinavia were first to pick up increased radiation levels. They alerted the world that something was terribly wrong at Chernobyl. Indeed radiation levels were so high that a Swedish engineer suspected something more sinister than an accident. 'My first thought was that a war had broken out and that somebody had blown up a nuclear bomb,' Cliff Robinson, a nuclear engineer at Sweden's Forsmark nuclear plant, told Reuters.

Before the end of 1990, 2,700 to 3,000 people had fallen seriously ill in the Chernobyl zone and the disaster would also destroy the lives of future generations. At Cherkassy, one in five babies are born with deformities. Limbs, eyes and ears are missing. Among children, the main types of diseases observed are grey cataracts, blood diseases, liver diseases, cancer and collapse of the immune system seen in children as young as three.

The Ukrainian government now says hundreds of thousands of people suffer from Chernobyl-related illnesses. And that may be just the beginning. Among scientists there is deep concern about long-term genetic damage to future generations.

In their own defence, the industry's proponents point to a long history of nuclear power generation all over the world and only a handful of disasters. The oldest commercial nuclear generating unit still in operation is the Calder Hall Unit 1 at Seascale in Cumbria, Great Britain. The United Kingdom has seven commercial reactors built in the 1950s that are still in operation. No other country has any reactors in operation that were built prior to 1960.

France began the development of its nuclear energy programme as early as 1945 with the creation of the Commissariat à l'Energie Atomique, or CEA, by the provisional government of General de Gaulle. The CEA has supervised the development of all atomic applications in France ever since.

In the 1970s and 1980s, a period during which the world experienced two oil crises, the French government decided to build 34 reactors of 900 MW capacity. The first programme was launched in 1974. Two years later it was decided to build 20 additional 1,300 MW reactors. A third programme to build four additional 'new generation' PWRs (a 1450 MW unit, called N4) has been implemented. The first N4 reactor (Chooz B-1) went critical in July 1996 and the last (Civaux-2) was connected to the grid in May 2000. These are the most powerful reactors in operation today.

The successful implementation of its civil nuclear programme meant that France would be able to entirely replace fossil fuel plants with nuclear units. With 58 PWRs and a net installed capacity of 63,000 MW, by 2000, nuclear energy would represent 75 per cent of the country's electricity production, satisfying national needs. France is the world's second largest nuclear operator in capacity terms, trailing the USA but well ahead of Japan, Germany and Russia.

In 1998 the most talked-about nuclear project in France was Civaux. EDF has put the cost of the Civaux units (including Civaux-2, which was already under construction in 1998) at $4.1 billion. It was scheduled to be the last nuclear installation of the N4 series and would give France more than 12,000 MW of excess generating capacity.

EDF sought to reassure the residents of Poitou-Charentes by explaining that the N4 unit at Civaux was the safest design in the world. The company highlighted an abundance of safety features, including the basic design. The reactor vessel's 23 centimetres of thick cast steel provided the first level of nuclear containment. This was then encased in a three-layer structure comprising 1.2 metres of concrete, a 50-centimetre compressed air gap and finally 60 centimetres of reinforced concrete. Reactor shutdown would take 2.15 seconds.

Civaux, said EDF, was fundamentally the safest and most secure nuclear power facility in the world. Due to these promises and comprehensive safety plans, the government had approved the construction of Civaux-1 over the concerns of the people of Poitou-Charentes.

But no matter how safe Civaux-1 was from mechanical, electronic or some other catastrophic failure, it would have been impossible to guard against the fate that was planned for it by the terrorists headed by Bin Laden during 1997. Bin Laden was fascinated by nuclear energy. His interest in obtaining nuclear materials for himself, in order to construct a nuclear device, led to his following the industry closely. Civaux was on his radar screen.

In the search for supplementary targets, the Al-Qaeda leader and his allies hit upon an audacious plan. Using a hijacked airliner, a suicide pilot could crash into a nuclear power station. At the very least, a hit that failed to cause a major accident would cause worldwide panic by the ease at which a nuclear power station could be attacked. Most likely, however, a hit on any part of the central nervous system of a nuclear power station would set off a chain reaction of calamities that could not conceivably be planned for, leading to a core meltdown and a major disaster of Chernobyl proportions.

Bin Laden and his team had been looking closely at France in preparation for the multiple hit. The country had a plethora of nuclear targets from which to choose, but Civaux-1 stood out. Scheduled to be operating in test mode until May 1998, shortly before the 15 June attack date set by Bin Laden, the facility would have a huge stock of low-enriched uranium oxide.

A direct hit on the reactor by a jetliner travelling at several hundred miles an hour in a crash dive, or alternatively a fatal hit on the reactor's central systems would, said those advising Bin Laden, create a disaster that equalled, if not surpassed, that of Chernobyl. It was also believed that an attack of this sort would surprise the French authorities so completely that the power station certainly would not be notified in time and the reactor would be on line and at its most vulnerable.

Air traffic in the Poitou-Charentes region revolves around three airports in Poitiers, Angoulême and La Rochelle, all of which had scheduled services with multiple connections to other parts of France and Europe. The best developed and most convenient from an operational standpoint was the Aéroport de Poitiers-Biard. The principal aerial gateway in and out of Poitou-Charentes, this airport was served by a handful of regular flights operated by Air France, Air Liberte and Buzz. The airport has direct scheduled routes to destinations such as Dijon, Marseilles, Nice, Strasbourg and London. Had a suitable scheduled flight not been available on 15 June, Bin Laden and his fellow conspirators considered stealing an aircraft from the Aero-Club du Poitou, which based its operations there.

Summer airline schedules would tell the plotters all they needed to know, allowing them to make the decision on which flight would be used in the operation. They preferred a larger commercial aircraft of the types operated by Air France, Air Liberte and Buzz as they carried a larger load of fuel on take-off and would reach a greater crash speed when sent into a dive.

With Civaux-1 decided upon as a target, operational planning for the hit on Poitou-Charentes began with Ahmed Zaoui, the GIA's head of European operations, and Kishk Samir, Bin Laden's most senior man on the continent. Only a couple of individuals were required for the operation, such was the limited security at Aéroport de Poitiers-Biard, a small provincial airport considered low risk in all security assessments. Therefore they recommended that the cleanest method of arranging a team in Poitiers was to enrol several young operatives at Poitiers University where they could disappear among the city's 28,000 students. Hassan Hattab quickly began preparing a cell in the region.

As for execution of the plan, it was simplicity itself. Ahead of time, they would simply purchase tickets for any flight from Poitiers-Biard on 15 June within an operational window that coincided with England's match in Marseilles.

Despite exhaustive efforts to uncover the names of the individuals involved in the Poitiers University cell, they were so well hidden that there is simply no trace. Operational documents only refer to 'the Poitiers cell', without offering needless detail.

One possible scenario is that two or more men, most probably of North African extraction, obtained places in Poitiers University for the scholastic year 1997 to 1998. This offered them ample cover to be living in and around the city. Going by what is known of the terror group's modus operandi, they would be model students, never missing lectures, completing work on time, hitting high but not notable grades.

Reference is made to the nearby city of Vivonne, making it likely that an apartment was maintained there. The men would have maintained a small home and lived quietly, causing no suspicion among the neighbours.

Also mentioned in GIA documentation, much of it written by a man called Abu Hamza, is that one of the Poitiers cell members used the Christmas break from his studies in 1997 to travel to attend flight training at a flying school. This course was completed with the minimum of fuss and the individual concerned returned to Poitiers with basic skills necessary to fly a civilian airliner into a nuclear power station. Certainly the tricky parts of a pilot's craft, taking off and landing, were not covered. After taking control of the aircraft after take-off, the hijackers would have to steer the aircraft in the direction of Civaux-1, before sending the plane into a steep dive into their target.

In early February 1998, the GIA coordinator Abu Hamza visited the men in Poitiers for two days, during which time they went over the plan. So confident were they of their cover that they went for lunch and dinner several times at the appropriately named Medina, an Arabic restaurant in the city. What emerged from this man's subsequent note to his superior, Zaoui, is that the Poitiers cell was essentially ready. However, he must have had some lingering shadow of doubt, perhaps alluding to the various temptations available to the young men in a French city, because mention is made of ensuring that the men did not stray. One passage reads:

> ... their time in France has not undermined their resolve. They still think in the way they taught them ... We must guard against this, as they are young and impressionable. Now that we have gone this far with them, they must be martyrs ...

The two or three men in Poitiers had been recruited from the Islamic hotbeds in the Algerian south by the GIA. They had been indoctrinated with the poison of the Islamists' creed – that women and children were legitimate targets, and that the West was Islam's prime enemy. In undertaking a mission on Islam's behalf, one that would definitely end in their deaths, they believed that they were assured a special place in heaven reserved for martyrs. In heaven, they would be received by 77 virgins, all waiting to sacrifice their bodies to them. It is a nonsensical promise, but nevertheless one trotted out by so many of the twisted Islamic groups and one that is believed by their human sacrifices.

The mission objective, they were told, would strike a blow against the West and kill hundreds of thousands of infidel Christians. It would also force the French government to step in to quell the civil war in Algeria and bring about fresh elections that would bring the Islamists to power.

The tragic young men sucked into this story were nothing more than pawns, however. Their lives were tokens that Bin Laden and his fellow conspirators were willing to sacrifice, while they themselves remained in the shadows, thousands of miles away in the safety of Afghanistan. The mission represented no risk to their lives, and was therefore a step they were only too willing to take.

For the men chosen as Bin Laden's sacrificial lambs, a promise of heavenly rewards and that their families left behind on earth would be helped financially for decades to come was enough. All were from poor families, the ghettos of Algeria's appalling inner cities being a ripe recruitment grounds for the GIA. Although they fervently believed they were Islamic warriors, privileged to have been selected to give their lives for the jihad, finance also proved an attraction for many. Coming from a society where family bonds were strong, a son could release his parents and siblings from abject poverty for a generation. And the GIA was as good as its word, providing a weekly or monthly payment to the family of a 'holy warrior' that was well above the average income in strife-ridden Algeria. The GIA also helped members of the families of its human sacrifices with job-hunting, health care and other social services

With such fringe benefits as an attraction, the GIA found that many young men rallied to its revolutionary message. As quickly as they died, more would be drawn from the fringes of the mosques and indoctrinated with the GIA's message. From there, many went on to be the GIA's foot soldiers in Algeria. But a special place was reserved for those who bought into the organisation's agenda without question and showed themselves able to see the Koran twisted so fully that they reached the depraved depths of Islamic fundamentalism thinking. Like the easily led youth of Palestine, Chechnya and other 'Islamic battlegrounds', they were the men who would deliver suicide bombs.

It was from this select niche that the group in the Poitiers cell were selected. The man chosen to lead this cell was allotted the pilot's role. Another would have been trained at an Al-Qaeda camp. But instead of the usual training in guerrilla warfare, he would have received specialist preparation with small arms. He was to be the point man in the hijack of the aircraft from Aéroport de Poitiers-Biard; the operation planners felt that only one handgun needed to be smuggled on board the aircraft for the hijack. After that was accomplished, possibly with another man for additional muscle, the success of the mission would be down to the pilot.

In a subsequent communication to Zaoui, the GIA coordinator wrote:

> The men you have sent to Poitiers are good men with stong faith who take their responsibilities very seriously. God willing, with such men on our side we will succeed in our task. It will be a glorious day for Islam when the poison that the infidels have created themselves [nuclear materials] is used against them. I have no doubt that God has given us the opportunity for a glorious victory that will be remembered for eternity.

Thirteen

The Import Business

In the wake of the events of 11 September 2001, Western governments seemed to wake up suddenly to the danger posed by Osama bin Laden and his terrorist network. In truth, it was nothing new. Governments had been at least partially warned by their intelligence services. Yet the cancer of Islamic fundamentalism had been allowed to spread its network of operatives and cells across Europe and into North America.

During the latter part of 2001, the authorities moved swiftly to neutralise at least the larger part of Islamist network that had been allowed years of open space in which to set down deep roots throughout Europe. Entrenched there, reaching out to the United States had been easy.

Evidence emerged of a number of plots simmering under the guidance of Osama bin Laden and his associates. Among the most advanced in 2001 was another Algerian and Al-Qaeda joint assault on the United States embassy in Paris.

The large Muslim, North African populations that called various countries of western Europe home harboured much festering anti-colonial sentiment. The US, although not directly implicated in the Algerian crisis itself, was nevertheless tarred by the same brush. Due to the dangers, the United States had always maintained high security around its premises in Paris. However, its fundamentalist foes saw the United States embassy at 2 avenue Gabriel as a soft target.

The plot moved into execution phase in late July 2001 when, according to published accounts, an Algerian-born Frenchman named

Jamal Beghal, who had undergone months of terrorist training in Afghanistan, was summoned to the home of a senior aide to Osama bin Laden. The aide, Abu Zubeida, told Beghal that the time for action had come. Beghal was instructed to return to France via Morocco and Spain and orchestrate a suicide bombing of the American embassy in Paris.

Beghal was well suited for such a mission. He had previously lived in Germany and London, where his activities had failed to attract any attention from the authorities there.

The *New York Times* added detail to the account: 'Mr Beghal shaved his beard, put on Western clothing, and, before leaving, was given three gifts from Mr Bin Laden: a toothpick, prayer beads and a flask of incense.'

Quoting a source in the French government, the newspaper said Beghal's plan fell apart in the transit lounge of Dubai International Airport on 28 July, six weeks before 11 September: 'With his name on a watch list, he was arrested for a forged visa extension. His lawyer said that he was tossed into a darkened cell, handcuffed to a chair, blindfolded and beaten and that his family was threatened. After some weeks he talked and out poured a wealth of information. Agents in half a dozen countries went to work.'

The information obtained from Beghal was insufficient to break up the cells that would orchestrate the evil of 11 September, although soon after the Twin Towers collapsed the intelligence services were able to trace Beghal to the same Hamburg apartment that had been home to Mohammed Atta, identified as the leader of the operation on the ground in America.

After senior French Judge Jean Louis Bruguiere travelled to Dubai to question Beghal, the French police arrested seven people in connection with the alleged plans. The seven were suspected of belonging to extremist Islamic groups and were detained in Bezon, Vigneux-sur-Seine and Chilly-Mazarin in the Paris area.

Within three weeks of 11 September, the Beghal connection had led to further police action. Europol announced that a continent-wide investigation had led to the discovery of suspected bomb-making chemicals in an apartment above a North African restaurant in Brussels. Two men were arrested. Officials said the terrorists had planned to bomb the US embassy in Paris.

That such a plot could cause such apparent surprise and alarm shows just how cynically successful several European governments had been in suppressing details of how close Al-Qaeda had already come to jeopardising the lives of those working in and utilising the embassy in 1998. But while the embassy in Paris was lucky in 1998, others were not. Almost three weeks after an attack had been planned for the French capital, the US embassies in Kenya and Tanzania were hit, with devastating consequences.

As early as mid-1994, Bin Laden had ordered that cells of sleepers be established in several East African cities. It is alleged by the FBI that Al-Qaeda's African project was handled from Britain by Saudi dissident Khaled al-Fawwaz, while the European operation was managed by an entirely different structure. It is likely that al-Fawwaz, a signatory on the bank accounts for Bin Laden's London-based Advice and Reformation Committee, was unaware of a parallel operation in France that was being timed to coincide with the 1998 World Cup finals, while Al-Qaeda's European head Kishk Samir and the Algerians involved in the French project were seemingly oblivious to the twin targets in East Africa. This was standard operational procedure, ensuring that if one of the two projects was smashed by the authorities, no one involved in either could offer details of the second plot while under interrogation.

Telephone records from London subsequently showed that al-Fawwaz almost exclusively dealt directly with cell leaders in Africa, while he remained in contact with the operational commander, Ayman al-Zawahiri.

Al-Zawahiri was also point man for the Al-Qaeda hierarchy on the World Cup project and was in constant touch with the GIA's Hassan Hattab, Ahmed Zaoui, and his own man in Europe, Kishk Samir. It is quite feasible that Bin Laden and al-Zawahiri, for the most part, kept even their most senior acolytes in Sudan, and later Afghanistan, out of the loop on one or both of the projects, meaning that only those at the very highest level of Al-Qaeda knew of the existence of two large operations during this period.

In Africa, the plot followed a pattern not unlike that which would be devised in Europe. Two cells were formed in Kenya and one in Tanzania in the city of Mwanza. As in Europe, Bin Laden's men were inserted into the African countries under the cover of employment. In Africa, this was within a cleverly constructed front of charitable organisations. The largest was Help Africa People, established in Germany, which opened offices in Kenya. Help Africa People was an operation headed by Wahid El-Hage. Born a Lebanese Christian, he later became a naturalised American citizen and converted to Islam.

Weakness – some would say incompetence – in the US intelligence services was highlighted by the African embassy bombings. Even when information on the potential for such a plot was effectively handed to them on a plate, they failed to act.

In the wake of the Khobar Towers tragedy in Saudi Arabia, a United States Justice Department grand jury in New York, in which both the FBI and CIA participated, heard from at least two sources that something was afoot in Kenya. One source was a Saudi businessman named Sidi Tayyib, who was married to a distant relative of Bin Laden. Tayyib's evidence led to the discovery of part of the Bin Laden financial network and several of the records uncovered showed funds being directed into Kenya.

Then, in August 1997, Kenyan operational head El-Hage was identified. During a sweep of his home, a laptop computer revealed information that fingered him as an active part of an Al-Qaeda cell in Kenya. The FBI told El-Hage and his family to leave the country. He returned to the USA and was only arrested in the wake of the embassy attacks.

Even more remarkably, further details were revealed to the authorities closer to the actual event and still nothing was done. In late 1997, Egyptian Mustafa Mahmoud Said Ahmed, an Al-Qaeda operative in Kenya, came to his senses and surrendered to the US embassy in Nairobi. Here he briefed a CIA agent about Bin Laden's plan to detonate a truck bomb in the parking garage of the embassy. After being interrogated a second time, by Kenyan police, he was deported, but no further action was taken as the State Department did not consider Nairobi a high-risk location. By any measure it was an extraordinary lapse of security.

In East Africa, plans called for the cells to construct simple truck bombs using readily available materials such as fertiliser and a quantity of TNT. During the attacks both groups would be armed with guns and grenades previously smuggled into the country. In France, the project was far more complicated due to the closer control of national borders and airports. Therefore, long-term planning for delivery of arms was required.

The GIA head of European operations, Ahmed Zaoui, began this process as early as 1996, after his acquittal by a Belgian court on charges based upon his terrorist activities. By the time he settled in Switzerland, he had already set in motion plans for smuggling arms into Europe. So successful was his scheme that there is no record of any major finds by the security forces disrupting the GIA's smuggling operation prior to the 1998 World Cup in France.

What is known, from the GIA's own documentation, is that despite Zaoui's near miss and the attentions of the police in Belgium, the Belgian port of Antwerp remained one of the key entry points into Europe for much of the heavier equipment and shipments of munitions, carefully hidden among more innocent cargoes.

For its sheer size and transport links into the European mainland, Antwerp was a wise choice for terror groups wishing to import their hardware. Long a centre for trade, after Rotterdam it has the largest port in Europe and one of the most important in the world. Cargo throughput in 1997 totalled around 33.5 million tonnes.

With such a high volume of traffic and the attendant commercial pressures to clear shipments quickly, Zaoui believed that cargoes arriving in Antwerp would receive less scrutiny than those arriving at other ports. Its efficient network of distribution routes also made Antwerp the ideal choice for anyone wishing to disperse a shipment rapidly throughout Europe.

The GIA and Al-Qaeda used Antwerp to bring quantities of terror materials and armaments that can only be guessed at into Europe. From Antwerp, they were dispersed primarily into Belgium, Germany and France and hidden in safe houses or buried in the fields of a couple of country estates that belonged to sympathisers. If they had not been sympathisers to begin with, they might have been 'persuaded'. The GIA had a long history of using intimidation and threats to convince those in the Muslim community to actively support terrorist actions. Many in Belgium, Holland and France were reportedly coerced into storing materials by threats that their families remaining in Algeria would be murdered if they refused.

So successful was Zaoui's network of supporters and hostages to the cause that only a very few of the GIA's or Al-Qaeda's shipments through Antwerp were ever discovered. One official catch came during the early months of 1998 when customs officers making a routine drugs check discovered a home-made mortar weighing 190kg, plus some 320mm shells, amongst a shipment of gherkins and garlic aboard an Iranian vessel. The freighter in which the mortar was hidden was en route to Hamburg, a well-known hub for Islamic fundamentalist operations in Europe. The Iranian named in documentation accompanying the shipment was subsequently arrested.

Terrorists had shown themselves willing to use the weaponry that they imported. In December 1995, a Belgian policeman was seriously injured during a car chase when a grenade was thrown from the car he was pursuing. The car contained two Bosnian men and a Moroccan. All were GIA members. Soon after a GIA network was uncovered that spread through Belgium and Luxembourg and evidence indicated that huge amounts of weaponry had passed through these countries.

Just a month later, in January 1996, Belgian police discovered a car full of explosives during a routine patrol. The two occupants of the car, identified as Algerians, started shooting at the police and escaped.

During 1998, the only major GIA/Al-Qaeda operation under way was the preparation for the World Cup attacks. Only one of this group of targets would require the assault capabilities offered by a mortar: the US embassy in Paris. Fortunately, it did not get that far.

Fourteen

Abu Hamza on the Ball

Weeks after the meeting of the Al-Qaeda and GIA operational heads with Osama bin Laden in Afghanistan in December 1997, Hassan Hattab dispatched one of his most trusted contacts to France to take a hard look at the targets that were being isolated. That man was the shadowy figure known only as Abu Hamza. His reports were thorough and provide much of the inside detail of the 15 June 1998 plot. Quite who Abu Hamza is, and where he fits into the broader picture, remains unknown.

What is known is that an Abu Hamza entered France during October 1997 on a forged passport. His mission was to report back to his bosses on the defence capabilities of proposed targets and the readiness of the men already in France for the operation. He followed in the footsteps of Al-Qaeda top man Kishk Samir, who had made a preliminary trip to France in mid-1997 in order to visit some of the proposed targets and visit the cell charged with the Civaux-1 nuclear power station attack.

Abu Hamza's instructions were to flesh out the wider plan and make specific recommendations. His subsequent letters to his superiors, despite being cryptic in places, give the clearest insight into the nature and scope of the plan that Bin Laden was developing.

Abu Hamza's itinerary covered checking the security and layouts of various US diplomatic embassies and consulates from an operational point of view. For this purpose he visited Paris, Marseilles and Strasbourg. The latter had a particularly strong attraction for Al-Qaeda, being a diplomatic post that had a high-profile second tier of responsibility. An important international crossroads during the days of Julius Caesar, since the Second

World War Strasbourg had also become a symbol of European unity as the home of the Council of Europe, the European Court of Human Rights, the Parliamentary Assembly of the Council of Europe, the European Parliament and the European Science Foundation.

For the USA, the Strasbourg consulate plays an important function in the US's dealings with the European Union. On the one hand it provides information on US policy to permanent representatives and observers to the Council of Europe, while on the other it relays European thinking on key issues back to Washington. The Consul General is the deputy permanent observer to the Council of Europe.

Abu Hamza, aware of Bin Laden's interest in targeting the Strasbourg consulate, was nevertheless honest in his appraisal of the difficulty in attacking it. On 10 October 1997 he wrote to GIA head Hassan Hattab:

In the name of God the Merciful

Leader,
I have studied the embassy [sic] in Strasbourg and I found that there is much potential for discovery. Due to its importance on a wider stage, the city of Strasbourg has strict security and the French have a high number of secret police operating there undercover. During my stay I saw much evidence of this. Therefore I would say that there was a better chance of success in Paris and Marseilles, although the embassies there are well protected.

I visited Sheikh Abdallah [GIA operative Sheikh Abdallah Kinai, arrested in 1998] and found him ready. But his men are not well prepared and are ignorant of their duties. They are from Strasbourg and Marseilles and have not been trained outside for fear of alerting the government here.

God willing, they are good men whose hearts belong to God and whose minds are with us. But it would be foolish to send them [into action] when they are simply unable to do what is asked of them.

Based on these facts, I would say that the mission would fail.

With God willing,
Abu Hamza
(see Figure 2)

His concerns would have been relayed to Bin Laden via Ayman al-Zawahiri. After this reference, Strasbourg does not appear again in documentation and seems not to have merited any further attention from the plotters. However, Bin Laden had made it clear that his support for the entire exercise depended on the GIA guaranteeing that a number of its cells could hit US targets. Naturally, the US's diplomatic buildings in France were the major focus of this effort.

As the decade ended, plans were under way to open five American Presence Posts in France: in Bordeaux, Lille, Lyon, Rennes and Toulouse. At the time of the 1998 plot, however, only the three primary US diplomatic targets were available. The plotters did not necessarily see this as a drawback, as one earlier document from Abu Hamza addressed to Ahmed Zaoui on 26 December 1996 reveals.

In the name of God the merciful

Leader,
[Pamela] Harriman is an interesting and important target. Although she is old, it is likely that she would be in the area of the embassy during the mission. Also, she will almost certainly attend a match should the American team qualify for France. Perhaps she could be killed there?

With God willing
Abu Hamza
(See Figure 3)

The extraordinary Harriman, at the time American Ambassador to France, was not in a position to be targeted by the Bin Laden plan, however. She suffered a stroke at the Ritz Hotel, and died at the American Hospital, near Paris, on 5 February 1997. Her replacement was Felix Rohatyn, appointed by President Bill Clinton on 7 July 1997.

In a document dated 10 December 1997, Abu Hamza wrote to Hattab referring to the new ambassador in a letter that also vaguely discusses what appears to be a shipment of arms through a port, probably Antwerp, and its delivery to Marseilles.

In the name of God the Merciful

Leader,
I received your instructions and spoke with Tunis [head of the Marseilles cell]. He will go to collect these personally, although I told him not do so because the risk is high and suggested that he send one of his men instead.

Tunis was pleased by the size of the shipment. He has two missions [Stade-Vélodrome and the US consulate in the city] and believes that this shipment will allow him to complete them successfully, ensuring a high degree of satisfaction for you and the Sheikh [Bin Laden], may God bless him.

With God's help, a new American ambassador was appointed to Paris. He will definitely be attending games played by the American team, at least the first game in Paris. Therefore we could be certain that he will be in the embassy prior to travelling to the stadium. He has an office facing the front of the building and this should be focus of the attack. The value of killing the ambassador cannot be underestimated.

With God willing,
Abu Hamza
(see Figure 4)

Marseilles is arguably the Islamic fundamentalist heartland of France. Thousands of workers and their families arrive in the city from North Africa every year. Many decide to settle there. And while most are genuine in their desire to live peaceable and productive lives, it would be near impossible to prevent the shadow of Islamic fundamentalism following them across the Mediterranean from Algeria, Tunisia and other former French-dominated states in North Africa. Such a massive, transient population makes it hard for the authorities to keep a watchful eye on elements within the community with hidden nefarious agendas.

Notable among this element was 'Tunis', an extremist whose pseudonym reflects his Tunisian birth. University educated, intelligent, multi-lingual and, most importantly, blindly loyal to the cause of Islamic fundamentalism, Tunis caught the eye of his GIA masters and was soon promoted.

Sometime in 1997, it appears that he was hand-picked by Hattab to head the unfolding operation in Marseilles. Tunis's posting would turn out to be inspired and downright lucky when the Tunisian national team was scheduled to play England in Marseilles on the day chosen for the attack. This offered him additional cover and a legitimate reason to be on the streets on 15 June.

The terrorist events of this day were planned to extend to two fronts for Tunis and his team. The first was Stade-Vélodrome, where England were to play Tunisia. The second, only a few kilometres away, was the American consulate in the city.

Abu Hamza joined Tunis in Marseilles soon after visiting Strasbourg in October 1997. The focus of the entire operation was shifting to Marseilles. Other cells might have had grander, more illustrious targets, but the attack on the England team would be in front of television cameras and a live global television audience numbering in the hundreds of millions. This was the cell that would deliver Bin Laden's message of defiance, the magnitude of which was unthinkable before 11 September 2001, on a global stage. A great deal was at stake in Marseilles, as detailed in Abu Hamza's letter of 19 October 1997:

In the name of God the Merciful

> Leader,
> I thank you for your telephone call. The man you spoke of will arrive next week and spend some time here.
> I am writing to you from Marseilles. I was impressed with what I have seen here, and in Tunis. You were entirely correct in your judgement of him. His men are organised and ready. They have been trained abroad [presumably at Al-Qaeda camps in Afghanistan], and Tunis continues to ensure that they are strengthening mentally and

physically for the missions that will be given to them.

He himself is delighted with the delivery received. He now has everything that he needs. He is thankful for the extra equipment. Ahmed [Zaoui] has promised that he will send him more whenever he has the opportunity.

Tunis has his men concentrating on football now. They attend all matches for Olympique Marseilles here and even travel around France watching the team when they play elsewhere. They have joined the club [presumably meaning the Supporters Club] and are trying very hard to make their faces known. With God willing they are waiting for the club to ask its supporters for help at the match. This will enable the three we need to be in position when the time comes.

The embassy in Marseilles [sic] has limited security. This is why some of the Brothers will be able to enter the vicinity with just light support [arms]. Therefore, a lot of Americans could be killed here and even the building could be destroyed easily.

Tunis needs only a couple of men for this and he himself would be quite well enough experienced to participate in the attack personally.

With God willing,
Abu Hamza
(see Figure 5)

This letter suggests that a handful of men had busied themselves in becoming associated with Olympique Marseilles. Coming so soon after the draw for the World Cup, and Bin Laden's decision to go for 15 June and the England–Tunisia match, this invites the thought that Islamists may have been active elsewhere in the country involving themselves at the football clubs hosting other championship matches.

A week later, Abu Hamza surfaced in Paris. Unusually, he referred to a man named Singh, suggesting that a Sikh was in some way involved. This was strange, but it was possible that the man had converted to Islam and slipped into fundamentalism. His involvement, if true, would have been a masterstroke. In the wake of the GIA's earlier campaign that had killed seven and injured many more in the French capital, the police were mindful and aware of Islamic fundamentalist groups and particularly watchful of Algerians. A Sikh would not attract their attention.

Singh was linked to the cell being asked to target the United States embassy. Of the other target, the US football team in their hotel, only an oblique reference was made by Abu Hamza in a letter of 29 October 1997. Interestingly, he also suggests in this letter that another cell might have been established in Paris.

In the name of God the Merciful

Leader,
I am leaving Paris a happy man today. Paris is still on alert [after the 1995 GIA bombing campaign] and we are proceeding slowly and with great care. Singh has rented a property outside Paris. This is in a quiet area, but close when the time comes. Ahmed [Zaoui] has sent some important supplies, but the main delivery [a mortar or perhaps TNT for a bomb like those used in the East Africa embassy attacks] will not be made for some months. With God's help, this last element will arrive here safely in spring.

Singh has bought a small truck for selling sweets, a common vehicle in Paris and will drive this himself. Some Brothers will be armed with guns to provide him with back-up and ensure our victory.

Singh is a good man and a fervent believer. The Holy God is in his heart.

I found those around him unclean in their hearts and in their appearance. Yet he assures me that they are strong men. If you trust his judgement, then I will also put my faith in him.

Singh is unaware of the others close to him [presumably meaning a second cell in Paris] and it is better that way. The two should be separated.

With God willing,
Abu Hamza
(see Figure 6)

Abu Hamza completed his time in France with a short visit to Poitiers, where he met with the head of the cell there and the man whose role was flying the aircraft eventually selected for the crash-dive into the Civaux-1 nuclear power station.

This cell was in a unique position as far as the operation was concerned. While the murders of the England team in Marseilles and attack on the US squad in their hotel would leave the world shocked, and the strikes against the United States diplomatic targets would create international furore, Bin Laden wished to leave a lasting reminder of his capability and determination. While the Paris and Marseilles cells, with four missions between them, would create an immediate impact, the Poitiers cell would leave a lasting legacy of death and destruction.

On 10 November 1997, Abu Hamza wrote to Hattab:

In the name of God the Merciful

Leader,
You were entirely correct regarding the situation in the west [Poitiers]. I found our man focused and ready. He is as committed to the success of this project as any of us and, with the help of God, you could not have selected a better man to take on this task. For one so young, he is an intelligent man.

I gave him the money which he will need to complete his mission [flight training] in December. He is impatiently looking forward to this and is preparing himself in advance by reading and collecting information. All the men in the west are nearing readiness for the mission that will be given to them.

They are monitoring air traffic and within 45 days will have a plan as to which [flight] they will choose. At this point he will inform me of the details. God willing, I will inform you.

With God willing,
Abu Hamza
(see Figure 7)

156

During his month-long tour of France, Abu Hamza had been able to appraise the entire GIA-led operation. His reports provide an extraordinary window into the genesis of the terrorist cells and the full extent of their planning.

Only the plot to attack the United States squad in their hotel remains largely unexpanded upon; it may be that a letter concerning Abu Hamza's impressions of that cell is missing. However, reference is made to this for a second time in a letter dated 11 December 1997. This was an end-of-trip overview produced by Abu Hamza just days before his leader was due to leave for Afghanistan for an Al-Qaeda/GIA heads meeting to discuss the project.

In the name of God the Merciful

Leader,
After one month in France, I was delighted to have some quiet time to reflect on the progress of our mission.

God has helped us a lot. All the Brothers I met, without exception, would be able to stand alongside me in our battle in Algeria. All of them are strong and committed. After my thanks to God, I offer my admiration to you for selecting this group of believers for our operation.

Although we are only now entering the crucial period, things are on the right course. Farid [Melouk] has helped us with the necessary documentation and the office [in Belgium] is efficient [in importing arms].

In Marseilles, Tunis has some strong and well-trained men with him for battle. In Poitiers I was impressed by the leader. In Paris both Brothers [cell leaders] are very well prepared. One has lived in Paris for more than a decade and is well established.

One weakness I see is that the men of the two cells in Paris are not experienced in battle. I know that the Pakistani Brother [El-Wed] is a believer, thanks be to God, and is claiming Martyrdom. And this [his secondment there] will benefit not only the operation but also all the Brothers who will be influenced by him in the future.

Please inform the Sheikh of my highest wishes for his continued health and inform him that his servants in France and Europe will not fail him.

With God willing,
Abu Hamza
(see Figure 8)

Fifteen

Bin Laden's Lions

Unarguably the most extraordinary facet of Osama bin Laden's plot against the World Cup finals and France itself was his personal input to the selection of targets. It shows both his knowledge of the game and the fact that he had followed football closely enough to be able to identify accurately the high-profile players who would be involved in the match in Marseilles and where they were likely to be at the time of the planned attack.

In December 1997, he hosted an extraordinary meeting of senior Al-Qaeda and GIA officials at a camp in remote Kandahar. The most senior European officials from both organisations were there: GIA European head of operations Ahmed Zaoui and Al-Qaeda's European director Kishk Samir. Also present was GIA supremo Hassan Hattab.

Both Zaoui and Samir had been into France during 1997, monitoring progress, making specific recommendations about targets and visiting each of the cells that had been planted for Bin Laden's masterpiece operation against the 1998 World Cup finals.

Hattab had also dispatched one of his senior confidants, Abu Hamza, into the country to oversee the entire operation as Zaoui was finding it extremely difficult to fulfil his duties while under increasing surveillance by the security services in his base in Switzerland. And it was to an unknown third party, possibly Abu Hamza, to whom Zaoui turned in January 1997, having returned to Switzerland following a face-to-face meeting with Bin Laden. Soon after leaving Afghanistan on 24 December 1997 he wrote:

May God bless you and smile upon your efforts,

Please inform Tunis [head of the cell in Marseilles] that the Sheikh [Bin Laden], may God bless him, has personally prepared a list of those who should be targeted in the operation at the stadium. It is needless for me to remind you that the Sheikh's support is very important to us and I therefore instruct you to follow these directives carefully. Ensure that Tunis is aware of the requirements, and that he fully understands the identities of the men they are to focus on.

The Sheikh, may God bless him, wishes you to ensure that three men are in position in the stadium. As agreed, they should be free to move around in order to carry out their instructions. He asks that we observe the movements of David Seaman, the goalkeeper of England, Alan Shearer, the most famous player, and the trainer, Hoddle. Also, thanks be to God, his attention has also been drawn to two younger players who are becoming well known, David Beckham and Michael Owen. They are not certain to be playing, but wil be visible with the others [reserves] at the side of the field.

Therefore, we suggest that the point man for the mission should make his way to Seaman and blow himself up next to him. This will be the signal for the other Brothers to start the rest of the operation.

The second Brother should throw a grenade at the reserve players at the side of the field. He should keep a spare grenade to throw at the English supporters if this is necessary.

The third Brother should carry a gun and shoot Shearer, who will be at the opposite end of the field to Seaman.

We understand that there will be armed gendarmes around the field at all matches. Inform Tunis that his men must act quickly. The Sheikh says that 500 million people will be watching this on television all over the world. It is therefore vital that all goes to plan. Inform Tunis that he will be given assistance with anything he requires. The Sheikh is resting all his hopes on Tunis and his Brothers to complete this mission and to deliver our message to the widest possible number of people throughout the world.

Ahmed
(see Figure 1)

Elsewhere, as 1997 turned into 1998, the countdown to 10 June – the beginning of the World Cup in France – was well and truly under way. French consulates around the world were scrambling to recruit additional staff. Their task was compounded by the fact that spectators from at least 12 of the 32 countries participating in the event needed visas to enter France.

The sheer number of hopeful World Cup visitors had taken French officials by surprise and visa applications far outnumbered the number of tickets available to foreigners. Among those most affected by the rules were fans from Asia, Eastern Europe and North Africa.

The French government planned to control the influx of foreigners by requiring travellers to present both their ticket to the games and their visa, which must both have the same number inscribed on them, to immigration officials upon arrival. To foil the inevitable counterfeiters, no tickets would be distributed abroad until mid-May, leaving consulates less than a month to do their paperwork.

The 32 teams were also preparing for their greatest test.

Four years after the United States had made such an impression when hosting the tournament, advancing to the second round, they had secured their third consecutive World Cup berth by finishing second behind Mexico in their qualifying region. In preparation the American squad had embarked upon a mini-tour of Europe playing friendlies against other national sides and a couple of engagements at home in America.

The squad were scheduled to leave for France on 4 June and train in Trévoux before their opener against Germany. They would be staying at the Château de Pizay in Belleville, about 50 kilometres north of Lyon. On 13 June, the squad would transfer – as anticipated by the plotters – to a location just outside Paris ahead of their clash against Germany, the European champions, at Parc des Princes in Paris on 15 June.

In England, while Beckham was being hailed as the man whose emergence could lead England to their first World Cup victory since 1966, the country was in the grip of a footballing identity crisis during the early months of 1998.

On 11 February, Chile froze England out at Wembley, beating them for the first time by a score of 2–0. One bright spot for the home side was the début of Michael Owen, who became the youngest player of the century in England's national team and the fourth youngest ever. He had a chance to score early and might have been England's best player.

In late March, Glenn Hoddle and his squad were on duty again, meeting Switzerland in Berne, where the best they could do was scramble to a 1–1 tie.

Just seven weeks before he was required to name a final squad for France, Hoddle's plans remained clouded ahead of a match against high-flying Portugal. He named a 34-man squad for the 22 April exhibition game at Wembley.

England had not beaten Portugal since 1969. Although Portugal had failed to qualify for the World Cup, they still represented England's sternest test in their preparations for the tournament. On the pitch it seemed a much more confident performance from England and they took just five minutes to get off the mark on their way to a three-goal victory.

The England team read Seaman (Arsenal), G. Neville (Manchester United), Le Saux (Chelsea), Campbell (Tottenham), Adams (Arsenal) Ince (Liverpool), Batty (Newcastle) Beckham (Manchester United), Scholes (Manchester United), Shearer (Newcastle), Sheringham (Manchester United). Substitutes: P. Neville (Manchester United), Merson (Middlesbrough), Owen (Liverpool).

All four of the players named by Bin Laden in his instructions to the GIA played a part in the game. and elsewhere there were other operational advances for the plotters.

By the time that spring was giving way to summer, the footballing world was turning its attention to the biggest show on earth. So was the Islamic fundamentalist world which, by now, was at an advanced state of readiness for what was intended to be its most important show of force on the international stage.

Sixteen

Bombs, Balls and Uranium Oxide

The danger has been present for a generation, yet only in the wake of 11 September did the idea of a terrorist attack on electricity-generating nuclear power facilities get a wide public airing. By the turn of the millennium, nuclear power plants were in operation in eight out of the fifteen nations of the European Union, generating about 35 per cent of the EU's electricity. A number of countries in Central and Eastern Europe, in line for EU membership, were also heavily reliant on nuclear-generated electricity.

In October 2001 in the European Parliament, Irish Green MEP Nuala Ahern spoke of the need for 'no-fly zones' and added that: 'Nuclear plants are a ticking time bomb in our midst and the only logical response is to close them all down and end this terrible threat.' However, even a no-fly zone with a 50-kilometre radius would offer the authorities an impossible two minutes to act should an average airliner be heading towards a nuclear facility.

Most reactor containment buildings have an outer structure, with as much as a metre of concrete containing large amounts of reinforcing steel. Inside is a steel lining that can be up to ten centimetres thick. The reactor is usually surrounded by thick holding walls and also has reinforced steel bars woven through it like wicker. The reactor vessel itself is made of high-carbon steel about 15 centimetres thick.

Today, most new reactors are designed in line with strict safety guidelines so that they can withstand the impact of a light aircraft. But no measurements or rules exist for a large modern jet loaded with fuel, deliberately flown at high speed. Experts say that such a scenario could result in a break in the reactor vessel.

Adding to the concern is the fact that security on the ground at nuclear power stations has been found to be lax. In the USA, nuclear regulators operated a highly effective security evaluation programme known as Operational Safeguards Response Evaluations, in which teams simulating attacks attempted to penetrate reactor sites. Former US Navy SEAL Captain David Orrick ran the programme and was often able to compromise sensitive areas within reactor sites, sometimes even gaining access to plants' control rooms. This was despite the fact that managers of the sites were frequently notified in advance of pending evaluations.

Nuclear power stations were an obvious target for Bin Laden if he could plan to have his men seize an aircraft and direct it into a nuclear site. There was a strong level of certainty that such an attack would create a major disaster.

Consultants Wise-Paris looked at the irradiated fuel-cooling ponds of La Hague in the north of France and estimated that a catastrophe there had the potential to release 60 times the amount of caesium-137 that leaked from the doomed Chernobyl power station. Cogema, the operator at La Hague, issued a statement on 19 September 2001 stating: 'A permanent overflight ban is in force at the site. Considering its geographical position, the French armed forces would have time to intervene if any breach of this ban were suspected.' The French government added that anti-aircraft missile batteries were to be stationed around La Hague. In their own ways, Britain, Germany and the USA took similar steps.

In light of 11 September, it could so easily have been all too late. Investigators looking into the hijack of United Airlines flight 93, which later crashed into a field in Pennsylvania, speculated that its target was Three Mile Island, site of America's most serious nuclear accident in 1979. US security sources indicated that Three Mile Island was the subject of surveillance by some of the hijackers and their associates in the months before the terrorist attacks.

During early 1998, the GIA's cells across France were beginning their countdown to the summer. Most of the arms and explosives required for the coordinated attacks on 15 June had been shipped into Europe via Antwerp and smuggled from safe houses and secret weapons dumps in Belgium, Luxembourg, Switzerland and Italy into France. The reason for such a roundabout method, especially via Italy, was to spread the load. GIA supporters in these countries would carry a single gun or grenade, easily hidden among their belongings. In this way there would be no great breakthroughs for the authorities should one item be discovered. Similarly, the courier would avoid stringent penalties by not being caught with a large arsenal about his person.

After crossing the border, the individual would post his illicit contraband to an anonymous post office box address, either in Paris, Marseilles or Poitiers. In this way, all cells were separated; again, if one was discovered there was no chance that the remainder would fall.

One revealing letter from Abu Hamza on 30 January 1998 illustrates the workings of this operation, a picture of the preparedness of the Poitiers cell and an insight into a near miss with the police. It is not clear if Abu Hamza had embarked upon a new tour of France during this period, or simply stayed in touch by telephone with those he had met earlier.

In the name of God the Merciful

Leader,
The Loire Valley is a beautiful area. I am pleased that this is the place where our cause will have its victory. Chirac will be forced to deal with the issue [of Algeria] in a proper manner when Poitiers is no longer so beautiful.

I spoke with the leader of the Poitiers cell today. His visit was successful and he is confident that he returns with the necessary skills [to fly the suicide aircraft]. The fools welcomed him and gave him all the necessary training knowledge, without realising that he was their enemy. His heart is burning with the desire to strike the Infidels in the name of Allah.

They are watching the airport and will shortly choose the flight he will utilise [hijack]. He also tells me that his man in the station reports that the fuel has been arriving continuously. Although there are operational difficulties, this will not affect the timing. With God willing everything will be ready when our day dawns [June 15].

He has also taken possession of a handgun. This arrived at the Post Office but when he was leaving with it his car was stopped by the police as he was speeding. He was taken to the police station but God smiled on us because the package was not discovered, although the police inspected his car. Thanks be to God.

With God willing,
Abu Hamza
(see Figure 9)

In the Poitou-Charentes region, work was continuing at the controversial and troubled Civaux-1 nuclear power station. The facility was well stocked with low-enriched uranium oxide and staff were operating it in test mode, which they were scheduled to do until May 1998. At this point, the nuclear reactor and its systems were to be off-line for final tests before going to full commercial operation, originally scheduled for July 1998.

On 7 May the reactor was taken off-line, but five days later 300 cubic metres of radioactive water leaked from the primary circuit into the reactor building. Subsequent investigation revealed a crack in the residual cooling system that is used to remove heat from the core when the reactor is shut down. The reactor was still off-line when the leak occurred.

Civaux-1 was scheduled to restart in early June but, even before the cracking in the residual heat removal system had been tackled, another problem beset the facility. The operators were required to install an ultraviolet treatment system to kill disease-bearing amoebae. The amoebae, which can cause a rare form of encephalitis, were first seen in cooling circuits at French nuclear plants at Chooz, Dampierre and Golfech. It was felt that a similar problem was likely to occur in Civaux's titanium condenser tubes.

Elsewhere, chlorine or peracetic acid had been used to disinfect the cooling circuits but this could not be used for Civaux because the flow rate of the Vienne river is too low to disperse the toxic chemical discharge. The Vienne, below the reactor, is the source of drinking water for several communities, including Châtelleraut.

But despite these problems, the plotters were consistently reassured. In his 30 January 1998 letter to GIA leader Hassan Hattab, Abu Hamza refers to the leader of the Poitiers cell informing him that his man 'in the station' was confident that, despite these well-publicised and highly damaging difficulties for the operators of the plant, Civaux-1 would be a viable target.

Osama bin Laden was left to enjoy the anticipation of his men exacting a terrible price from the West for its perceived anti-Islamic stance. From the remote safety of Afghanistan, thousands of miles away, Bin Laden believed that they were going to pay with a nuclear holocaust.

Seventeen

Nutmegging the GIA

October 1994 was a critical time for the Algerian Armed Islamic Group, the GIA. In the second week of that month, many of the most senior leaders of the GIA attended a secret summit in Algiers. The GIA's ruling council, the Majlis ech-Choura, was meeting in crisis. It had been thrown off balance by the military-backed government of President Liamine Zeroual, which was making attempts to bring the Islamist opposition into talks aimed at ending the civil war. Ultimately this would lead to a split within the grouping, with some smaller entities breaking away and others taking a more autonomous route, although still existing within a wider GIA framework.

At the meeting was Hassan Hattab, his sponsor within the group had been GIA leader Mourad Sid Ahmed, whose death in an ambush by Algerian security forces on 26 February 1994 had sent the Islamists into a tailspin.

Sherif Ghousmi, head of the judicial commission of the GIA and leader of the death phalange, a group of Arab-Afghans charged with the assassinations of officials in Algeria, had then taken over as acting head, but on 26 September he too was killed in a shoot-out with police. His death damaged the government's peace moves as Ghousmi was believed to be in favour of a deal. His leanings towards peace meant, however, that the conservatives in the GIA hierarchy would not confirm him as leader.

With its well-respected leader Ahmed dead, and the government making peace overtures, the GIA had been destabilised. The October meeting was called in order to appoint a new boss and to debate a unified response to the government. On 10 October, the Algerian daily newspaper *An-Nahar* reported that leaders of the GIA had appointed Abou Khalil Mahfoud as their new head. The London-based *Al-Hayat* daily also announced Mahfoud's appointment as 'emir' of the organisation.

Observers believe that in fact Djamel Zitouni was the real leader of the Islamists, but that he remained in the shadows. Mahfoud was allowed to be publicly named as leader, probably because Zitouni was seen as too valuable an asset to lose – both previous leaders had been killed in quick succession.

Mahfoud, whose real name was Mahfoud Tadjine, had previously served as guerrilla chief in the so-called Triangle of Death, a GIA-held area outside Algiers where there had been many massacres of civilians, and had been considered a success story. Just 36 years old, according to the *An-Nahar* story, he resided in secret in the pro-Islamist Eucalyptuses area of Algiers and had been a GIA member since its foundation.

A year earlier he had been sentenced, *in absentia*, to life imprisonment by an Algiers special court, for his violent actions. Mahfoud's trademark was a particularly gruesome method of execution, inflicted on soldiers and government workers, which involved binding their hands above their heads, usually from a tree, and then cutting a main artery. As the victim began to bleed to death, he would be brutally tortured and maimed. As the civil war became more savage, Mahfoud broadened his horizons to killing ordinary civilians, including women: on one occasion he used a knife to remove the foetus of a pregnant woman as she bled to death in front of him. The body of a Mahfoud victim would then be left to hang as a warning to others, with Mahfoud promising death to anyone removing it. In this way, sometimes weeks would pass until an army unit could recover the body.

Mahfoud was a hard-line Islamic conservative and his appointment sent a message to the Algerian government. The GIA would not negotiate. Its bloody campaign would continue. But Mahfoud was not what he seemed. Indeed the Majlis ech-Choura, even the wily Hassan Hattab who supported his elevation as leader, had been hoodwinked. Mahfoud was a double agent.

Details that only emerged in 2001 indicate that Mahfoud worked for the French intelligence service. At the time of his elevation to leader, he had been working for the French intelligence service for some time, covertly supplying them with information in return for money and a guarantee of immunity from prosecution for himself. Using intelligence that he provided, the Algerians had uncovered several dangerous GIA terrorist operations – including several assassination attempts against President Zeroual – and Mahfoud had even sold details of safe houses that led to the removal of some of his superiors through ambushes. It is believed that both his predecessors, Mourad Sid Ahmed and Sherif Ghousmi, had been killed in army raids resulting from information supplied from Mahfoud. Ironically, he had risen unexpectedly to his new position, having helped the authorities to clear his path forward.

The first public revelation about Mahfoud's complicity was made by Omar Chikhi, former head of the Z'Barbar guerrilla movement in Algeria, who had surrendered to the authorities in Algeria after brokering a deal for his men if they laid down their arms. In several newspaper interviews, Chikhi cited Mahfoud Tadjine as an informant to an officer of French intelligence.

After Mahfoud's appointment in 1994, the GIA's fortunes took a nosedive. Several senior officials were arrested along with dozens of minor fighters, some large caches of arms were discovered by the authorities and a handful of GIA operations were quashed. Those in the higher echelons of the group began to believe that there was a traitor among them.

For some six months, the GIA was put on the back foot by a string of government successes, along with several events on mainland Europe in which GIA operatives were discovered. One of the biggest blows to the group was the discovery and arrest of its European head, Ahmed Zaoui, in Belgium, using information supplied by Mahfoud. Zaoui was subsequently found not guilty in a Belgian court.

Eventually, those at the heart of the Majlis ech-Choura could link only one man to all these failures. Their conclusion was almost unthinkable: only the group's leader and its operational commander were privy to information concerning all operations, and Zitouni had an unquestionable reputation. Mahfoud had to be removed and, apparently in late spring of 1995, he was invited by Hattab and Zitouni, to a secret meeting. The French informer arrived and was tied to a tree, where he was dispatched in the same evil method that he had meted out to so many innocents during his bloody career.

But although Abou Khalil Mahfoud was dead, his ghost would continue to cast a long shadow over the GIA.

While it was Zitouni who had been working closely with the GIA's paymaster, Osama bin Laden, for a time Mahfoud had been in the loop and it seems certain that he must have known of the proposal from Bin Laden in Khartoum to target the 1998 World Cup. Sometime before his death in the spring of 1995, he went alone to a debriefing house set up by the French in the suburbs of Algiers. It was to here that Mahfoud, a man with the blood of hundreds of people on his hands, would go to sell information to the GIA's avowed enemies. It is almost certain that he provided the first tip-off about the 1998 World Cup scheme.

One name that was sold to the French was that of Farid Melouk, a French-passport-holding Islamist who was already operating in France at the time. Melouk was subsequently linked to the GIA's bombing campaign in Paris during 1995 and would be the key that French intelligence used to unlock the events of 1998. 'Melouk is an expert forger. He provided logistical support to a group accused of massacres in Algeria and bombings in France,' commented Bart van Lysebeth, a spokesman for Belgium's state security service.

In late January 1998, Melouk was identified crossing the border between France and Belgium using a forged passport. No arrest was made but it was easy for the Belgian police to follow Melouk. He was quickly sighted around a mosque in Brussels that was a known haunt for GIA Islamists and his movements were tracked.

Melouk had been convicted *in absentia* by a Paris court on 18 February the same year and sentenced to seven years in prison for criminal association with a terrorist group and falsification of administrative documents. Investigations into his activities owed much to information received from Mahfoud.

However, Melouk had consistently evaded the French authorities. His sighting in Belgium was a remarkable, if lucky, breakthrough. Melouk made the mistake of not taking enough care with his communications. He used a GSM telephone line maintained in France and the French intelligence services went to work. He was found to be in contact with Ahmed Zaoui, and gradually a picture emerged before incredulous investigators of a massive plot against the World Cup.

The authorities in Belgium and France quietly built up a picture of the operation they had stumbled upon in Brussels. Unaware that he had been uncovered, Melouk met with associates and spoke to others on his telephone. The house where he was staying in the suburbs of Brussels, sharing with others who were ultimately shown to be involved in the plot, was now staked out and intelligence officers were allotted to follow his associates.

After nearly two weeks of monitoring him, police heard Melouk speak of returning to France. They could not risk losing him and a decision was made to move in on the house in Brussels.

On 3 March, nearly 50 officers, many of them armed, took part in a major raid. Just before morning prayers, when some of the Islamists could have been expected to be awake, police descended upon the house. Most were caught unawares, but Melouk swiftly made for the loft of the building. He barricaded himself in there for 12 hours, occasionally trading fire with police officers with a .44 Colt pistol. The Belgians decided to bring in a negotiator instead of storming Melouk's hiding place. This gave him the chance to destroy documents. After half a day, the police moved in anyway, overwhelming him with tear gas. But by this time he had succeeded in burning a wealth of documents that perhaps would not only have blown open the plot in France, but have laid bear entire GIA and Al-Qaeda networks in Europe.

Inside the house, seven men were arrested. A large quantity of liquid explosives was found, a bag of Islamist videotapes, five detonators, mercury – used in delayed-action explosive devices – a Kalashnikov rifle, several handguns and the equivalent of $16,670 in cash.

Police also recovered dozens of fake passports and papers that Melouk had been unable to spirit away to his hiding place. These offered an insight into the plot at hand. There were brochures and documents relating to the World Cup, maps of several French stadiums, a large quantity of photographs of football grounds and street maps of many major French cities. Also exposed were GIA plans to assassinate Dalil Boubakeur, the imam of the great mosque in Paris. His crime? He had been appointed by the military-backed government in Algeria.

According to the director of Interpol, Raymond Kendall, those in custody were a support group. Another house in Brussels was raided soon after and more arrests made, although no more equipment or information were seized.

The Belgian judge who was appointed to oversee the investigation into the plot, Christian Valkeneer, commented: 'You don't need to be a big specialist on terrorism to realise that very many people will be gathering together for the World Cup. It is a good opportunity for anybody who wants to attack France.'

The *Sunday Times*, which broke the story of the raid in Brussels, wrote on its front page: 'Security sources believe a threat therefore remains to the World Cup.'

The loss of Melouk was a blow to the GIA and in particular to Ahmed Zaoui, who had built much of the World Cup plot around one of the finest operatives available to him. But after an assessment of the damage caused by the police action – and assured that Melouk would not talk – Bin Laden, from his lair in Afghanistan, ordered that the operation continue.

Now on the offensive, the European authorities adopted a game of stealth. The information gleaned from documents culled in Brussels was enough to make a string of arrests, but was considered not the full extent of the plot that they believed was afoot. A watching brief was adopted, while the network of Islamists was fully explored. In taking a cautious approach, the full extent of Bin Laden's plot, they hoped, could be exposed.

The GIA terrorists now found themselves going head to head with a new group, and for the first time Europe worked together as a highly effective unit. Europol was the replacement for the ineffective TREVI agreement (the French acronym for Terrorism, Radicalism, Extremism, and International Violence), which had come into being through the European Community in 1976. This provided the relevant ministers and other senior officials with a regular opportunity to meet and discuss the various security issues. One success for the TREVI agreement had been a French, Italian, and West German joint operation in 1987 that had smashed a Hezbollah network in their countries.

In 1992 the Maastricht Treaty between the European Union membership created, among other things, the European Police Office (Europol). It was designed to bring together international police forces and to provide a system that would boost information sharing. The EU feared that terrorist groups were exploiting European integration by improving their cross-border networks, while complementary law enforcement and counter-terrorism agencies were still splintered along national lines.

Technically, Europol was not due to come into operational status until October 1998, and with a meagre £12 million budget and only 155 staff it was thought that the grouping would have limited scope. However, in March 1998, an as-yet only partially staffed Europol swung into action at a time of continent-wide concern among the counter-terrorism branches of several European police forces. Collating a series of cross-border surveillance missions, Interpol and Europol worked in tandem with police forces in every EC state and others outside the grouping.

The Islamists seem to have recovered quickly and returned to their work as normal, in part due to the fact that the lack of arrests elsewhere seemed to suggest that the house in Brussels had thrown up no leads.

In Afghanistan, Bin Laden finally put the finishing touches to plans for a double-continent wave of attacks that he hoped would devastate the world. His GIA allies had done extremely well in Europe with their organisation and their smuggling of weapons into France.

But there was more for the world. Bin Laden's own Al-Qaeda network had succeeded, against all odds, in surviving a series of gaffes and security lapses to come within sight of another mission objective: synchronised attacks against the US Embassies in Kenya and Tanzania.

In May 1998, Harun Fazhl, an employee of Help Africa People, rented an estate home in a high-class residential neighbourhood outside the centre of Nairobi. The building was notable for its high walls, making the house and its grounds a secluded spot in which to work. Another feature was a gated driveway, large enough to accommodate large trucks, as was the garage. Fazhl was a member of the Kenyan Al-Qaeda cell and this house, according to subsequent reports, was where the bomb used to destroy the US embassy in Nairobi was constructed and stored.

In June 1998, Khalfan Khamis Mohammed of the Tanzanian cell would rent a similar large detached home in the Ilala district of Dar es Salaam. Much the same sort of activities were planned there.

Some observers have speculated that the African project was in place simply as a fall-back position for Bin Laden should the project aimed at his prime target, the 1998 World Cup in France, come apart. But all indications are that the East Africa plot was proceeding at full tilt alongside its European counterpart. The movements of operatives on both continents indicate that the East Africa operation was viewed as a second kick at the United States in the wake of the French attacks.

Back on Valentine's Day, three weeks before the Brussels arrests, Abu Hamza was asked to offer an overview of the entire project. He wrote:

In the name of God the Merciful

Leader,

At your request I have called all our leaders in France and found them at an advanced state of readiness. Please be reassured. The men that you have entrusted to carry out your plans are capable and will not fail you, God willing. This day [June 15] will be a glorious one that will never be forgotten.

Tunis [head of the Marseilles cell] has had a notable success. Three of his men are now employed [at Stade-Vélodrome] and have freedom of movement within the stadium. They have taken care to learn of the men named by the Sheikh, may God bless him. They have focused on Beckham, who is extremely popular among the English. They have looked at the American embassy [sic] and found it an easy target.

Our situation in the west [Poitiers] is good and our men are well trained. They believe that the day will leave a sour taste and poison the land of the enemies of Islam. Also in the west we have found worthy Muslims and I have asked the Brothers to warn them of the danger of radiation, but only after the victory.

I have been to Paris many times and I found some of the weak points. The men have willing hearts but their missions are complicated. Singh [head of the cell charged with attacking the US embassy] has a small farm where his things are stored and he has a truck. The equipment arrived in January and is suitable for the mission. I have asked him , if he is stopped before getting to the target, to blow up the bomb when as many policemen are there as possible.

176

The other Brother [leader of the cell to attack the US hotel outside Paris] was proposing to hide the equipment in the hotel. But I have stopped him out of caution. The French are already nervous, but with God's help they have left many holes in their security and are unaware of us.

I would ask that you convey my best wishes to the Sheikh, may God bless him. His men in France are ready for martyrdom. We will meet together in Heaven, God willing.

With God willing,
Abu Hamza
(see Figure 10)

Eighteen

Selling Bin Laden a Dummy

The discovery of a command cell and safe house in Brussels in March had been a significant blow to the Islamist plot against the World Cup in France. Belgian authorities briefed police and intelligence officials from seven countries, including Britain, in the wake of the raid. The Metropolitan Police's anti-terrorist branch and MI5 were quietly investigating links between Algerian exiles in London and the GIA.

Raymond Kendall, the British director of Interpol, hurriedly visited Algeria to discuss the issue with the Algerian intelligence services. Later he told journalists: 'It is very clear that we need to be vigilant. Any successful police operation will have a disruptive effect on the channels a network has put in place. But we can never presume that those networks won't be recreated in another form.'

For a time, it seemed that Osama bin Laden might have cancelled a project that had been four years in the making. But while events in Belgium had been reported in the media, the Belgians, French, Interpol and Europol took a decision to play down the discovery. While significant information was garnered from documents found in the safe house, it was the Islamists' house of cards that the police needed to bring down.

What was clear from the information the authorities now had in their possession was that an extensive network of cells had been established in France. However, much of what they had was written in cryptic fashion, making it impossible to be sure of names and places. It was, therefore, impossible for the intelligence services to be sure that they had obtained enough knowledge to smash every cell that was working on the project. Any holes might leave GIA operatives at large in France and result in an attack.

Soon after the Belgian operation there were signs that cells were actively pressing ahead regardless. In late March, a bomb was discovered on a Paris sidewalk outside a France Telecom building. Its design was similar to those used in the GIA's 1995 campaign. The device was defused by the bomb squad and there were no injuries.

The decision to hold back from making a wave of arrests, giving the Islamists time to show themselves, was a brave one in the circumstances. But it appeared to be working and lulling the GIA and Al-Qaeda into a false sense of security. After an understandable period of nervousness, with no arrests being made, Bin Laden signalled to the GIA to proceed as planned.

In addition to information gained in Brussels and through interrogation of the arrested Islamists, another source of intelligence now came on line. France had long sought to arrest Mohamed Kerouche, a French citizen of Algerian origin, who was believed to have been intimately involved in the 1995 bombing campaign in Paris. In the wake of this GIA operation, French police had arrested nearly 100 suspects in an attempt to smash the Islamist network, but Kerouche had escaped across the English Channel. He had been held in London, charged with illegal entry into the country and, after a lengthy extradition process, had been handed over to French authorities on 19 December 1997.

Despite his beliefs – strong enough to be part of a killing spree of innocent civilians in France – Kerouche 'sang like a bird' to the police in order to save himself. Thanks to information that he gave them, the French police made it known that they believed that the 'brains' behind the 1995 GIA operation were being sheltered by sympathisers in north London. During the first week of May, Scotland Yard officers followed up information passed to them from their French counterparts and arrested eight suspected Islamic militants in London who were alleged to be part of the World Cup plot. These, though, were men known to be connected with Kerouche and the bombing campaign of 1995, and as such would have caused no great panic among the Islamic fundamentalists in mainland Europe. However, the Islamists' house of cards was shaking.

Around this time the French Minister of the Interior Jean-Pierre Chevènement, told the media that security surrounding the World Cup was his greatest concern. The French police had been 'preparing for months for a whole range of possible eventualities,' he said. René-George Query, the man charged with heading police efforts for the championships, said: 'Every possible security danger is being scrutinised.'

But while comforting noises were being made in public, behind the scenes there was panic among those whose job it was to ensure that the Islamic fundamentalists were not able to attack France. As early as mid-March, there were firm indications that the GIA was at the forefront of a carefully planned and massive plot to disrupt the World Cup. A clearer picture began to emerge as Belgian authorities tracked the previous movements of the Islamic fundamentalists that they had arrested in Brussels. For the most part they had arrived in the Belgian capital having spent time in Denmark or Sweden. There were copies of documents detailing the arrival of cargoes of foodstuffs at the port of Antwerp, indicating that a widespread smuggling operation had been under way. And there were letters that made cryptic references to cells in Paris, Marseilles and elsewhere in France.

Despite outward appearances, the authorities were anything but confident.

At this point, both French President Jacques Chirac and FIFA supremo João Havelange entered the picture: two men with remarkable synergy, two men looking to enhance their personal reputations.

Chirac was in his third year as president of France at this point and like his predecessor, François Mitterrand, was just as consumed with leaving a legacy from his time in office. As prime minister between 1974 and 1976, and as mayor of Paris from 1977 to 1995, he had dreamt of winning the presidency. Twice an unsuccessful presidential candidate, in 1981 and 1988, he served as prime minister for a second term between 1986 and 1988 under Mitterrand. From this vantage point, he watched Mitterrand's extended effort to leave his mark on France and the world.

There could have been no better teacher on the importance of legacy. Mitterrand had hoped to live to see the World Cup, one of 'his projects', but he died in 1996. Meanwhile, Chirac again once ran for president in 1995, and this time he was elected.

Chirac had championed the European Union and was a driving force in efforts to integrate the grouping. As far as the World Cup was concerned, he had 'picked up the ball', placing tremendous emphasis upon a successful event as a personal statement. His personal prestige was tied to the championships.

Matters of national security are high on the agenda of all world leaders. It is inconceivable that Chirac was not regularly briefed by his interior minister, Jean-Pierre Chevènement, during this period on the size and scope of the plot that was being exposed. A web of Islamic fundamentalists was emerging, one which extended throughout western Europe and was shown to have been in place for some time. Thanks to the permeable nature of Antwerp's harbour, the cells in France were fully equipped to do serious damage.

Everything that emerged through March and April 1998 indicated that the GIA was on the verge of a massive campaign in France. Yet there were no official statements, no warnings to the public to be vigilant, nothing to suggest that their lives might be at risk – which they were. It was as though a conspiracy of silence existed at the highest levels. It was nothing short of incredible.

The outgoing FIFA president, Jose Havelange, was almost certainly also fully briefed on the security risks and, if so, also culpable of risking the lives of the general public. Havelange's reign was officially to come to an end when he handed over the World Cup trophy to President Chirac at the end of the 12 July final in the Stade de France, before it was handed to the captain of the winning team. 'My mission will be over,' he said.

In the weeks remaining until he stepped down, Havelange was working furiously to ensure that his own legacy was set in stone. In media briefings, he was boasting about leaving FIFA with a bulging bank account of around $4 billion. At a press conference prior to the championships, Havelange boasted: 'Soccer is the greatest employer in the world.' When he had taken control in 1974, he said, 'We had two competitions: the World Cup with 16 teams and the Olympic competition. Now we have 10 and the World Cup has 32 teams.'

During the press conference, Havelange was interrupted by a phone call from Chirac – a blatant public relations exercise. Both men should have had more on their minds than swapping footballing banter before the press. The fact that, four years later, much of the detail of the Islamic fundamentalists' actions are still hidden gives an indication as to the priorities of those charged with public security and heading the World Cup.

A threat to the World Cup presented a devastating scenario for Havelange in particular. The 1998 event was the biggest money-spinner in his corporate empire. His official sponsors – Adidas, Budweiser, Canon, Coca-Cola, Fujifilm, Gillette, JVC, MasterCard, McDonald's, Opel, Philips and Snickers – were between them ploughing hundreds of millions into FIFA coffers, purchasing exclusivity, pitch-side advertising and marketing associations with the sport. Television rights worth hundreds of millions more were contracted, Disney alone paying a reported $24 million for US rights. Estimates of FIFA income from the 1998 World Cup ranged between $600 million and $750 million. A great deal was certainly at stake.

Whether Chirac and Havelange made the decision themselves to proceed with the World Cup, against a backdrop of secret revelations that Islamic fundamentalists had constructed a massive network to hit the championships, remains obscured. What is clear is that both would almost certainly have known of the threat. The tournament proceeded regardless.

Self-importance and image problems beset Osama bin Laden as well. For one with an ego and a need for the spotlight, the isolation of Afghanistan was always hard to bear. His desire for attention was well served by the notoriety of being a hero of the masses, fighting the Soviets, a freedom fighter. But in remote Kandahar he was stifled and sidelined. In a country isolated by its Taleban leadership, Bin Laden was out of the spotlight and he didn't like it.

During the early months of 1998, he and his operational number two, Egyptian Islamic Jihad leader Dr Ayman al-Zawahiri, had overseen both the European and African plots and become convinced that both were entering the critical state with every chance of success.

The loss of a GIA safe house in Brussels was seen as a hiccup. It seemed to Bin Laden that Farid Melouk had been able to destroy most of the evidence during his stand-off with Belgian police. As Bin Laden's confidence grew, so did his desire to be seen and this led to an extraordinary press conference in early May. The conference was staged in the wilds of northern Pakistan, where a grandstanding Bin Laden, with al-Zawahiri by his side, appeared before members of the international media: 'The Islamic world is facing a period of trouble; we are entering a period of danger. I refer to the presence of Christian forces in Arab lands. The Christians are attempting to establish full control over our region. For the first time since the rise of our Holy Prophet Mohammed, peace be upon him, we see a situation where the sacred places of our religion – the Kaabah [in Mecca], the Nabvi Mosque [in Medina] and the Al Aqsa Mosque [in Jerusalem] – are under the open and covert power of non-Muslims. It has now become obligatory for Muslims, wherever they are in this world, to begin the struggle to oust the infidels from our sacred places. Mecca is the place where God sent divine revelations to the Prophet Mohammed, peace be upon him. There has never been such a difficult period for the Kaabah as there is now, with it surrounded on all four sides by the United States . . . '

For the crisis that Islam was facing, Bin Laden laid blame squarely on the House of Saud. He announced that Muslim scholars had issued a fatwa calling for a jihad, stating: 'Muslims should sacrifice their lives and resources . . . We pray to God that he may provide courage to Muslims to raise up in the name of jihad. The United States is supporting the infidels and the Christians and Jews have together gained control over more than one-third of the Muslim nation. We will halt this now.'

He went on to announce an all-out war against 'the infidels', highlighting his own successes against the Soviets in Afghanistan as an example how jihad could defeat the strongest military machine. 'I have decided that national boundaries have no importance. We are good Muslims and we wish to be martyred. We do not allow any discrimination on the basis of colour or race; all oppressed Muslims are our allies. We pray to God to provide us with the strength to support every oppressed Muslim.'

Amid a plethora of rhetoric and Bin Laden's normal rehashed version of his manifesto of hatred, the reason for the press conference emerged almost at the end of this event when he stated: 'By the grace of God, we have established an organisation named Islamic Front with the help of jihad organisations all around the world. The purpose of the Islamic Front will be to fight America and Israel. An important leader of this organisation is here with me, Dr Ayman al-Zawahiri. We have received offers of support from many Mujahid organisations. Everything that is happening has happened according to our expectations.' When one journalist finally asked the leader of the new Islamic Front how long he believed it would be before the grouping would begin its campaign, he replied: 'Within weeks . . .'

The 1998 World Cup was just weeks away and Al-Qaeda's cells in East Africa were also making their final preparations.

Nineteen

A Game of Two Halves

Even as Osama bin Laden was broadcasting his grand, but ultimately doomed, plans for jihad, in Europe the noose was being tightened around his GIA fellow conspirators. Even Bin Laden could apparently not see it coming.

After a two-month surveillance programme that stretched throughout western Europe, by the third week of May, the intelligence being shared among European police forces seemed to be throwing up less and less new leads pertaining to the danger area – France. The World Cup was set to burst into life with an opening gala set for 9 June in the Place de la Concorde in Paris, and before that time the threat had to be eliminated.

While the overlapping networks of Al-Qaeda and the GIA would continue to be picked apart thanks to interrogations and good detective work, immediate efforts were directed towards removing the danger hanging over the World Cup. Interpol and Europol were orchestrating one of the largest police operations ever on the continent. It is a credit to the excellence of so many members of the police and various intelligence services that throughout this period it seems that not one of the hundreds of Islamists being monitored – all of them jumpy because of the Brussels incident – suspected a thing.

A vast body of information was being collected and much was being quickly passed through to the French authorities. Over ten weeks between the arrests in Brussels and the second half of May, the French secretly pinpointed and then conducted massive operations to monitor the cells they had discovered in Paris, Marseilles and Poitiers.

By the weekend of Saturday, 23 May, consultations between the heads of the counter-terrorism branches of half a dozen European nations led to a decision. The following Tuesday a concerted and synchronised sweep of cells and Islamist sympathisers would be launched with a joint police operation in France, Germany, Italy, Switzerland and Belgium.

Over the next three days, specialist teams were formed and prepared for one of the largest joint police actions ever attempted on mainland Europe. The element of surprise was vital.

Before dawn on Tuesday, 26 May, the police and the intelligence services in France and its neighbours struck with startling precision.

In Belgium, heavily armed squads of police descended on 13 private residences in Brussels and another in the southern city of Charleroi. All had been identified through telephone records and the limited evidence that was discovered in the GIA safe house in Brussels. During the intervening period, the Belgian intelligence services had watched the comings and goings at these 14 locations, used mostly by men of North African extraction. Later the same day, a spokesman for the Belgian prosecutor's office said ten people had been detained and interrogated.

In Germany, police across the country raided seven apartments belonging to Algerians, searching for evidence of links to the GIA. They struck homes in Bonn, Munich, Berlin and the port city of Hamburg. Among those detained for questioning were two Algerian men described as senior aides to GIA leader Hassan Hattab: Abdel Mechat and Omar Saiki.

The German Federal Prosecutor's Office announced that in addition to these arrests, the police had seized computer disks, video cassettes and documents. The information gained from these would later lead to a wider series of arrests. A statement read from the Federal Prosecutor's Office in Karlsrühe declared that investigations were focusing on 'Algerian citizens suspected of belonging to a group which provides explosives and logistical support to Islamic extremists . . .'

In Italy, eight police teams were in action in a number of sites across the north of the country. Italian police insensitively code-named their raids 'Operation Crusade', creating needless antagonism with the Muslim community. Based on information from the testimony of Mohamed Kerouche, the Italians had unearthed a deep support network for the GIA that was providing the French cells with false documents. Following a wide surveillance operation, six Algerians were arrested in northern Italy and fifteen others were taken in for questioning. In a number of private homes, police discovered forged documents and machinery that was used to produce fake passports, French identity cards and travel papers.

An Italian police statement said that the move was closely linked to 'investigations carried out by police in other countries into a vast organisation traceable to the GIA'.

In Switzerland, Algerians Tesmin Aiman and Resus Huari were arrested, They were two more senior GIA officials connected to Hassan Hattab and to GIA European boss Ahmed Zaoui who had been based in Switzerland. This pair were accused of integral involvement in a network that delivered East European arms to the GIA.

French authorities immediately requested the extradition of four of those detained elsewhere in Europe – Mechat and Saiki in Germany and Aiman and Huari in Switzerland – for urgent questioning. The four were recognised as senior members of the terror hierarchy and might have had vital information on the French cells that were already poised to strike. Mechat was later convicted of supplying weapons and equipment to GIA underground cells and of providing shelter to GIA operatives.

But it was in France that most action occurred on 26 May. Minister of the Interior Jean-Pierre Chevènement and René-George Query, the most senior police official directly in charge of protecting the World Cup finals, had remained in a huddle over the preceding weekend.

Working with Interpol and Europol, French anti-terrorist and intelligence organisations had spent the previous ten weeks in an intensive effort to develop a full picture of the Islamist forces ranged against them.

The telephone records for mobiles and landlines used by Mechat, Saiki, Aiman and Huari had been used to pinpoint contacts in France. Those of master forger Farid Melouk, arrested in Belgium in March, had been similarly illuminating.

As their contacts had been discovered, these in turn led to other individuals in France who were connected to the plot. The French discovered a rat's nest of Islamic fundamentalist operatives and supporters, spread among a network of safe houses and militant-leaning mosques in several major cities. Hattab's Salafist Group for Preaching and Combat was linked to two previously unknown cells in Boumerdes and Dellys.

Secret surveillance had allowed the French to monitor those connected with the plot and from there they had been able to paint a clear picture of the Bin Laden plan. The French were, quite rightly, horrified at the depth and scope of what lay before them.

In the early hours of 26 May, several dozen crack police units left their bases and headed for a target belonging to the Islamists; it was the biggest campaign to root out the GIA and Algerian terrorists that France had ever seen.

A total of 43 locations, mainly in Paris, Lyon and Marseilles and on the island of Corsica, were targeted. Elsewhere around France, the intelligence services had identified several key points in the Islamist network. The entire operation was completed so swiftly and successfully that there were no reports of resistance from the men who were arrested.

Later that day, the media was clamouring for information when French government spokesman Daniel Vaillant gave a clear indication of the importance of the morning's events, although the wall of silence that stifled any information on the scope of the plot from entering the public arena remained: 'It was a matter of urgency. Now we can approach the World Cup more serenely,' said Vaillant.

One British newspaper quoted a French police source as saying that 'preparations were under way to mount terrorist attacks during the World Cup'.

A statement by the French Interior Ministry said the operation had been carried out after several months of surveillance that led police to 'suspect the preparation of terrorist activity in the run-up to the World Cup'. A spokesman for the ministry stated that the operation 'was aimed at dismantling a network of dissident extremists' and hinted that the French believed these men to belong to the GIA.

One reliable news service carried a report that quoted another police source as saying: 'We confirmed that attacks were being planned, and were able to nab the people who were planning all this, both here and abroad. That will make continued preparation – at least by these people – impossible.' As another French police official put it, the police operation aimed to 'kick the anthill' of Islamist support networks.

On the streets of France, most notably in Paris, the French government ordered a strengthening of the 'Vigipirate' plan, a security operation that had been in existence since the 1995 bombings in the capital. For the World Cup, 'Vigipirate' threw a security cordon around all ten footballing venues. The ministry announced that it was to assign 1,000 extra troops to the 15,000 already on World Cup duty.

For Osama bin Laden, Al-Qaeda and the GIA leadership, the news from France and Europe got worse as the day went on and information filtered through of the massive success for the authorities. Of the 55 men detained in France, 25 were still in custody a day later; most of those would eventually be charged or deported.

The overall operation had an effect like dropping a stone in a calm pond. Interrogations, telephone records and paper and electronic documents found in safe houses across Europe threw up a wealth of information on which the police continued to act. While newspapers carried news of the initial wave of raids, for the most part there was no reporting of the arrests of the hundreds of Islamic fundamentalists plucked off the streets over subsequent months.

Unfortunately, this overwhelming operation prompted scathing criticism among ordinary Muslims, even though the GIA at this point was a highly unpopular organisation among the moderates due to its complicity in Algerian civilian massacres. Many Algerians abroad dismissed the GIA as a gang of criminal murderers using the civil war as a cover for butchery and crime.

The London-based Muslim media condemned the Europe-wide operation saying 'their joint criminal action, still unfolding, is religious in nature, directed as it is against Islamic activists and also designed to bail out the corrupt and anti-Islamic junta in Algeria – a country whose vast gas and oil resources the "Christian democrats", incidentally, have no compunction plundering'. The police raids were 'typical of totalitarian states and in clear violation of EU and United Nations conventions against racism, religious discrimination and violations of personal freedoms, including the freedoms of thought and belief'.

Muslim-orientated media were dominated by comment on the fact that the police operation did not uncover any explosives. Therefore, Muslims were told by their leaders, the governments of Europe were simply attempting to bully the Islamic community into submission and send a message to future Muslim immigrants of 'how unwanted Muslims are in Europe'.

Despite this, intelligence services plunged deeper and deeper into the murky world of Islamic terrorism. In France especially, new cells were discovered and smashed, video cassettes, computer disks and written material seized that in turn led to more discoveries.

During the summer of 1998, while the rest of the world cheered as the French side, led by an inspirational Zinedine Zidane – a French superstar of Algerian heritage – marched on Paris to claim the greatest prize in football, the intelligence services were quietly winning a war against the Islamic fundamentalists. The European networks of Al-Qaeda and the GIA were smashed. Osama bin Laden's cause was turned on its head.

In Africa, however, things went differently. It was a brutal reminder that safety from terror attack can never be guaranteed. Two US embassies were being targeted by Al-Qaeda, and on several occasions American intelligence had been gifted information on the project but no one had acted. This attack was allegedly managed from London by Khaled al-Fawwaz, a Saudi dissident. Documents supplied by Barclays Bank show that al-Fawwaz was the signatory on the account for Bin Laden's European mouthpiece, the Advisory and Reformation Committee, and his telephone records show his contacts with all parties involved in East Africa.

In May 1998, Al-Qaeda member Harun Fazhl had rented an estate home in a high-class residential neighbourhood outside the centre of Nairobi. One month later, 24-year-old Khalfan Khamis Mohammed rented a similar large, detached home in the Ilala district of Dar es Salaam. Inside these safe houses cell members could work in seclusion.

While reconnaissance efforts continued – in Nairobi, two operatives were working for a company that sold fresh fish to hotels throughout the city, so that they could spy on the US embassy – inside these innocent-looking suburban homes two sets of men were working on massive truck bombs.

On 7 August 1998, two light-coloured vehicles left the villa in Nairobi. The first was a pick-up truck, the second, a truck carrying suicide bomber Mohammed Rashed Daoud Al-Owhali and driven by Jihad Mohammed Ali. These trucks rumbled into the city toward the US embassy. The plan was to park outside the embassy building, scare as many Kenyan civilians away from the site as possible with a gun, and then detonate the bomb.

This did not happen, however, and none of the hundreds of civilians nearby were warned. Inside the cabin of the truck, Jihad Mohammed Ali manually detonated the bomb. The blast tore through the embassy building, the Co-operative Bank, and reduced the seven-floor Ufundi Co-operative House to a pile of rubble, on the heads of hundreds of Kenyans.

Gruesome film footage showed the horror of the moments following the Nairobi blast. The passengers of a bus passing the embassy at the wrong moment were incinerated in their seats. Children sat on the road in shock, staring at the bloody stumps that moments earlier had been their arms or legs. A pregnant woman held the body of her husband, whose head had been removed by shrapnel.

In total 213 people were killed. Hundreds more were cut by flying glass as the blast shattered windows in office buildings five blocks away, or by flying metal from the blast site. As night fell, rescue workers were still frantically trying to dig their way into the rubble, desperately seeking survivors. But for the most part they were lifting only corpses from the shattered structure.

Osama bin Laden had struck. Five American embassy employees and a child were dead, but Al-Qaeda had managed to massacre hundreds of Kenyans and injure many hundreds more, the irony being that many were the Muslims in whose name Bin Laden was claiming to fight.

Around 450 miles away, four minutes after the explosion in Nairobi, Hamden Khalif Allah Awad, also known as Ahmed the German, detonated a massive explosive in his truck, parked outside the US embassy in Dar es Salaam. The force of the blast was so strong that the top half of his body, still holding on to the steering wheel, was slammed into the embassy building and later found embedded there in the masonry. Eleven people died.

At 5.30 a.m. Washington time, US President Bill Clinton was woken in the White House with news of the attacks. In a statement he later said: 'These acts of terrorist violence are abhorrent. They are inhuman.' Later the same day, Clinton condemned what he called 'the cowardly attacks'. He vowed that the United States would bring the bombers to justice 'no matter what or how long it takes'.

Twenty

Extra Time

The coordinated attacks on France in June 1998 may have been prevented, but the events of 11 September 2001 showed that Al-Qaeda had not been defeated. If anything, it had resurfaced stronger than ever. Whether the allied effort to wage a new and broad-based 'War on Terrorism' will have the desired long-term effect remains to be seen. Meanwhile, detective work continues to bring the accused to justice.

Following the arrest in Dubai of Algerian-born Frenchman Jamal Beghal in July 2001, other breakthroughs were achieved. Under interrogation at the Palais de Justice in Paris, he implicated a cell in Holland. Dutch police soon had a four-person cell under surveillance in Rotterdam, when they learned of a fresh cell in Brussels. The head of the cell was Nizar Trabelsi.

Trabelsi, a former Tunisian footballer, was to be the martyr in another operation against the American embassy in Paris, penetrating the embassy with explosives strapped to his body. He was arrested in Brussels on 13 September. Under interrogation he provided information that led to the arrest of Mohamed Belaziz, Mohamed Boualem Khnouni, Ocine Khouni, Madjid Sahouane, Yasin Seddiki and Hakim Zerzour, six alleged GIA operatives, in Spain. All were detained over alleged plans to attack the US embassy in Paris. The material seized in Spain included three sets of night-vision glasses, forged identity papers, credit cards and knives. Belgian police also raided an Egyptian snackbar in the heart of Brussels, where they found 220lb of sulphur and 13 gallons of acetone, the basic ingredients for a bomb big enough to blow up a building.

In a raid on Trabelsi's apartment, police recovered an automatic pistol and ammunition, detailed plans of the US embassy in Paris and chemical formulae for bomb-making.

Others implicated in the 1998 World Cup plot have also found themselves in custody or on the run. In Italy, Kishk Samir, one of Al-Qaeda's most senior figures in Europe and the head of the GIA's Lombardy cell in France, was arrested on 30 November 2001. The 46 year old was detained at Rome's Fiumicino airport en route from Cairo to Paris. Italy had issued a warrant for his arrest on 5 October.

Investigators had been trying to catch Samir for several years without success, their break being the arrest of senior Italy-based Al-Qaeda operative Essid Sami Ben Khemais. Khemais had been arrested the previous April following an investigation into suspected Islamist terrorist cells in Milan, according to a statement issued by the Italian Interior Ministry.

Samir was accused of trafficking in arms, explosives, toxic chemicals and false documents to support Al-Qaeda cells all over the continent. Italian investigators dubbed him 'head of the main branch of the GIA network in France . . . providing logistical support for militants preparing to leave for Al-Qaeda training camps'.

Police said they believed Samir's arrest would deal 'a decisive blow to a complex terrorist structure with bases in northern Italy, which has connections in numerous European countries and direct contacts with members of Osama bin Laden's organisation'.

Another who has been put out of action is the GIA European commander Ahmed Zaoui, although he has thus far escaped the long arm of the law. In the wake of the May 1998 wave of arrests across Europe, the Swiss government was left with a political hot potato on its hands. Despite being the puppet master, Zaoui has kept himself well hidden from underground activities and lived a public life as a high-minded politician wishing a peaceful end to the crisis in Algeria. Senior officials involved with investigating the plot in France, Belgium and Britain believed that the rat's nest of cells working in the 1998 project was his work. The French were understandably keen to see Zaoui in custody and available for interrogation and, ultimately, trial.

With nothing coming to light that could be used as grounds for arrest, pressure began to mount on the Swiss government. Fearing that Zaoui might later be implicated in an attack plotted by the Islamic fundamentalists as revenge for the collapse of their plans, the Swiss panicked. On 28 October 1998, Zaoui was at home in Sion when at 6 p.m. there was a knock on his door. A squad of ten police officers, some of them armed, entered the building and informed Zaoui that he and his family were being expelled immediately. Despite his arguing that his wife was sick and that his four children were in school, the family were given one hour to pack. They were then driven straight to a private airfield.

With his lawyer frantically attempting to win Zaoui a stay, the GIA European head and his family were placed aboard an aircraft and flown to Ouagadougou, the capital of the poor African state of Burkina Faso. The former French colony, formerly known as Upper Volta, borders Côte d'Ivoire, Ghana and Mali, and was the only destination available to the Swiss.

Despite the fact that Zaoui had known terrorist links, astonishingly Amnesty International leapt to his defence. In an open letter dated 5 November, Alan Bovard, the head of the group's Swiss office, attacked the decision. Bovard claimed that the expulsion was a violation of the rights of asylum, that it was a political decision. He also fretted that Zaoui would be mistreated in Burkina Faso, which, although it had retained its ties with France, also has relatively good ties with the military-backed government in Algeria.

In Ouagadougou, Zaoui found that the roles were reversed. For years he had been content to hide in the shadows and orchestrate the killing and maiming of ordinary people that had nothing to do with, and had no knowledge of, his fundamentalist agenda. In Burkina Faso he was exposed. The French would have liked nothing more than to incarcerate him and throw away the key. But more than this, many Algerians, victims of the GIA, would have been delighted to see such a man dead – and the regime in Algiers was also well versed in political assassinations. His well-publicised arrival in Ouagadougou made Zaoui the hunted instead of the hunter. As news spread of his presence, he went into hiding.

In the city there were reports of hit squads making discreet inquiries as to his whereabouts. Elsewhere, the French ambassador visited several ministers in a bid to see him arrested and initiate extradition proceedings.

For a time it looked as if Zaoui's future would depend simply upon who got their hands on him first. But true to form, he had a keen measure of self-preservation. Within one month of arriving in Ouagadougou, under cover of darkness he had disappeared from his rented house in the suburbs of the city. Almost unbelievably, the Algerian left alone, leaving his wife and four children to an uncertain fate.

Since then, Ahmed Zaoui has lived a life on the run, making fleeting appearances in Algeria and other North African states. Knowing that the French want him alive, and that Algerian death squads are also in pursuit, most of Zaoui's friends in the Islamist cause will not touch him for fear of encountering the wrath of his enemies.

Life has changed a great deal for the architects of the plot against the 1998 World Cup. Osama bin Laden is on the run; Ayman al-Zawahiri is on the run, believed by some to be dead. Kishk Samir is incarcerated and Ahmed Zaoui is living life as a shadow, in hiding. However, that is not to say that this sorry saga has ended.

Twenty-One

A Golden Goal for Al-Qaeda

Wherever he is, Osama bin Laden remains a marked man. It is impossible to believe that the United States will not find and 'neutralise' him at some point. But would that halt the rising tide of global terrorism? Would that put an end to audacious attacks on high-profile targets?

In a particularly sobering commentary, terrorism expert Brian Jenkins stated an obvious fact that many have chosen to ignore: 'I think we have to presume that even before 11 September, [Al-Qaeda] realised that that would provoke a response from us. And so, in addition to the actual terrorist attack itself, there was probably something like a business continuity plan that they would put in place.'

Al-Qaeda was known for meticulous planning of operations, sometimes over a period of years. 'So there may be operations that are in training right now that we don't know about,' Jenkins said.

In the wake of 11 September, several small plots have come to light. Evidence has also surfaced that suggests these plots were merely the tip of the iceberg.

An amateur video discovered by the Northern Alliance forces at an Al-Qaeda training camp in Kabul purports to show fighters rehearsing assassinations with live ammunition and hostage-taking. One scene shows an attack on what appears to be a set-up of a motorcade in Washington, on a road system in the District of Columbia.

The footage also shows Al-Qaeda men practising an attack on what appears to be an international golf tournament. They are shown on the tape hiding guns and rocket grenades in their golf bags as they rehearse the attempted massacre.

However, the most obvious operation, given the terrorists' thirst for publicity, would be something on a global stage. Such a platform could have been found at the Winter Olympics in Salt Lake City, Utah, but this event was far too obvious a target and surrounded by far too much security for a full-blown assault. However, just months later comes an equally tempting occasion at the 2002 World Cup in Japan and South Korea. Where better to strike than on a stage that Bin Laden has already shown a liking for?

Inevitably, considering that England and the United States were always likely to reach the 2002 finals, there is a clear danger to the event in view of the close shave that the 1998 finals had. Although this possibility has hardly been raised in public, a growing body of evidence suggests that Al-Qaeda could be in a position to mount such an offensive.

While Japan and South Korea initially celebrated and began pumping billions of dollars into the event, after 11 September both began to get nervous. In October 2001, Sepp Blatter, the new president of FIFA, announced that a new cancellation insurance contract for the 2002 World Cup finals had been secured.

The contract, with the US-based National Indemnity Company, follows the decision by the French company AXA SA to withdraw from insuring the event. FIFA declined to say how much the contract would cost. However, they had agreed to pay AXA $17 million to protect against the possibility of having to cancel the event, prior to 11 September.

Japan's World Cup Organising Committee (JAWOC) announced that it had redoubled efforts to strengthen security for the 2002 World Cup in the wake of terrorist attacks in the United States. The committee said the assaults on New York and Washington showed terrorism was changing and they were being forced to re-examine safety measures. 'We will have to revise ways in which we approach the prevention of terrorist acts,' JAWOC director Kazuhiko Endo told a news conference.

The 64 games of the 2002 World Cup competition will be played in 20 stadiums dotted around Japan and South Korea, from 31 May to 30 June. It is the first time the event has been co-hosted and the first time it has been staged in Asia.

In Daegu, Korea's biggest World Cup venue nestles on a lush green hillside that provides a spectacular backdrop for the white concrete and steel sci-fi construction which holds 66,000 fans. By comparison, the 1997 International Stadium in Yokohama, Japan, seems almost old, but with its 72,350 capacity, it is imposing enough to host the World Cup final on 30 June.

The cast for the championships are much the same as in France, with only a few surprise qualifiers and non-arrivals. The Islamic and Arab world will be represented in the Far East by perennial qualifiers Saudi Arabia, Tunisia and Turkey, while the Islamists' old foe, the United States, also made it to the finals with relative ease.

England, under Swedish manager Sven-Goran Eriksson, open their campaign against Sweden in Saitama, Japan, on 2 June, and follow up with a game against Argentina, old World Cup adversaries and championship favourites, in Sapporo on 7 June. Also in the group are the gifted Africans of Nigeria.

In mid-May, before the official deadline of 21 May, Eriksson has said that he will name the 23 players he will take to the Far East, before flying them and their partners to Dubai for a private break to recuperate from the rigours of the demanding European domestic season.

Osama bin Laden would not have difficulty recognising most of the players aspiring to make the trip to Dubai. Many were in the squad that he targeted in 1998. The notable exception is England's captain in France, Alan Shearer, who insists that he is not available. But the England goal is still likely to be kept by David Seaman, its midfield will be inspired by the new national captain, David Beckham, and an attacking position looks a certainty for Liverpool's Michael Owen.

While Al-Qaeda had never been shown to be as organised in the Far East as it was in Europe, post-11 September events revealed that the group had grown significantly there in more recent times. According to a report by *Jane's Intelligence Review*, a respected authority on defence and security, the Al-Qaeda network remained virtually intact in Asia. The *Jane's* report indicated that terrorist attacks on the region's non-Muslim countries such as South Korea and Japan were well within the group's capability. The publication also noted the vulnerability of Malaysia, Singapore, Indonesia and the Philippines, countries with large Muslim populations, and suggested that Asian governments should 'take pre-emptive action against known Al-Qaeda members and supporters currently living in these countries'.

It stated: 'Al-Qaeda's network in the United States, Europe and East Africa has been disrupted significantly as a result of investigations and widespread arrests . . . In Asia, however, a network of cells and support structures remains virtually intact after 11 September . . .'

Jane's Intelligence Review also claimed that Al-Qaeda had extensive links with groups in the Philippines, Indonesia and Malaysia in South-east Asia, as well as groups in Pakistan, India and Bangladesh in South Asia. Non-Muslim countries and nations that have supported the US-led anti-terrorism campaign are the most likely targets of any campaigns supported by Bin Laden.

As events on the ground in the Far East have shown, governments in the region were only beginning to get to grips with the Islamic fundamentalism in their midst. On 22 January 2002, Thailand became the fifth nation in the region to detain Al-Qaeda operatives within its borders. Arrests had been reported during January in Singapore, Malaysia, Indonesia and the Philippines.

Police swooped on Bin Laden's men in Thailand after the Thai embassy in Kuwait was supplied with intelligence that airline offices of the US and its allies in Thailand, Malaysia and Singapore could be targeted by Al-Qaeda. *The Nation*, a major daily newspaper published in Bangkok, said in a major report that security had been increased around 'sensitive areas'.

In Malaysia more than 50 Islamists were detained during January, including members of the Kumpulan Militant Malaysia (KMM). The KMM has a long-standing association with Al-Qaeda and many of its fighters are known to have trained in Bin Laden's camps in Afghanistan. Malaysian police raided a number of safe houses, unearthing clear evidence that the Al-Qaeda network extended through Singapore, Indonesia and the Philippines.

In neighbouring Indonesia, the world's most populous Muslim country, although moderates dominate, the country faces tremendous instability in arresting men who may be terrorists but promote themselves simply as guardians of the faith. American defence analysts believed that Indonesia was a country where Muslim terrorists would potentially find sanctuary. It was one thing to speculate, but quite another to do so publicly, an action that did not help the situation. Indonesian Foreign Minister Hasan Wirayuda defended his country, saying: 'It seems that with the arrest of alleged terrorists in Singapore and Malaysia the pressure is on us to produce something.'

The most sensational revelation in the Far East emanated from Singapore, which had been pinpointed as an area of Al-Qaeda infiltration in intelligence gathered in Afghanistan. On 7 January, Singaporean police announced that they had broken up a network of militants that was preparing to target the US embassy and American businesses. Defence Minister Tony Tan revealed that those picked up in the arrests, which were made in December, were aiming to launch missile attacks on embassies and some military installations.

A total of fifteen men – fourteen Singaporeans and one Malaysian – were arrested in an initial swoop, while intelligence in the state beefed up low-key security for some embassies. On 6 January, 13 of those suspects were ordered to be detained for two years under the country's Internal Security Act. There was evidence that eight had trained at Al-Qaeda camps in Afghanistan.

As a result of searches in the homes and workplaces of those arrested, several days later roadblocks were erected around the Israeli embassy, which had been a focus point for the plotters. The searches also uncovered detailed information on bomb construction, Al-Qaeda literature, falsified passports and forged immigration stamps. The Ministry of Home Affairs issued a statement saying: 'We believe that the network has been disrupted. There is no information of any imminent threat. American establishments, including the US embassy and commercial entities, were the principal targets for attack.'

Just as Bin Laden forged an alliance of terror with the GIA to execute his plot against France, it is plausible that an assault on the 2002 World Cup could be planned along the same lines. There is no shortage of terrorist groups in the Far East with which Al-Qaeda has been linked.

Perhaps the most notorious among these is the Abu Sayyaf group, the smallest and most radical of the Islamic separatist groups operating in the southern Philippines. Many members have studied or worked in the Middle East and developed ties to Al-Qaeda while fighting and training in Afghanistan. After their leader, Abdurajik Abubakar Janjalani, was killed in December 1998, his younger brother, Khadafi Janjalani, took his place. Their sister is one of Bin Laden's wives.

The Philippines was the location of the first significant expansion outside Afghanistan of President Bush's worldwide war on terror, when Bush ordered US special forces to the island nation to support the government's efforts against Abu Sayyaf. A joint operation was planned, targeting Abu Sayyaf strongholds in Basilan and Zamboanga.

The Abu Sayyaf have been active for well over a decade, carrying out bombings, assassinations, kidnappings, and extortion to promote an independent Islamic state in the southern Philippines. They also have a well-established capability to mount large-scale offensives. More recently, observers have witnessed an expansion of the group's capabilities. Previously, the furthest from its heartland that the Abu Sayyaf operated was Manila, but in 2000 the group appeared in Malaysia, where it abducted foreigners from two different resorts.

Also in the Philippines is the Alex Boncayao Brigade (ABB), a small group that has on occasion been linked with Al-Qaeda. The ABB is a breakaway urban hit squad of the Communist Party of the Philippines New People's Army, formed in the mid-1980s.

Bin Laden and the Islamist cause also has highly established contacts with two groups from Japan. Foremost among these is the Japanese Red Army (JRA). The JRA is known to train its members in Syrian-controlled areas of Lebanon and has a long history of cooperation with Islamic groups. In 2000, Lebanon deported to Japan four members it arrested in 1997, but granted a fifth operative, Kozo Okamoto, political asylum.

Formed around 1970, the JRA was led by Fusako Shigenobu until her arrest in Japan in November 2000. The JRA's historical goal has been to overthrow the Japanese government and monarchy and to help foment world revolution. Details released following Shigenobu's arrest indicate that the JRA was organising cells in Asian cities, such as Manila and Singapore. The group also has a history of close relations with Palestinian terrorist groups, and intelligence has implicated Al-Qaeda in supporting the Japanese.

In April 1988, JRA operative Yu Kikumura was arrested with explosives on the New Jersey Turnpike, apparently planning an attack to coincide with the bombing of a United States Officers (USO) club in

Naples, a suspected JRA operation that killed five, including a US servicewoman.

Less well known, but believed to be stronger than the JRA, is Japan's Chukaku-Ha. Active on and off since its formation in 1957, this group was established in protest to Japan's imperial system, Western imperialism, and imperialist actions such as the Gulf War. The Japanese government believes this to be the largest domestic militant group, and again links have been established with Al-Qaeda.

Some, if not all of these groups have the operational capacity and on-the-ground presence that would enable them – with the right backing – to mount a campaign against the World Cup. Supporting such outrages is what Al-Qaeda has shown it does best. Its leader, wherever he may be, alive or dead, has laid down a blueprint for action with his own failed attempt to hijack the 1998 World Cup in France.

Bin Laden could have been an exemplary football fan, revelling in the successes and moaning over the failures of his team. Instead he chose a twisted path. He chose to destroy that which he loved as a player, corporate sponsor and enthusiastic supporter, in the name of global Islamic revolution. He targeted star players and ordinary fans alike with callous disregard for the spirit that united them. What he really tried to attack in France was the soul of a sport that unites millions around the world. There can be no greater treachery, nor any scheme so utterly doomed to failure.

Acknowledgements

Writing about the activities of Osama bin Laden and an organisation so ready to commit acts of violence and murder as the Armed Islamic Group is not an easy process. Al-Qaeda and the GIA remain operationally viable. They would think nothing of killing a journalist or writer who opposes them. Indeed, it is GIA policy to do so.

Many journalist colleagues and friends around the Middle East have, therefore, possibly risked their careers and even their lives in supporting my research, asking questions where information has been buried for sometimes years. This may seem melodramatic, but I assure you that it is not.

My special thanks go to Ahmed Nasr for taking so many hours to explain crucial background and pull apart the modern history of Algeria and the GIA.

My researcher in Saudi Arabia, Hassan Abdul Malik, is more responsible than anyone for discovering priceless information on the childhood of Bin Laden in Jeddah. This offers an insight into his psyche – which was especially important for my first book on the subject, *Bin Laden: Behind the Mask of the Terrorist* – and a fascinating portrait into the origins of his interest in football.

In Lebanon, much the same can be said for Rashid Ghosson, who risked the hostility of the authorities and walked a fine line between completing his work and being 'detained for questioning'. Both Hassan and Rashid not only did an extremely good job but also put themselves at some risk in the process, not only from Islamic fundamentalists but from the authorities in both countries who would prefer such chapters in history to be forgotten.

Jean Tankoano's work in Burkina Faso was important and illuminating, while hours spent with Mohammed Ali Khan, a journalist in Peshawar during the days of the Soviet occupation in Afghanistan, have formed the backbone of much of the information in this book.

Thanks too to my editor and friend Trudeau who, as always, was both a rock and a sounding board. I must also mention my colleagues at Mainstream Publishing whose professionalism makes the process a pleasure and whose dedication adds much to a difficult and complicated undertaking of this nature.

Much of the background information herein has come from sources who understandably wish to remain disassociated with a book such as this. Nevertheless, the men and women who have given me their time, and most importantly their trust, should know that this was gratefully received.

Background

In the summer of 1999 I had the good fortune to be introduced to a former Assistant Chief of Staff in the office of President Mohammed Boudiaff, the Algerian Head of State who was assassinated in June 1992. He later left the side of the military-backed government, tired of the corruption and nepotism, to join the political wing of the Islamic Salvation Front (FIS), the legitimate Islamic opposition.

In the face of death threats from the military, as it tried to wipe out all political dissent, my friend left Algeria. In September 1999 he arranged a meeting for me in Beirut with Abdelkader Hachani, one of the most senior leaders of the FIS, as I wished to write a book about the unique struggle of the organisation as it attempted to bring about change in Algeria. For his troubles, Hachani was assassinated before the end of that year.

But this was not the end of my interest in the FIS. Hearing that I was attempting to put together my first book on Osama bin Laden, *Behind the Mask of the Terrorist*, through the same channels that brought me to Hachani, I was offered a handful of Armed Islamic Group (GIA) communications that had fallen into the hands of the FIS. They were to prove a starting point from where Bin Laden's lifelong association with football became more apparent.

Long before I began, some wonderful researchers and talented writers had already looked hard at the seedy world of Islamic fundamentalism, the situation in Algeria, the GIA and Al-Qaeda. They left in their wake an invaluable body of information that is eye-opening, should one be able to absorb it, and makes for a disturbing read when one considers that someone, somewhere in authority should have done so before 11 September. The men and women to whom I refer are recognised below and I humbly commend them for their efforts.

Notes

Osama's World Cup
This chapter is based on GIA communications and is entirely fictional, portraying the nightmare scenario which might have occurred had Osama bin Laden's plot against the 1998 World Cup finals and France not been interrupted.

The Goalkeeper
Information on Bin Laden clan history was provided courtesy of a member of the family who was interviewed on a number of occasions. Other background was sourced from articles that appeared in *Time*, *Newsweek*, *The Times*, The *Sunday Times* and *The Independent* in the period immediately after 11 September. Details on Bin Laden's involvement with Ittihad Club as a youth goalkeeper were investigated by Hassan Abdul Malik who interviewed several former administrators, players and coaches from the late 1960s and early '70s.

Sex, Lies and . . . Pelé
Research conducted by Rashid Ghosson, supported by articles appearing in *Al Anwar*, *An Nahar* and *L'Orient-le Jour* in Lebanon during the years preceding the civil war in that country in 1975, and in some later articles. Background on Broumanna High School came from former pupils at the school during the period. The family of 'Rita' granted an interview on condition that no photographs appeared linking them with this publication and that her name was changed.

Information on Nejmeh Sporting Club was provided by a former player.

A New Playing Field
Research in Jeddah was carried out by Hassan Abdul Malik. Information on Afghanistan was culled from media sources including *Newsweek*, *Time*, The *New York Times*, *Washington Post* and *Al-Hayat*; also from an interview and notes provided by Mohammed Ali Khan, a Pakistani journalist based in Peshawar during this period.

An Own Goal in Algeria
Most information on the history of Algeria and the origins of the civil war was gathered from various books and newspapers, notably *Le Jeune Indépendant*, *El Khabar*, *La Liberté*, *La Tribune d'Alger* in Algeria and *Le Parisien* in France and *Al-Hayat*. *Jane's Intelligence Review* was also an important source.

Corporate Sponsorship, Terror Sponsorship
The Sudan Football Association provided information on Al-Ahli Football Club and the scope of the sport in that country. Details of Bin Laden's business interests in Sudan and background on the election process in Algeria were provided by Ahmed Nasr. These were corroborated through newspaper articles that appeared in the French media in 1991 and 1992.

Football and Fatwas
Information pertaining to Bin Laden's visit to the United Kingdom came from an interview with a Yemeni intelligence official. Allegations concerning the activities of Sheikh Abu Hamza Al-Masri are drawn from various British news agencies and newspapers and his statements reported in *Christian Science Monitor* and the BBC. Bin Laden's affiliation with Arsenal was reported by a family member.

All the World's a Stage
Background from *al-Wasat*, GIA communiqués and press releases, also articles from *Le Monde*.

The Baron

Information collected from FIFA press releases, The *Financial Times*, biographies of João Havelange and the speeches of Jacques Chirac.

Hoddle's Italian Job

Footballing content drawn from a variety of newspapers and news agencies. Other information from official GIA communiqués, reports that appeared in *La Liberté* and subsequent details that emerged following the Europe-wide crackdown on Islamists, widely reported in the mass media in May 1998. The movements of Ahmed Zaoui were detailed during interviews with Ahmed Nasr, as were details of the Islamists' network in Switzerland, subsequently dismantled in 1998.

The Road to France

Algerian and Islamic background courtesy of Ahmed Nasr. Cornell University's *Algeria: A Bibliography of Events Since 1991* was an important source. Ayman al-Zawahiri's paedophilia was touched on during an interview with a Yemeni intelligence officer.

Bin Laden's $4.1 Billion Bomb

Electricité de France press communications provided background on Civaux-1, while information on the plot against the facility came from GIA communications. GIA communiqués provided background into the direction of the group during this period.

The Import Business

GIA communications were a leading source as to the plot, while recent events contained within this chapter were culled from the major news services. The writings of Yossef Bodansky were particularly important in uncovering the underworld of the Islamists. Reports of GIA smuggling activities in Belgium taken from *Gazet van Antwerpen* and *La Libre Belgique* at various times between 1996 and 1998. The arrest and investigation into Jamal Beghal taken from the *New York Times*.

Abu Hamza on the Ball

This chapter is based upon GIA communications from this period and

European Union media briefings dealing with the EU's relations with the US.

Bin Laden's Lions
Again GIA communications were a leading source, while football content was gathered from various British newspapers. European Parliamentary records, press statements by Cogema and Electricité de France, and newspaper reports from *Le Monde* all provided information.

Bombs, Balls and Uranium Oxide
Much background for this was drawn from US Nuclear Regulatory Commission statements and other nuclear-related information was drawn from international media coverage after 11 September. Also used were details from GIA communications. Electricité de France statements covered operational troubles at Civaux-1.

Nutmegging the GIA
Internal information on the GIA and the election of Abou Khalil Mahfoud came from interviews with Ahmed Nasr, the testimonies of Omar Chikhi and articles that appeared in *An-Nahar*. Statements made by Interpol and Europol, the justice departments of several governments, a variety of police sources across Europe and reports carried in dozens of European newspapers across the continent were used to form a collage of 3 March 1988.

Records of the Al-Qaeda operation in East Africa came from various US Government enquiry reports and the works of Yossef Bodansky and Jeffrey Richelson.

Selling Bin Laden a Dummy
Reports produced by Interpol and Europol offered a keen insight into the workings of the continent-wide inquiry into Islamic fundamentalist activities, between March 1998 and May 1998. As did French Interior Ministry communications. Material on French President Jacques Chirac and João Havelange came from personal statements they made and biographical works on the two men. Reportage of Bin Laden's press conference was drawn from reports that appeared in the Egyptian newspaper *Al-Ahram*.

A Game of Two Halves
Record of the events of 26 May 1998 were drawn from newspaper and news agency reports produced in the wake of the raids. Additional background into the blow dealt by the GIA was produced from interviews with Ahmed Nasr. Source material from Interpol and Europol. Several May and June editions of *Muslimedia* commented on the issue.

Subsequent US Government enquiry reports were used to collate information on the East Africa disasters.

Extra Time
The arrest of Islamic fundamentalists was covered by several Italian police statements and in reports that appeared in *l'Unita, la Repubblica*. The fate of Ahmed Zaoui was learned through an interview with Ahmed Nasr, reports in *La Tribune de Genève* and statements issued by Amnesty International. Background on Burkina Faso was garnered from an interview with Jean Tankoano and through articles that appeared in *L'Observateur Paalga*.

A Golden Goal for Al-Qaeda
Information gathered from post-11 September media reports. Background on Al-Qaeda's ties with Far Eastern Islamic fundamentalist groups and other terrorist organisations was drawn from CIA statements, *Jane's Intelligence Review* and newspapers in the Philippines and Japan.

Bibliography

Newspapers and periodicals

Algeria: *Horizons, Le Jeune Indépendant, El Khabar, La Liberté, El Moudjahid, Le Quotidien d'Oran, La Tribune d'Alger, An-Nahar*

Belgium: *Gazet van Antwerpen, Het Volk, La Libre Belgique*

Burkina Faso: *L'Observateur Paalga*

Egypt: *Al-Ahram*

France: *Le Monde, Charente Libre, Le Droit, L'equipe, Le Figaro, France Daily, Le Parisien*

Germany: *Bild, Die Zeit*

Italy: *L'Espresso, Il Gazzetta, Gazzetta di Mantova, I'Unita, la Repubblica*

Lebanon: *Al Anwar, An Nahar, L'Orient-le Jour, The Daily Star*

Saudi Arabia: *Arab News, Al Sharq Al Aswat*

Sudan: *Sudan Globe*

Switzerland: *L'Essentiel, La Liberté, Swiss Daily, La Tribune de Genève*

Yugoslavia: *Blic, Borba* and *Politika*

UK: The *Sunday Times*, The *Times*, The *Financial Times*, The *Observer*, The *Daily Mail*, The *Daily Telegraph*, The *Sunday Telegraph*, The *Guardian*, The *Independent*.

US: *Time, Newsweek*, The *Washington Post*, The *New York Times*, The *Wall Street Journal*

Also: *Al-Hayat, Al-Wasat, Al Khaleej, New Scientist, Muslimedia, Christian Science Monitor*

CNN, ABC News, BCC and other major television channels and their websites.

Books and papers

Aburish, Said K., *Arafat: from Defender to Dictator* (Bloomsbury, New York, 1998)

Adams, James, *The Financing of Terror* (Simon and Schuster, New York, 1986)

Al-Khalil, *Samir, Republic of Fear* (Hutchinson-Radius, London, 1989)

Almana, Mohammed, *Arabia Unified: A Portrait of Ibn Saud* (Hutchinson-Benham, London, 1980)

Ayubi, Nazih, *Political Islam: Religion and Politics in the Arab World* (Routledge, New York, 1991)

Bedjaoui, Youcef, *Abbas Aroua & Méziane Aït-Larbi: An Inquiry into the Algerian Massacres* (Hoggar, Geneva, 1999)

Bedjaoui, Youcef, *An Inquiry into the Algerian Massacres* (Hoggar Books, Geneva, 1999)

Abdalhaqq, Hajj and Aisha Bewley, *The Noble Qur'an* (Madinah Press, Granada, 1999)

Bodansky, Yossef *Bin Laden: The Man Who Declared War on America* (Random House, New York, 2001)

Burgat, François and William Dowell, *The Islamic Movement in North Africa* (Center for Middle Eastern Studies, University of Texas, Austin, 1993)

Carew, Tom, *Jihad! The Secret War in Afghanistan* (Mainstream Publishing, Edinburgh, 2001)

Cantwell Smith Wilfred, *Islam in Modern History* (Princeton University Press, Princeton, 1957)

Cornell University, *Algeria: A Bibliography of Events Since 1991* (Cornell University Library, 1997)

Esposito, John L., *Political Islam: Revolution, Radicalism, or Reform?* (Westview Press, Colorado, 1997)

Cooley, John K., *Unholy Wars: Afghanistan, America and International Terrorism* (Pluto Press, London, 1999)

Esposito, John L., *The Islamic Threat: Myth or Reality?* (Oxford University Press, New York, 1995)

Field, Michael, *A Hundred Million Dollars A Day* (Sidgwick, London, 1975)

Fuller, Graham E. and Ian O. Lesser, *A Sense of Siege: The Geopolitics of Islam and the West* (Westview Press, Colorado, 1995)

Gowers, Andrew and Tony Walker, *Behind the Myth: Yasser Arafat and the Palestinian Revolution*, (W.H. Allen, London, 1990)

Guazzone, Laura (ed.), *The Islamist Dilemma: The Political Role of Islamist Movements in the Contemporary Arab World* (Ithaca Press, Reading, 1995)

Heradstveit, Danie,l *Political Islam in Algeria* (NUPI, Oslo, 1997)

Hoffman, Bruce, *Inside Terrorism* (Colombia University Press, New York, 1998)

Labévière, Richard, *Dollars for Terror: The United States and Islam* (Algora Publishing, New York, 2000)

Lacey, Robert, *The Kingdom:Arabia and the House of Saud* (Avon Books, New York, 1981)

Laird, Robbin 'France, Islam and the Chirac Presidency: Strategic Choices and the Decision-Making Framework', *European Security* 5, no.2 (Summer 1996)

Laqueur, Walter, *The New Terrorism: Fanaticism and the Arms of Mass Destruction* (Oxford University Press, Oxford, 1999)

Maddy-Weitzman, *Bruce a*nd Efraim Inbar, *Religious Radicalism in the Greater Middle East* (Frank Cass, London, 1997)

Nielsen, Jorgen S., *Towards a European Islam* (Macmillan, London, 1999)

Pedersen, Lars, *Newer Islamic Movements in Western Europe* (Ashgate Publishing, Aldershot, 1999)

Pillar, Paul R., *Terrorism and US Foreign Policy* (The Brookings Institution, Washington, DC, 2001)

Raviv, Moche, *Israel at Fifty* (Weidenfeld and Nicholson, London, 1998)

Reeve, Simon, *The New Jackals: Ramzi Yousef, Osama Bin Laden and the Future of Terrorism* (Northeastern University Press, Boston, 1999)

Richelson, Jeffrey T., *The U.S. Intelligence Community* (Westview Press, Columbia, 1999)

Rich, Paul B. and Richard Stubbs, *The Counter-Insurgent State: Guerrilla Warfare and State Building in the Twentieth Century* (Macmillan, London, 1997)

Shahin, Emad Eldin, *Political Ascent: Contemporary Islamic Movements in North Africa* (Westview Press, Colorado, 1998)

Simonsen, Clifford E. and Jeremy Spindlove, *Terrorism Today: The Past, The Players, The Future* (Prentice Hall, New Jersey 2000)

Willis, Michael, *The Islamist Challenge in Algeria: A Political History* (Ithaca Press, Reading, 1996)

Index